Challenges to Morality

PHILOSOPHICAL TOPICS
PAUL EDWARDS, GENERAL EDITOR

Challenges to Morality

Edited, with an Introduction,
Notes, and Bibliography by

JONATHAN HARRISON

UNIVERSITY OF NOTTINGHAM

Macmillan Publishing Company
New York
Maxwell Macmillan Canada
Toronto

Editor: Maggie Barbieri
Production Supervisor: Bert Yaeger
Production Manager: Rohnda Barnes
Text and Cover Designer: Angela Foote

This book was set in Caledonia by Digitype, Inc., and printed
and bound by Book Press.
The cover was printed by New England Book Components.

Macmillan Publishing Company
866 Third Avenue, New York, New York 10022

Macmillan Publishing Company is part of
the Maxwell Communication Group of Companies.

Maxwell Macmillan Canada, Inc.
1200 Eglinton Avenue East
Suite 200
Don Mills, Ontario M3C 3N1

Library of Congress Cataloging-in-Publication Data

Challenges to morality / edited, with an introduction, notes, and
    bibliography by Jonathan Harrison.
        p.   cm. — (Philosophical topics)
    Includes bibliographical references and index.
    ISBN 0-02-350591-5
    1. Ethics — Controversial literature.   I. Harrison, Jonathan.
II. Series: Philosophical topics (New York, N.Y.)
BJ1031.C48   1993
170 — dc20
                                            92-26225
                                               CIP

Printing: 1 2 3 4 5 6 7   Year: 3 4 5 6 7 8 9

To Toni

ACKNOWLEDGMENTS

I wish to thank the publishers and living authors of the pieces I have included. My special thanks are due to the general editor of this series, Paul Edwards, for giving me the benefit of his great experience, sound judgment, and philosophical acumen; for his patience; for many discerning criticisms; and also for suggesting some of the selections (in particular, the one by Bertrand Russell) for a piece of work which must have given him more than the usual amount of trouble. I have learned a great deal. I am grateful to Charles Pigden for his attempts to guide me in areas he knows better than I; to an anonymous reader for helping me make this book more intelligible; to the staff of the Nottingham University Library for the trouble they have taken to obtain necessary books; to Pauline Davis, whose administrative ability was invaluable in keeping track of the surprisingly large volume of correspondence necessary to produce a work of this kind; and to L. V. Harrison for the care and vigilance with which she has read the proofs.

CONTENTS

PART V
BEING GOOD INVOLVES BEING THE DUPE OF SOMEONE ELSE

PART VI
MORAL BELIEFS: THE IRRATIONAL
PRODUCTS OF EVOLUTION

PART VII
MORAL BELIEFS IMPOSSIBLE TO JUSTIFY

Challenges to Morality

Introduction

The challenges (or threats) to morality considered in the following pages are of different kinds. According to the simplest, ethical egoism, my only duty is to seek my own happiness, which would mean that the ordinary belief that we ought sometimes to sacrifice ourselves to others is mistaken (Part II).

But ethical egoism is *itself* a moral view. A more far-reaching challenge (discussed in Part VII) comes from philosophers who have held that moral beliefs are all false or, if not false, at least irrational. (Some philosophers have held that the reason these beliefs are all false is that morality presupposes religion, which is false because there is no god [see Part IV].)

If all our moral beliefs are false, an explanation is needed of how we came to have them. Some have held that the reason is that we have been duped by those who benefit from them (e.g., the bourgeoisie or the establishment) (see Part V). Others have held that it is because alternative moral beliefs have been weeded out by a process of natural selection (Part VI).

Not only can morality be challenged on the grounds that moral beliefs are false or irrational. It can also be challenged on the grounds (discussed in Part I) that although moral beliefs themselves are both true and rational, *acting* on them is not rational. The most common reason for this belief is that it is not rational *not* to seek one's own interest, and morality conflicts with interest.

Less obvious challenges to morality (see Part VIII) result from certain accounts of moral judgments. To take just one example, some philosophers have held that when we *appear* to be making moral *judgments* that certain things are wrong, all we are doing is issuing *imperatives* telling people not to do these things. Since imperatives can be neither true nor false, morality is threatened because it becomes impossible to adopt moral beliefs on the grounds that they are true.

It should not be forgotten that one can challenge some moral beliefs without challenging others. For example, it is possible to maintain that although it is a delusion that human beings are bound by duty, it is a *good* thing that people have this delusion. Without it, life would be nasty, brutish, and short. This view implies that although the belief that human beings have duties is false, the belief that their having this false belief is a good thing is true. There must then be at least one good thing, namely, people's delusion that they have duties.

Part I: The Impossibility of Altruism

Psychological hedonists hold that people are incurably selfish; the only thing they are capable of desiring is their own pleasure (or according to *psychological egoism*, which holds that there are goods other than pleasure, their own good).

Psychological hedonism should not be confused with *ethical hedonism*, and psychological egoism should not be confused with *ethical egoism*. The first are *factual* theories about what men and women *do in fact desire*, whether or not they ought to. The latter are *ethical* theories about what they *ought to do*, whether or not they actually desire to. There is all the difference in the world between holding that human beings in fact desire only their own pleasure and holding that this is the only thing at which they ought to *aim*.

Psychological hedonism has been thought to present a challenge to morality because it has been supposed to entail that human beings have no duties. Philosophers have thought that people cannot do their duty if they are not able to want to do it, and if their only desire is a desire for their own pleasure, they will not be able to want to do their duty. (Whether the fact that people do not want to do something is a reason for thinking they are unable to do it will be discussed in the third section.)

If psychological hedonism is true, all men, "good" and "bad" alike, are actuated by one and the same desire. The priest and the prostitute will have only one motive—a desire for his or her own pleasure. It is just a vagary of fortune, for which neither can claim credit or deserves blame, that desire for pleasure leads them in different directions. It is supposed to follow from this that the priest is not really any better than the prostitute. If one's being a good person depends on his or her having dutiful or altruistic motives, then it will be false that there are any genuinely good people. There can, if psychological egoism is true, be no such motives. All humans, indeed, will be equally bad or indifferent because they will all be actuated by one and the same motive, a desire for their own pleasure.

Because experience of life shows that people, although fairly selfish, are not completely, inevitably, and equally so, psychological hedonism must rest on confusions, a list of which follows:

1. It is a confusion to suppose that because every desire gives some pleasure when satisfied, the desire in question must be a desire *for* the pleasure it gives. On the contrary, as Bishop Butler held, there must be a desire for sex or food or fame in the first place, if having sex or food or fame is to give us any pleasure. To suppose that we desire food for the pleasure it gives is to put the cart before the horse. Food gives pleasure because we desire it. If we do have an *initial* desire for food, however, we can then have a resultant, second-order desire for the pleasure we get from satisfying it.

(It is for this reason that the behaviorist view associated with B. F. Skinner is incorrect. It is not the case that all desires are the result of positive or negative reinforcement (reward or punishment). Having something can reinforce behavior only if there is a desire for it in the first place; that there is such a desire is due to nature, not to reinforcement. For example, we can make children desire to be good (or at any rate, to conform) by giving them sweets, but not pebbles; however, this presupposes that children by nature want the sugar in sweets but not the stone in pebbles.)

2. Some philosophers seem to have supposed that an unselfish action would have to be an action motivated by someone else's desire, which is impossible. It is a confusion to suppose that, because we cannot act from other people's desires but only from our own, all our behavior must be selfish. It must be conceded that if we try to satisfy someone else's desire, we ourselves must *want* to satisfy it. And a want to satisfy someone *else's* desire is as much a want of *ours* as any other want. But an action is not made selfish simply because the agent wants to do it. It is *why* he or she wants to do it, or what the motivating desire is a desire for, that determines whether or not the action is selfish. A mother sacrificing herself for her children *is* doing what she wants to do. But her action is nevertheless altruistic because the object of her desire (i.e., *what* she wants) is the welfare of her child, not her own welfare.

(Similarly, when we provide now for the satisfaction of desires that we will have — in our old age, say — we are not acting from no desire at all. We are acting from a desire not to have unsatisfied desires at a later date. For example, a man who is not hungry may desire to provide for the hunger he knows he will later feel.)

In trying to gain the maximum amount of pleasure from satisfying one's desires, one should take altruistic desires into consideration as well as selfish ones. Satisfying altruistic desires often gives more pleasure than satisfying selfish ones. It would be extremely foolish, for example, for a woman not to seek the pleasure of her children on the grounds that her desire for their pleasure was a desire for the welfare of someone else, when in fact she would get more pleasure from spending time and money on them than from spending it on herself. The fact that a mother gets pleasure from seeing her children happy does not mean that she is acting selfishly when she tries to make them happy. Rather she is *un*selfish because one of the things from which she gets happiness is the happiness of her children.

(We shall see later [p. 188] that some philosophers have thought that inculcating a love of honor or virtue was a device for getting people (perhaps irrationally) to do what is not in their interest. This may be so, but given that we do love honor, however, it is rational and in the interest of people trying to maximize their satisfactions to take into consideration the pleasures of being honorable as much as any other kind of pleasure. The same applies to our desire to be virtuous.)

3. It is a confusion to suppose that a desire is a desire for the effects of satisfying it. For example, a desire to eat food is a desire to eat food, not a desire to avoid the bad effects — falling ill, for example — of not eating food.

It is a manifestation of this confusion to suppose that, because satisfying a desire has effects that are of benefit to the agent, the desire from which the agent is acting is a selfish desire for those effects. For example, a desire to help others in need is a desire to help others in need, not a desire for the effects of helping others in need, which may be that they help you when you are in need.

It is another more edifying confusion to suppose that because satisfying a desire has effects that benefit someone else, that desire is a desire for that benefit. It so happens that for excellent biological reasons (see Part V) we have evolved as creatures whose desires prompt them to perform actions that are of benefit to others, although this is not what they are desires for. For example, a man who starts a factory in an area of high unemployment may be actuated only by a desire for profit, although it so happens that his enterprise is of great value to the locality. His employees may work hard to produce something that is of benefit to the community, not from a desire to produce that benefit but simply because, from a variety of motives, egoistic, altruistic, and neither, they need the money.

Hence people have been created (or have evolved) with reciprocal desires. For example, if everybody were to have (as they do to some extent) a desire to help others in distress, we ourselves would sometimes help others when they were in distress. We would also sometimes benefit, when we were in distress, by others helping others in distress. It does not follow, however, that when we help others in distress, we do so *in order* that they will help us. Indeed, it may be that God (or nature, through the medium of natural selection) has found a more efficient way of seeing that others are helped than entrusting it to an egoistical calculaton. Children are brought up more efficiently if nature has planted in men and women an altruistic and spontaneous desire to care for offspring than they would if their parents had to work out whether they would gain more than they would lose from looking after them.

4. It is well known that human beings, for good or ill, knowingly act in such a way as *not* to maximize their own *distant* pleasure. I would maximize my own remote pleasure by giving up smoking, but from weakness of will I deprive myself of an enormous long-term benefit to retain a troublesome short-term satisfaction. If my only desire were for pleasure, this could not happen. The idea that someone tempted by a strong desire for pleasure would imprudently throw away pleasure is absurd. I do not smoke from a craving for pleasure, but from a craving for nicotine.

Part II: Virtue Does Not Pay

Ethical egoists hold that the only thing we ought to do is try to produce as much good or pleasure as possible for *ourselves*. (An *egoistical hedonist* thinks, on top of this, that pleasure is the *only* good, but we shall ignore this refinement.) It is true that, since ethical egoism is itself a moral view, it would be undermined by any attack on the truth or rationality of moral beliefs as such. But if *no* moral beliefs were true or rational, there could be no *moral* reason for *not* seeking one's own good at the expense of other people's.

Since ethical egoists hold that the only thing we ought to take into consideration in deciding what we ought to do is the amount of good performing an action produces for ourselves, ethical egoism implies that we would have no obligation whatsoever to produce pleasure for thousands (or millions) of people unless doing so was a means to our own pleasure. For example, even if I could save thousands of people from starving in Ethiopia by forgoing a single meal, I could not be under an obligation to forgo it unless it could be shown that I myself would not lose anything by doing so. It also implies that if circumstances were to rise in which one could obtain a very small increase in pleasure (or good) for oneself by letting millions of people die in agony, one positively *ought* to let them die. Ethical egoists have a number of answers to these objections, but they are unsatisfactory.

The first answer is that a conflict between one's own good and that of others can never arise. Only a moderate experience of life, however, shows that this is mistaken. Even if such conflicts never occurred in fact, one could imagine circumstances in which it would be one's duty to sacrifice one's own good, if they *were* to arise. A moral theory ought to be true in all *imaginable* circumstances.

The second answer is that if it is my duty to make a sacrifice, and I do, I become a morally better person as a result. Therefore, although it looks as if I am sacrificing something in order to do my duty, in fact I am not. I am actually increasing my own good by the sacrifice because this makes me a better person. It has been held (perhaps by Immanuel Kant and certainly by Cardinal Newman) that even the smallest amount of moral goodness outweighs in value anything necessarily sacrificed to obtain it.

This answer, too, is unsatisfactory. For one thing, *moral* goodness is not the kind of goodness that egoistical hedonists are talking about when they hold that one ought to maximize one's own good. (Furthermore, this answer begs the question against ethical egoism and assumes the very thing that it is trying to prove.) Unless I have a duty to make the sacrifice in the first place, I would not gain in moral goodness by making it. But according to ethical egoism, it never *could* be my duty to make such a sacrifice.

In defense of ethical egoism, it has even been suggested that the pleasure one gets from doing what one ought is so great that it will compensate one for the consequences of any sacrifice, however large. Alternatively, a person will suffer so much painful guilt for *not* making the sacrifice that he or she would have been happier if he or she had made it.

This defense fails because, though men certainly both do get pleasure from contemplating their own virtue, and pain from contemplating their own vice, this is usually not enough to make up the loss which an action involving a large sacrifice would entail. I personally doubt very much whether the pain I would get from realizing that I had *not* thrown myself on a grenade to save the lives of my colleagues would so blight the rest of my life as to make my refusal to sacrifice myself not worth it. Self-deception (an undervalued human propensity) would undoubtedly come to my rescue. In any case, if egoistical hedonism were true, it would not be meritorious, but positively blameworthy, to make the sacrifice in the first place. Self-sacrifice, according to egoistical hedonism, is wrong. A strong-minded egoistical hedonist would simply have to learn to live with what he or she ought to consider to be irrational guilt, in order to abide by his or her professed principles.

Egoistical hedonism may well be wrong, but it is not inconsistent, although it has been held to be so. (It is wrong to hold that the earth is flat and not round. It is inconsistent to hold that it is both flat and round.)

For one thing, it has been alleged that it is inconsistent for egoistical hedonists to hold that only their *own* pleasure is good; the pleasures of others have, it is said, as much claim to be considered as good as theirs. But egoistical hedonists need not hold that only their own pleasure is good. All they need maintain is that (although everybody's pleasure is *good*) it is *right* for people to pursue only their own pleasure. Analogously, one might maintain that, although other people's countries were as good as one's own, it would be right to fight only for one's own country.

Some critics of egoistical hedonism have also supposed that it is inconsistent because what egoistical hedonists are maintaining is that *everyone* ought to pursue his or her pleasure (i.e., the pleasure of the egoistic hedonists themselves). If one thinks that egoistical hedonism is true, one must also think that anyone who believes it will be believing what is true. Then if Smith is an egoistical hedonist, he must think both that everyone ought to seek his (Smith's) pleasure and that what Jones thinks when Jones thinks that everyone ought to seek his (Jones's) pleasure is true. But it is inconsistent to hold that everyone (including Jones) ought to seek Smith's pleasure and that everyone (including Smith) ought to seek Jones's pleasure.

One way around this difficulty might be for the egoist — let us call him Smith — simply to maintain that everyone ought to promote Smith's pleasure and that the equally egoistic Jones is wrong when he thinks that everyone ought to pursue Jones's pleasure — although this might mean (I am not sure) that Smith would have to point to some relevant difference between himself and Jones which would explain why it is right for everyone to seek his pleasure but not Jones's.

In any case, egoists need not maintain anything so absurd as the view that opponents say is inconsistent. All they need maintain is that everybody should pursue only his or her own pleasure (i.e., that each person should pursue only the pleasure of that person). To suppose otherwise, as in the above objection, is like supposing that when a man says that everyone should sleep with his own wife only, he means that everyone should sleep with *his* wife only. The difficulty arises because it is not clear what person the word "he" refers to. A person who thinks that every woman ought to fight for her country means that every woman ought to fight for the country that she (where "she" refers to the woman faced with the decision) belongs to, not that every woman ought to fight for the country that she (where "she" refers to the holder of the view that every woman ought to fight for her country) belongs to. Hence, if the holder of the view is an Englishwoman and the person to whom the view applies a Frenchwoman, the view implies that the Frenchwoman ought to fight for France, not that she ought to fight for England; only the Englishwoman ought to fight for England.

It has also been held (recently, by Gilbert Harman; see bibliography) that egoistic hedonism is unsatisfactory because the fact that something produces pleasure for me is, if egoism is true, a reason only for *my* doing that thing. Genuine moral reasons for performing an action, however, are always reasons for *anybody's* performing it. For example, that something produces the greatest happiness of the greatest number would be a reason (if utilitarianism is true) for *anybody's* doing it. That it produces happiness for me would be a reason only for my doing it.

There is yet another unacceptable reason for rejecting egoistical hedonism. Immanuel Kant thought that some moral principles could be rejected because they would be self-defeating if everybody were to adopt them. (Being self-defeating may be a kind of inconsistency.) Breaking promises is thought to be self-defeating, for the people doing it aim to benefit from others' keeping their promises, while they themselves break theirs. This object would be defeated, however, if everyone were to break their promises. Egoism is self-defeating in that if everybody were to become an egoist, the aim of a person who adopts egoism, which is to gain from others without giving anything in return, would be defeated. *Everyone* cannot take from others without giving anything in return.

It is doubtful, however, that the fact that egoism would be self-defeating if universally adopted is a good reason for rejecting it. A conscientious would-be seducer might reject the principle (which I am told is old-fashioned) "Seduce attractive women when you have the opportunity, so long as they are not virgins" on the grounds that, if everybody were to act on this principle, there would be no nonvirgins for would-be seducers to seduce. He might amend it however, so that it became "Seduce an attractive woman when you have the opportunity, whether she is a virgin or not." This maxim would, unlike the first, not be self-defeating. It is doubtful, however, whether the latter maxim is any less immoral than the former. Some would say that it was more immoral. (For what this fact is worth, the principle "Give without taking" is as self-defeating as the principle "Take without giving.")

Some philosophers have also thought that ethical egoism could be rejected because it prescribes actions one would not be in favor of if one were in the position of the person adversely affected by the egoist's egoistic actions. For example, it is frequently supposed that hurting someone else is wrong because one would not be in favor of it if one were in the position of the other person. (It may be that this is what people are emphasizing when they say "How would you like it if you were he?")

The answer to this objection is that an action is not shown to be wrong by the fact that one would not be in favor of the agent's doing it if one were in the position of the person affected by it. A judge cannot conclude that it is wrong to sentence a murderer because he or she would not be in favor of the judge's doing this if their roles were reversed. Putting oneself in the position of other people affected by the action is at best a way of avoiding bias and of quickening one's imagination to the hurt one is causing. It does not necessarily mean that it is *wrong* to cause hurt. (Sometimes it is right to perform actions that hurt others.) It is not necessarily a successful way of avoiding bias, for the person in whose place I put myself may be as liable to bias as I am.

In any case, my action is likely to affect more people than myself and another person (for example, the judge and the prisoner), and so putting myself in the place of the other party will not be very helpful. I ought, perhaps, to put myself in the place of all the affected parties, which may affect me differently for each one of them. Some will gain and some will lose by what I do. Some philosophers have supposed that I then ought to try to maximize the interests of those affected by my action, counting my own interests as being of no greater (and of no lesser) importance than the interests of any of the others. If so, egoistical hedonism would have to be rejected in favor of something more like utilitarianism, the view that we ought to try to produce the good of everybody.

It could be argued in defense of egoistical hedonism (and against utilitarianism) that this recommendation is unrealistic. I have a special responsibility to my own wife, my own children, and my own country. (For example, I ought to try to get my child a place in school, even if this means excluding other people's children.) If I go about too assiduously looking after other people's wives, other people's children, and other people's countries, the result will be chaos. (It should be noted that this is a *utilitarian* argument against utilitarianism.)

It could then be argued that I also have a special duty to *myself*. It is better that each man should look after himself, and that others should look after themselves, than that everybody should go about looking after everybody in a disorganized way. It may be that more overall happiness is brought about if everybody puts him- or herself to some extent first than if everybody gives equal weight to his or her own interests and to the interests of everybody else. That is, perhaps one ought to be allowed to count oneself for more than one (but not for infinity). If so, there is something to be said for egoistical hedonism, exaggerated though it is. (Again, this is a utilitarian argument in favor of egoism, a nonutilitarian view.)

Finally, there is a sense in which, although ethical egoism itself is not inconsistent, the *action* of asserting it out loud to others (but not the "action" of thinking it quietly by oneself) *is* inconsistent. Telling others that they ought to act in such a manner as to maximize *their* pleasure is not a good way of maximizing one's *own* pleasure. Hence, if egoistical hedonism is true, one ought to hide the fact that it is true. Consistent egoistical hedonists will tell other people (insincerely) that they ought to act in such a way as to bring about the pleasure of others. They will preach altruism but practice egoism. Such egoists are being pragmatically inconsistent if they assert ethical hedonism out loud, for they are doing something that they should not do if ethical hedonism is true. This does not mean, however, that it is not true. Shouting in a library that one ought not to shout in libraries is pragmatically inconsistent, but this does not mean that it is not true that one ought not to shout in libraries.

Part III: Virtue Not Within Our Power

The Delphic oracle predicted that Oedipus would kill his father and marry his mother. Many philosophers have supposed that the prediction meant that neither Oedipus nor his unhappy family were able to avoid this fate. For if the oracle *knew* that he was going to kill his father and marry his mother, nothing Oedipus nor anyone else could do could prevent it.

Even if the Delphic oracle did not know that Oedipus was going to kill his father, the mere fact that he *was* going to do it seems to make his doing it inevitable. What will be, will be. So if Oedipus' killing his father is what will be, Oedipus must kill his father.

But if Oedipus could not avoid killing his father, it seems to follow that he should not be blamed for doing something he ought not to do. As Kant said, *ought* implies *can*. So when Oedipus discovered that the woman (Jocasta) he had married and by whom he had had three children was his mother, and put his own eyes out in an agony of remorse, he was acting irrationally. If everything we do is, as the fatalist supposes, fated, then it is irrational to bother about morality (or even about prudence). The wicked things we are fated to do we will do whether we try to avoid doing them or not. Praise and blame, reward and punishment, must all be ineffective.

I do not know whether the ancient Greeks supposed that the Delphic oracle knew everything. But Christians do usually suppose that God is omniscient. If so, He knows all our future acts of wickedness and whether or not we will be damned as a result of performing them. If Oedipus was not able to avoid the fate the oracle foresaw for him, does it not follow that we are not able to avoid the salvation or damnation an omniscient god foresees for us? In that case is not God acting unjustly if He damns us at all? For it is unjust to make people suffer for what they cannot help.

God is made to seem even more unjust if we suppose that He not only *foresees* which of his creatures will be damned, but also *decides* which of them (the elect) should be damned. But this is just what the doctrine of predestination holds that He does. It is very difficult to believe that an omnipotent omniscient being could not prevent our damnation if He wished. So, on an extreme view, perhaps it follows from the fact that the world is governed by an omniscient and omnipotent God that He, not humans (or He as well as humans), is responsible for sin.

For this reason, most Christians suppose that humans have free will. They regard this as the power to decide for oneself what one does, without one's decision being caused by anything else (by the will of God, for example). One's decision's having such causes would mean that the causes, not the human beings, were responsible for their actions. Because human beings have free will, they have the power to decide whether to sin or not to sin. Hence they, not God, are responsible for sin. According to this view, God could prevent people's sinning only at the cost of limiting his freedom. But a person who was not free would be something subhuman. So God, in choosing to give people freedom, despite the mischief He knew they would make with it, was choosing the lesser of two evils. He could have made humans so that they always acted rightly, but then they would have been mere automatons.

Few people nowadays believe in fate, and only a minority believe in a Christian god. But almost everybody believes in modern science, and, if modern science is right, it may well be that it is possible in principle (although obviously not in practice) to predict everything that will happen in the universe, including the supposedly free actions of human beings, just as it is possible to predict the behavior of the planets for many thousands of years in the future. Scientists believe that there is an explanation for everything. But if there is an explanation of everything —the person who thinks that there is is called a *determinist*—then there must be an explanation of why one person is a criminal and another is a respectable citizen. Their genes were different, perhaps, and one of them came from a good home, whereas the other did not. However, if their behavior can be explained, it can be predicted, and we have the same problem about foreknowledge that was produced by the existence of God or the fates. But if so, is not the person with the defective genes or the poor environment going to be a criminal, he or she and therefore whether we punish that person or not? Hence, perhaps, crime should be treated as a medical condition and its causes understood and eliminated, rather than that the criminal should be punished (ineffectually) for what he or she cannot help.

Things seem worse if we regard a cause as *necessitating* its effect. Perhaps if shooting oneself through the head causes death, then it must necessitate death (see the reading from Hume). If it necessitates death, there is nothing that can be done to prevent someone from dying if shot through the head. Hence, if defective genes cause crime, then defective genes necessitate crime, and there is nothing that anyone can do to stop someone with defective genes from being a criminal.

Hard determinists accept the arguments I have adduced. They think that it follows from determinism that human beings cannot help doing what they do. Many philosophers do *not* think that it follows from these premises either that our fates are unavoidable or that we cannot help performing the actions which result in our fates being what they are. (Such philosophers are called *soft determinists* or *compatibilists*.) When Cassius says

> The fault, dear Brutus, is not in our stars,
> But in ourselves, that we are underlings.

Soft determinists believe that Cassius is under a misconception. There is, they think, no reason why the fault should not lie both in our stars and in ourselves.

If it seems that soft determinism is a contradiction, it may be because of an ambiguity in the word "free" as it is used in philosophical discussions. In one sense the word means simply "not determined." In that sense, freedom is certainly incompatible with determinism. But in another sense an action is said to be free if the agent could have done something other than what he or she did. In this sense, it is a matter for philosophical investigation whether or not freedom is compatible with determinism. A compatibilist thinks that freedom and determinism are compatible.

There is much to be said for compatibilism. Let us consider the unavoidability alleged to follow from *determinism*. The assertion that an event is avoidable is what is called an unfulfilled conditional proposition. It says something about what *would* have happened *if* something else, which did not in fact happen, *had* happened. An example would be the statement that, *if* there had not been a hurricane, the tree at the bottom of my garden *would* be standing now. There is, obviously, no incompatibility between the fact that such a statement is true and the fact that the occurrence of the hurricane was necessitated and itself necessitated the falling of my tree. Both events were caused, they are explicable, and both are in principle capable of being predicted by anyone with enough knowledge of botany and meteorology. But this does not mean that there are scientific reasons for thinking that it is not true that my tree would not have blown down had there *not* been a hurricane. Rather, it means that there are scientific reasons for thinking that it is *true*.

If we apply this conclusion to the fate of a human being, we can see that some fates are avoidable and others are not. This is because the statement that a fate is avoidable is also an unfulfilled conditional proposition. If a fate is avoidable, then there are certain human actions which are such that *if* they had been performed (although they were not), the fates in question *would* have been avoided. For example, my dying of cancer will have been unavoidable if there were no actions that could have prevented it had they been performed. But all my money's going to my second cousin twice removed *is* avoidable in that there is some action (my making a will) such that *if* I had performed it, my money *would* have gone to my mistress. On this view, roughly, a fate is avoidable if one of the events in the chain of causes necessary to produce it is the action of a human being, because then the human being might have prevented it by not performing the action in question. Eclipses, then, are unavoidable, because there are no human actions among their causes; but hangings are avoidable. (Fatalism, therefore, is quite certainly untrue, for many things could have been avoided by taking precautions that were not actually taken.)

There is a serious difficulty with this attempt to reconcile causation, necessitation, and predictability on the one hand with avoidability on the other. It is that it is a logical truth that if a fate is going to occur, none of the actions which would prevent it, if they *were* to be performed, can be performed. (Similarly, if my tree would not have fallen down had there not been a hurricane, but *is* going to fall down, it follows that it cannot be that there will not be a hurricane.) If it was foreknown that Oedipus was going to kill his father, for example, it does follow that it cannot be that he will perform any of the actions which would result in his not killing his father. And, it may be said, it is poor consolation to be told that one's being hanged can be prevented, in that there are human actions which *would* result in one's not being hanged, *if* they were to be performed, if we are also told that it cannot be that any of these actions *will* be performed.

The compatibilist has an answer to this difficulty, however. It is that some of the actions which would result in my not being hanged are within my power. This fact is compatible with determinism, because the statement that an action is within my power is another unfulfilled conditional, and so it, too, is compatible with determinism. (Those who think otherwise are confusing the statement that I am unable to do something with the statement that it cannot be that I will do it. The statement that it cannot be that Smith killed Jones — perhaps because he had no motive — is compatible with the statement that he could have killed him because he would have done so if he had had a motive.) On this compatibilist view, the statement that an action is within my power is the unfulfilled conditional statement that *if* my wants and/or beliefs *had* been different from what they were, I *would* have performed it.

For example, it is not within my power to stop breathing (for long, at any rate). This is because I will go on breathing, even if I badly want to stop breathing and regardless of my beliefs about the disadvantages of breathing. Even if I am hidden in a cupboard in a house that is being searched by enemy agents, and I *believe* that I will be discovered if I breathe and *want* not to be discovered, I nevertheless go on breathing just the same. Hence not breathing is not within my power. However, if in the same circumstances I believed that I would be discovered *if* I did not stop talking and wanted not to be discovered, I *would* stop talking. Hence stopping talking is within my power.

It is obvious that there are some actions which would have been performed if the desires and the beliefs of the agent had been different. So, according to soft determinism, the actions that would have avoided our fates if they had been performed are sometimes really within our power. Indeed, according to soft determinists, to say that they would not have happened if our wants or beliefs had been different is just what it means to say that they are in our power.

According to soft determinism, freedom is compatible with necessity in that there are certain links in the chain of causal necessitation (i.e., free human actions) such that (a) the fates that are avoidable would have been avoided had these links been otherwise, and (b) these links would have been otherwise if someone's desires and beliefs had been different. But it must not be forgotten that, on this view, it is necessitated that all the links in the chain should occur precisely as they do. For a free action (i.e., one the agent is able not to do, is not an unnecessitated action, but an action that is necessitated by a special kind of cause, namely, the beliefs and desires of the agent).

One might, then, wish to distinguish between "full" and "partial" avoidability. Many fates are partially avoidable, in that they *would* have been avoided *if* certain actions within the power of the agent had been performed. They are not fully avoidable, for the events which would have resulted in these actions being performed (e.g., the agent's coming to desire something different from what he or she did) cannot happen. A compatibilist holds that certain fates are our own fault because they are partially avoidable. The hard determinist holds that our fates are never our own fault because they are never fully avoidable.

The fact of partial avoidability explains why it is possible to alter people's behavior by punishment or exhortation (or to alter our own behavior by strenuous endeavour). Actions that agents could have helped are precisely those which they would not have done if their desires or beliefs had been different. Hence one can try to make people behave differently by attempting to alter their desires and beliefs or by appealing to the desires and beliefs they already have. By moral exhortation, for example, one can arouse a desire that was not there before, and by threatening punishment one can create a belief (that may be true) that one will suffer pain, financial loss, or imprisonment if one performs the outlawed action. The difference between a happening which is a human action and a happening to an inanimate object, therefore, is not that one can modify the former, but that one cannot modify the latter. The difference consists in the *way* in which it is possible to affect them. Inanimate objects, for one thing, cannot be affected by reward or punishment, but people can. In both cases, however, it is determined (although by different factors) whether or not they will be affected, and whether or not the actions that would affect them will be performed.

According to *libertarianism*, when I perform certain actions, like resisting almost overwhelming temptation, I am conscious of exercising a power within myself that sets aside all the causal factors working on me, which power enables me to do my duty in spite of them. Sometimes libertarians say that since what produces a human action is not an event, it is exempt from the law of cause and effect, which applies only to events. What causes human action is an *agent* (i.e., a person, not an event). Libertarians think that there is no chain of cause and effect which is such that it is a matter of necessity that I perform the actions I do.

An objection to libertarianism is that it is an illusion that my action is not determined by the factors acting on me. The illusion is caused by the fact that I am usually not determined wholly by those factors of which I am conscious at the time of acting. But I can become conscious, retrospectively, of the apparently missing factor *after* I have acted. In any case, it would be a mistake to suppose that the fact that I act from honor or duty means that what I do is free in the sense of being uncaused. There must be an explanation of how it comes about that I love honor or duty when others do not. I have been better brought up than they, perhaps. Moreover, to say that something is caused by an agent (not an event) is just another way of saying that it is caused by an action of the agent, which *is* an event. To say that a boy (a person, not an event) broke the window is to say no more than that the boy's throwing the stone with the intention of breaking the window (an event) caused the window to break. (The boy's action will itself be caused by a number of factors, the desires and wants of the agent, among others.)

If the compatibilist's above outlined account of freedom is correct, morality is not challenged by determinism. Determinism does *not* imply that humans are unable to help doing any of the things they do. For the same reason, the fact that I (or God) can know what someone will do does not imply that the person in question is unable to do anything else. The fact that I know that Smith will accept the drink that I am offering him does not imply that he would not refuse if he were less thirsty or less addicted or less polite. (It may imply that I have to know that he is thirsty, addicted, or polite in order to predict that he will not refuse.)

If compatibilism is true, we are able to solve two well-known problems: (a) Although it is true that if Harrison is going to be hanged he is going to be hanged, this does not mean that he would still be hanged even if he had not committed murder. It does *not* follow, therefore, that it is not worth bothering not to commit murder. (b) Although it is true that if God knows that Harrison is going to be damned he is going to be damned, it does not follow that he will be damned even if he does not commit mortal sin. It also does not follow that he will commit mortal sin even if he does not have the base inclinations or erroneous theological beliefs that result in his committing it.

Compatibilism has serious difficulties, however. If they cannot be answered, morality *is* challenged by determinism. A few of these difficulties follow:

1. It is frequently objected that compatibilism makes me free only in a hypothetical sense. It makes me free only *if* I have the desires and beliefs which caused the action that is alleged to be free. This objection

confuses a conditional assertion with asserting something conditionally. One can assert, quite unconditionally, that something is a request bus stop, even though the assertion that it is a request bus stop is only the *conditional* assertion that buses will stop at it only *if* asked.

2. For this kind of compatibilism to work, it is essential that the statement that I could have done something other than I did should be genuinely hypothetical. It has been argued, however, that the statement that I could do something if I want is no more hypothetical than the statement that there are biscuits on the table if you want some, which asserts categorically that there are biscuits on the table, whether you want some or not.

3. Sometimes I find it impossible to do something (say, give up heroin) *because of* my wants. I want heroin so badly that I am unable to give it up. It may then be true that I would not take heroin if I did not want to. But no more does this mean that I am able not to take heroin than the fact that I could run if weights were not tied to my feet means that I am able to run.

4. It is not enough, for an action to be free, for it to be caused by an agent's desires and/or beliefs. It is further necessary that the agent should have control over the desires and beliefs which cause it. Mrs. O'Farrell, in the last reading in this section, did not have control over her wants. Dr. Svengali controlled them. Hence many will suppose that her actions were *not* free, although they *were* caused by her wants and beliefs.

5. This objection can be reinforced by the consideration that our wants may be, and perhaps always will be, the result of the condition of our brains. For example, there are certain substances secreted by our glands that cause sexual desire when in the bloodstream. In that case, it may be argued, it could be true that one would not be sleeping with one's neighbor's husband unless one wanted to, but nevertheless false that one could avoid it. We cannot help our brains being in the condition that causes us to have the wants we have.

6. It is very doubtful whether the assertion that I cannot bend my arm backward only *means* that if I were to try to bend it backwards, I would fail. Rather it is the way my joints are constructed that *explains why* it is impossible for me to bend my arm backwards.

Even if compatibilists are right, and we can help the things we do, there is nevertheless a sense in which it is a matter of chance, over which we have no control, that some people are good and others bad. This is because it is a matter of chance that human beings have the nature and motivation that result in their freely choosing the good rather than in freely choosing the bad. This will especially follow if the desires, which cause people to act in one way rather than another, result from the state of their glands, nervous systems, and brains, because that we are in these states is largely a matter of chance, in that sense of chance in which something happens by chance if it does not happen by design. (In that sense of chance in which something happens by chance if it is not *caused*, nothing, according to determinism, happens by chance.)

The fact that so much of what we do depends on the state of our brains must lead one to speculate whether in the very distant future all serious immorality might be cured by brain surgery. If so, exhortation and punishment may become even more useless than they are now, because more efficient ways will have been found of accomplishing one of the things we use them for. (This will not please those philosophers who think that to tamper with a person's brain, even with that person's consent, is to infringe inalienable rights.) This same fact — that whether we freely choose to be wicked depends on the state of our brains, over which we have little or no control — makes it quite realistic to think of every wicked man or woman "There but for the grace of God go I."

Part IV: Goodness Not Demanded by God

Atheism has been supposed to present a challenge to morality because it has been thought that, first, if there is no God, nothing will be immoral, and second, if people believe that there is no God to enforce morality, they will behave immorally. There is some tension between these two views. From the first, *nothing* will be immoral if there is no God. Hence it will not be possible for people to behave immorally in the event of there not being one. The best they will be able to do will be to behave in ways they wrongly suppose to be immoral.

View 1. Whether the first contention — that no action will be right or wrong if there is not a God — is true will depend what is the correct view of the relation between God's commands and humanities' duties (i.e., between God's law on the one hand and the moral law on the other). There are three main possibilities.

THEORY A

The moral law is identical to the commands of God; an action's being right or wrong is no more and no less than its being commanded or prohibited by God. If this view is correct, then it would follow that, if there were no God, nothing would be wrong. A nonexistent god could not command or prohibit anything.

This view must be rejected for the following reasons:

1. If it were true, the fact that an action was wrong would be identical with the fact that it was prohibited by God. Hence no one could

without inconsistency hold that there were actions (burning babies alive, for example) that were wrong and at the same time hold that there was no God to prohibit such actions. Atheists, however, believe precisely this, without any apparent inconsistency. Moreover, many theists also believe that such actions would be wrong, even if there were no God.

2. If no mention is made of goodness in the definition of "God," this view turns moral judgments into a species of factual judgment (about God's commands), and so leaves out what is distinctive about such judgments (i.e., that they say that something ought to be done or would be good).

3. On the other hand, if mention *is* made of God's (perfect) goodness in the definition of "God," the theory becomes circular: rightness will be defined as obedience to the commands of a being who always commands what is right.

4. God could be perfectly good, in that His will was always guided by the moral law, only if there was a moral law, independent of what God willed, for His will to be guided by. But if Theory A is correct, there is no moral law distinct from those actions God commands. If, however, God's will is not guided by the moral law, there is no guarantee that He will not command things like human sacrifice. For such things will not be wrong until after God has prohibited them, and if He were to command human sacrifice, it would (according to Theory A) become right.

5. On this view, we could know what was right only by first finding out what God has commanded. We could not argue, for example, that it *must* be that God prohibits human sacrifice because human sacrifice is wrong. If Theory A is correct, we could not know whether or not human sacrifice was wrong until we had first discovered whether or not God had prohibited it.

Theory B

One could think that the only reason any action was ever wrong was that it was prohibited by God. This view implies that Theory A is wrong, for if what makes an action wrong is that God prohibits it, it cannot be that an action's being wrong and its being prohibited by God are simply the same fact about the action put in different words.

Theory B, like Theory A, would have the consequence that if there were no God, nothing would be wrong, and that we could only find out what was wrong by first finding out what God commanded. It would also entail that an action (like burning babies alive) could not be wrong just because performing it would cause some human being an enormous amount of unnecessary suffering. There would, in addition, have to be a God who forbade human beings to cause one another suffering.

It seems obvious to me that (if anything is wrong) it would be wrong to burn babies alive, whether God had prohibited people from burning babies alive or not. It could, indeed, be wrong, even if God had *commanded* people to burn babies alive. Moreover, if Theory B is true, there could be no moral law independent of God's commands for God's will to be guided by, and so His godness could not prevent him from commanding us to burn babies alive (although his benevolence might prevent him).

Theory B is a theory about the supreme principle of morality, holding that what is common (and peculiar) to right actions is that they are all commanded by God. Having not more than one wife (for example) will be only *derivatively* wrong (i.e., wrong *because* God has prohibited it). On the other hand, if he allows four wives, having more than one wife will not be wrong (although in Britain and the United States it will be illegal).

Theory C

Theory C is the converse of Theory B. According to Theory C, God commands certain actions only because they are *already* right. They cannot, then, be right (as Theory B holds) *because* God has commanded them. Theory C preserves the belief that God is guided by an antecedently existing moral law which is independent of His will, which Theory A and Theory B do not. Consequently Theory C is favorable to God's morality because it holds that God will not command us to burn babies alive, if this is (antecedently) wrong. Theory C also makes it proper to argue from the premise that something is wrong to the conclusion that God must have prohibited it. For example, according to Theories A and B, it is proper to argue that, because God has prohibited killing, euthanasia is wrong. According to Theory C, it is proper to argue that, because euthanasia is not wrong, God cannot have prohibited it. Because, however, Theory C holds that the moral law is independent of God's will, it has the disadvantage (for theists) of being difficult to reconcile with God's omnipotence, because God will then be *unable* to make human sacrifice right.

Although Theories A, B, and C are incompatible with one another as they stand, it is possible to combine variants of them. One view would be that some things, murder for example, would be wrong whether God had prohibited them or not. Other things, like working on Sundays, copulating without having performed the appropriate ceremony, or believing that there is not a God, would not be wrong if God had not prohibited them. (This would correspond to the distinction in jurisprudence between *male in se* (those things that are wrong in themselves, for example, killing people) and *male prohibitas* (those things that are wrong only because prohibited, e.g., parking on a double yellow line).

If there was a God, everything that would be wrong if there were not a God could then be wrong on two counts instead of one. Burning babies alive could be wrong in the first instance because of the pain it inflicted on the babies. It would be wrong for this reason whether there was a God or not. But it could, in addition, be wrong because, since it *is* wrong, God forbids it, and it is wrong to do what God forbids. Other things, like copulating without having performed the appropriate ceremony, would be wrong only on one count. According to such a view, it would make a considerable difference to one's duties whether there was a God or not (but not as much difference as would be made by Theory A or Theory B).

If there is no God, then it is unlikely that we will suffer for our wicked acts in an afterlife, although Buddhists maintain that it is still possible. Of course, we may suffer for such acts in this life, but human punishment, as compared with divine, is relatively inefficient, because we cannot possibly escape detection by an all-seeing God. It is impossible for an omniscient being to forget what we have done. The means of enforcement at his disposal are unlimited, and we can never hope to be wrongfully acquitted. He can afford whole armies of devils, whom he does not have to pay by levying taxes, just to make miserable the afterlife of a single sinner. Moreover, one might even be sufficiently well disposed to the deity to dislike his witnessing one's performing wicked acts, even if he does not punish one. Belief in God strengthens the moral attitudes one thinks one ought to have.

On the other hand, punishment in an afterlife, although allegedly extremely severe, is remote, whereas effective punishment is supposed to be *immediate*. It is also *uncertain*, because God might not exist or might, one hopes, forgive one. And the possibility of obtaining absolution, which is beyond the power of an unauthorized human to give, or the possibility of obtaining relief by confession might even make one *less* reluctant to sin.

It is sometimes supposed (especially by believers) that morality is always on the side of the believer, but there are moral failings characteristic of belief as well as of unbelief. The major ones are irrationality, excessive conservatism, and a degree of intolerance that can amount to criminal lunacy.

1. The irrationality consists in believing propositions (not necessarily ones about the deity) without or against the evidence. Irrationality in thought (as opposed to irrationality in behavior) must always be a vice, because it leads us to adopt beliefs that are false and so to take courses of action which, because they are based on false belief, are generally useless or positively harmful to ourselves and our friends. (Our having false beliefs is beneficial to our enemies.)

2. Most of the great religions were founded some time ago and tend to have moral precepts which do not respond to increasing knowledge

and changing circumstances. Jews still condemn eating pork, although to eat pork has been quite safe in cold climates for many centuries. Christians accept a sexual morality, the elements of which were established by Saint Paul two millenia ago. This morality takes no account of modern knowledge about the danger to mental health of excessive chastity. Islam has an attitude toward punishment which is both barbarous and known to be counterproductive. But, with the exception of eating pork, which is a minor matter, all Western religions have the faults about which I have been complaining. All three have an attitude toward male domination which must become increasingly unacceptable. (The aforementioned defects, however, do not seem to be essential to religion.)

3. Intolerance leads us to persecute people with beliefs different from our own. This is a vice because, if we are mistaken, which in view of our human frailty we ought to be humble enough to think possible, we are persecuting people for having *true* beliefs. Even when the beliefs for which we are persecuting people are false, our doing so must prevent their using their own powers of judgment in such matters. Hence it inhibits a habit which people must have in order to acquire knowledge, and without knowledge human beings would relapse into barbarism. Persecution is also wrong because it leads the persecuted themselves to persecute when they have the opportunity, which makes civilized life impossible. The barbarism produced by religious intolerance, which can easily become fanaticism, is (along with nationalism and racism, which unfortunately often go with it) one of the greatest ills of modern times.

Closely connected with intolerance is refusal to compromise. Compromise is essential if people with different beliefs are to live together. Religious people find compromise difficult when they believe that their doctrines and practices are ordained of God. An intelligent God, however, would see the necessity for compromise and enjoin it upon his creatures. Compromising one's moral principles—something often unjustly denigrated—may be produced partly by a confusion between the propositions (a) that if it *is* wrong to do something it is wrong to do it, however much others may think it right, and (b) that, if it is wrong to do something, it *would* be wrong to do it even if a many other people thought it right.

That those who believe in God are more than usually reluctant to believe themselves mistaken is due partly to the fact that they suppose that because their beliefs have been revealed to them by an inerrant being, these beliefs must themselves be inerrant. They overlook the fact, however, that although it is true that *if* a belief has been revealed to one by an inerrant being it must be right, the belief that it *has* been so revealed may be wrong. Even if it were true, it could not be certainly true.

I find it impossible to generalize on the question of whether belief in God makes the believer better or worse than the unbeliever. More often than not, I suspect it makes little difference. When religious fanaticism is combined with nationalism and racism, we have an evil of a very high order. Moreover, a very large number of scientific and moral advances (including those of Copernicus and Darwin), and also the legitimization of homosexuality (and eventually, I hope, euthanasia), have been and are opposed by religious people. The official Catholic prohibition of contraception in an overpopulated world is absurd and would cause even more suffering than it does were it not usually ignored. Religious people have often shown a devotion and self-sacrifice which may well be impossible without the support of religious belief, but such beliefs strengthen attitudes which the believer supposes to be right, not necessarily the ones that are right. Too often this devotion has been lavished on trivial causes, such as abstruse points of theology, signing the cross one way rather than another, or not eating pork.

I sometimes have an ideal religious attitude that I both admire and envy. It includes, among other things, kindness; devotion to truth; a breadth of vision; serenity; detachment; and a sense of proportion concerning the littleness of oneself and one's own achievements, if any, compared with the enormity of the universe. Such an attitude may be possible to some people only if they believe themselves to be in contact with a being from whom they draw strength and perhaps also wisdom, provided they do not accept its apparent guidance too uncritically. Whether there is such a being is, of course, another matter.

Part V: Being Good Involves Being the Dupe of Someone Else

The view that moral beliefs are produced by strong people in their own interest may be divided as follows:

1. It could be held that people's moral beliefs are *delusions* produced by the strong. This view has two subclasses.

1a. There is the view that there is a truth about morals to be had, but that the strong have prevented us, in their own interest, from seeing what it is. Thrasymachus would think this if his view was that the rulers have deluded people into believing that it is right for us to act on a set of rules that are in fact conducive to the interest of the *strong*, whereas the truth is that the only thing that is right is for people to act in their *own* interest.

1b. It could be held that all moral beliefs are delusions and that although the strong have deceived us into thinking that it is right for us to perform acts which in fact benefit them, any other moral belief would be equally false (although perhaps not equally conducive to the interest of the strong).

2. It could be held that the moral beliefs which have been produced by the strong in their own interest are not delusions but *true* beliefs. Thrasymachus's view would fall into this category if he thought that justice consisted in obeying the law. From this view, it is *true* that it is right or just to do those things which the law enjoins, even though the law is made by the strong in their own interest. This is because "just" means simply "enjoined by the law."

There is no reason to suppose, incidentally, that the tendency in others to make rules in their own interest is necessarily a conscious one. The strong will naturally be inclined to think that what is in their interest is ordained by God.

It does not have to be held that moral beliefs are delusions produced by the strong. It could be held that moral beliefs are delusions produced by everybody in order to restrain everybody else, or by the weak in order to restrain the strong.

Part VI: Moral Beliefs: The Irrational Products of Evolution

A very interesting and comparatively recent challenge to morality comes from the new discipline of sociobiology. Sociobiology applies evolutionary theory to human social behavior. We are all familiar with the fact that giraffes got long necks because, since a long neck was advantageous to giraffes—they help them reach the parts that other giraffes cannot reach—giraffes with long necks were more likely than giraffes with short ones to reach maturity and so pass on their necks to their offspring. (These offspring then pass on to their offspring even longer necks.)

However, evolutionary theory can explain not only the physical features of living organisms, including human beings, but also many aspects of their behavior. Mother partridges, for example, fly noisily away from their nests when disturbed, which distracts the attention of predators from their chicks. This behavioral pattern has survived and been handed down from one generation to the next, because it is advantageous to partridges; the chicks of the partridges who stayed and guarded their nests, or slunk quietly away, did not survive.

Perhaps people are not much different from partridges in this respect. Mothers do not ponder the immorality of eating their own babies, and, if they did, would be unable to prove by the light of pure reason that eating their own babies was immoral. They grow up with a totally irrational feeling of horror at the idea of eating even babies they do not particularly like. This feeling has been favored by natural selection because mothers who had it have been more likely to rear their offspring to maturity, and so pass the feeling on to their grandchildren and great grandchildren, than mothers without it. Perhaps a woman's moral horror at the idea of eating her children can be explained, rather than justified, by its facilitating the survival of the human species. But if

our having the belief that eating babies is wrong cannot be justified —
and I have spent a large part of my working life trying to justify such
beliefs, without success — is it not irrational not to eat them when we
are sufficiently hungry and can eat them without being detected, especially when they are interfering seriously with our sleep? Wondering
why one does not meet anyone prepared to maintain that it is rational
to eat one's children would be like wondering why, if nicotine is so
dangerous, one does not come across anyone who admits to having died
of smoking it.

The doubt cast by sociobiology on the rationality of ethics cannot be
answered by a comfortable appeal to the distinction between causes
and reasons. The causes of a belief, it is sometimes said, are one thing;
the reasons for it another. The fact that a belief has causes does not
entail that it does *not* have *reasons*. Hence the fact that sociobiologists
can name the causes of the prevalence of our moral beliefs does not
show that these beliefs are irrational. However, although it is true that
if people had electrodes planted in their brains intended to cause them
to kill those who did not believe that Mrs. Thatcher was God, this
would not show that Mrs. Thatcher was *not* God; it would entail that if
she was, the truth of the prevalent belief in her divinity would be pure
coincidence. (However, that there were not many people around who
did not believe that Mrs. Thatcher was not God might then be because
there were not many people around.)

The theory that humankind has the moral beliefs it does, not because
it sees the reasons for having them, but because the alternatives have
not survived, is, although as old as Darwin, quite different from some
old-fashioned evolutionary theories. Such theories deduced moral conclusions about the way people *ought* to behave from supposed facts
about evolutionary biology. They often claimed such things as that we
should not limit competition between individuals, since it was by means
of a struggle for existence that human beings had become the godlike
creatures they were. Some believers thought that evolutionary biology
would justify a program of rational eugenics. Some even thought, most
implausibly, that words like "right" and "wrong" could be defined as
meaning "conforming to the direction of evolution."

It was usual, too, for evolutionary theorists to regard the evolutionary process, which they seemed to think (prematurely, if only because
homo sapiens is not an endangered species) had culminated in human
beings, as one of progress. But although that humans are descended
from apes is a judgment of fact, that they have *ascended* from apes is a
judgment of value, and it may well be that apes would think differently.
If one considers how much harm humans, the dirtiest of the animals, do
to the other animals who have the misfortune to share the world with
them than do apes, one may think they have reason. And it can be
argued that there is an inevitable illusion of progress. For when we look

back, from whatever point evolution takes us, it must seem to us that we have progressed.

The evolutionary theories of sociobiology are not moral theories at all, but explanations of how it happens that we have our moral beliefs and attitudes. A good sociobiologist, indeed, should think that he or she could have predicted that human beings would not hold evolutionary moral theories, for it would not be conducive to the survival of humankind for people to believe that the only thing that was right was to further the survival of mankind. (Such a belief would be much too complicated to be practicable, for one thing.) What people need in order to survive is to have beliefs condemning incest, aggression against fellow members of the same group, promise breaking, laziness, lack of altruism, cowardice, neglect of offspring, lack of leadership in leaders, disobedience in those led, failure to cooperate in necessary enterprises, and so on. There is no need for those who have them to *know* that these beliefs are conducive to the survival of humankind, even though they are.

There is a way, however (which sociobiologists sometimes overlook), in which the fact that we do *not* have certain moral dispositions, because they have been weeded out by natural selection, does not explain how it comes about that we have the ones we *do*. The fact that there are no cars on the roads without license plates, which is partly explained by cars without license plates being eliminated by the police, does not mean that the *presence* of license plates on cars must not also be explained, presumably by reference to manufacturers making them, car dealers fastening them on cars, and criminals replacing them by false ones, and by facts such as that metal nameplates retain their shape over long periods of time — longer than cars, at any rate. Similarly, the fact that we do not have certain items in our moral code because members of the species *homo sapiens* that did *not* have them did not survive does not mean that the process of our coming to *have* the moral codes we do have does not need explanation.

There are two major explanations of this (which may and probably ought to be combined). One theory is that there are certain congenital moral beliefs (or innate moral ideas). Just as baby deer have the (true) congenital belief, which they did not have to learn from experience, that a shadow resembling a hawk signifies danger, so humans are born with a congenital tendency to believe that having sexual intercourse with a near relative is wrong. Such a belief, it is said, is as much conducive to the survival of humans as the baby deer's belief is conducive to the survival of baby deer. Once upon a time there were societies whose members did not believe that copulating with a near relative was wrong, but these societies became unhealthy and did not survive.

The other theory is that our moral beliefs are inculcated rather than congenital (although our inherited natures may make us readier to accept some moral beliefs than others). What is inherited is a disposition to feel moral approval or guilt when subjected to certain kinds of pressure by our parents, teachers, or friends, for example. (Freud seems to exaggerate the extent we get guilt from our parents.) We disapprove of lying or eating pork or beans because this disapproval was inculcated by others. It was inculcated by people evincing, for a variety of different reasons, signs of disapprobation and disgust in our presence when we lied or ate pork. (The first reading by Mandeville [p. 190] is relevant here.) We *may* suppose that at some stage some people saw the disadvantages of lying or eating pork, and used the fact that humans had evolved as suitable subjects for the arousal and transmission of moral disapproval to cause them to disapprove of these things, without explaining why.

However, we need not suppose this, for it really does not matter *why* tribes believe that incest is wrong. They may believe that it is wrong because it is forbidden by the great god Shong. This belief is irrational, for there is no great god Shong, and it is unknown what he would or would not prohibit if he existed. But, since his supposed disapproval stops those who believe in him from committing incest, they will flourish while tribes with gods who do not condemn incest die out. Hence belief in Shong and his condemnation of incest will spread and may eventually cover the world. We congratulate ourselves that Jehovah is superior to Huitzilopachtli (the god of the Aztecs) because Jehovah did not approve of cannibalism, whereas Huitzilopachtli demanded it. Our congratulations may, however, be inappropriate, because the Jews, unlike the Aztecs, were not short of protein, which meant that to have a god who demanded cannibalism was of no biological advantage to them, whereas it was of advantage to the Aztecs. Indeed, the only reason the Aztecs' belief in human sacrifice has not conquered the world may be that not everyone is as short of protein as they were.

Other peoples may disapprove of incest because they think committing it weakens their hunters or is unlucky. But, whatever the reason for the disapproval, the tribes that have it will produce healthy offspring, or competition within the family for mates would lead to its breakup. Those that do not will, other things being equal, produce unhealthy offspring and have relatively harmonious families, although neither is in any way related to the content of their belief. It is not necessary, therefore, for the fact that people's moral codes are useful to them to be explained by any perception on the part of those people that their moral codes *are* useful to them. Even some quite distinguished moral philosophers seem blind to this fact.

These theories challenge morality because they produce what may be called "*evolutionary skepticism.*" Human beings no more need a rational appreciation of the advantages of morality in order to have it than birds need a rational appreciation of the advantages of having wings in order to fly. People do not disapprove of incest for the conscious reason that incest increases the probability of their producing deformed children or even for the reason that it would lead to the breakup of the family. Although these would be good reasons for disapproving of it, most people do not know it has these tendencies. They disapprove of incest simply because they have been born to develop such a belief on attaining a certain age, or with an innate tendency unreflectingly to copy other people's belief, produced for whatever reason, however trivial, that incest is wrong.

Hence people are the slaves of an irrational (or nonrational, because I do not condemn it) behavioral disposition which they had no hand in acquiring. They obey such rules as those proscribing incest and promise breaking and fight for their countries in time of war, because of something like programming. It is not as rigid a programming as that of bees, who at the cost of their own lives instinctively sting intruders to the hive without nature's having given them the option of behaving in any other way. Most humans are *able* to do something other than what they feel morally impelled to do but are constituted in such a way as to feel so unhappy if they do that they can allow themselves only relatively infrequent and minor lapses. Otherwise they will be made miserable by their consciences and fear of the censure of their fellows and will lose that degree of self-respect necessary for their mental health. Of course, people *are* prone to sin, but their proneness to sin can be understood only as a deviation from an endowment of original virtue that is one of the most valuable parts of their evolutionary inheritance.

According to this view, people owe their survival to nonrational moral dispositions which have been honed, by forces outside their control and over an enormously long period of time, to be conducive to their survival. It is a growth rather than an invention. Human beings no more invented morality than the leopard invented its spots, and that morality is no more rational than human prehensile fingers.

The nonrationality of moral behavior is also suggested by the fact that some of it (e.g., fighting for one's group or country against others) persists after the circumstances in which it evolved — living together in small communities and having only primitive weapons or none at all — have disappeared. One hopes that perception of the disadvantages of certain parts of our morality will cause people to set these parts aside and either turn morality against itself by rejecting its defective parts for moral reasons or, if this proves too difficult, ignore those parts. I suspect that these aforementioned parts of morality are so deeply ingrained that doing so will be enormously difficult.

Given, too, that there are things that it is rational for society to have done collectively, but that it is not rational for any individual member of society to do, a nonrational tendency to do them from *duty* would have enormous survival value. This is probably one biological reason that a sense of duty has developed in humankind.

It is true that the necessary behavior can be, and is, to some extent enforced. But it helps if people have evolved with moral sentiments approving enforcement and disapproving the prohibited actions, because these two sentiments must have survival value if enforcement does. Since enforcement is inefficient, feeling guilt when we deviate from an only partially enforced rule helps make us keep the rule. We feel the guilt even when we are unlikely to be found out.

Unfortunately, this device (morality) does not always work. It is in the interest of all nations that they all disarm, but not in the interest of any nation to disarm by itself. In this case, however, individual nations do *not* feel that it is their duty to disarm. We have not evolved as creatures who tend to feel that their own group should ever take an altruistic risk or make a significant sacrifice; quite the reverse, indeed, and with disastrous results. The solution I favor is to have a world government, having sufficient power to compel the performance of those actions which are in no individual nation's interest. Then the sense of duty *would* come to the aid of enforcement. The trouble with this solution is that the very tendency, nationalism, that world government would be designed to remedy prevents its establishment.

Part VII: Moral Beliefs Impossible to Justify

The most interesting challenges to morality that we have considered come from two views. The first, *ruler indoctrinationism*, holds that morality is created by the machinations of those who govern us. The second, *evolutionary skepticism*, holds that morality is created by natural selection.

It is, however, necessary to explain how a ruler or natural selection can create morality (i.e., make actions right or wrong when they were not so before). After all, neither a ruler nor natural selection can make it the case that the earth does not go around the sun, although a persevering ruler might try to persuade subjects to *believe* this if it was in his or her interest to do so.

Theories that explain how a ruler can make an action right are not hard to find:

1. *Naive subjectivism* holds that when we judge that an action is wrong, we are making the judgment that this kind of action or merely think about it arouses in us a personal *feeling* of moral disapprobation. Ruler indoctrinationists can adopt this theory, and then add that the reason we have the sentiments of disapproval we do (toward disobeying or overthrowing rulers, for example) is that our rulers have inculcated

these feelings into us in order to make us more loyal and more docile. In the absence of the activity of rulers, we would not approve of anything. Evolutionary skeptics can say that we have our present moral feelings because we have copied them from our parents with slight variations, and natural selection has bred out those members of the species *homo sapiens* who did not have the advantageous variations when they occurred.

2. According to *conventionalism*, to judge that something is wrong is to judge that human conventions prohibit it. (This view is sometimes known as *relativism*, as it is supposed that it makes "wrong" a relational term.) There are three main varieties of conventionalism.

(i) To say that an action is wrong is to say that it is contrary to the laws or conventions of the *agent's society* (a view that Thrasymachus might have held).

(ii) An action is wrong if it is contrary to the conventions of the society of the *person making the judgment* that it is wrong.

(iii) An action is wrong if it is contrary to the conventions of the *society in which the judged action is performed*.

These apparently similar theories lead to very different conclusions. According to *i*, cannibalism will be right because it agrees with the practices of the community of the cannibal (who is the agent). According to *ii*, cannibalism will be wrong if it does not agree with the practices of the community of the person making the judgment that it is wrong. (If this person is a British missionary, then he or she is saying that cannibalism is contrary to the rules that govern such matters in Great Britain.) With *iii* it will be right to eat people if eating people accords with the practices of the community in which the person performing the action is *residing*.

(Theory *i* is naturally favored by cannibals; theory *ii* by missionaries; theory *iii* will be favored by those wishing to escape from their own community to one whose morals are more congenial to them. For example, if *iii* is true, it would be legitimate for a dietetically adventurous missionary to practice cannibalism when living in a society which permitted it. (When in Rome, do as the Romans do.)

Only theory *i* has the difficulty constituted by the fact that the action and the rules that judge it might be incommensurable. To judge an action performed in one society by the rules of another might be like judging a move in chess by the rules of backgammon. The most commonly held and most plausible of these theories, *ii*, does not have that difficulty, for an agent's action must always be commensurate with the rules of his or her own society, just as a move in chess must always be commensurate with the rules of chess. According to theory *iii*, the actions of someone from another society trying to conform to the rules of the society in which he or she is living probably must always be commensurate with those rules — to the extent, anyway, that he or she gets those rules right.

All that ruler indoctrinationists need do, if they accept conventionalism, is to add that these conventions are brought about by rulers in the rulers' own interest, as many of these conventions obviously are. Evolutionary skeptics can say that conventions themselves have evolved because they are of biological advantage to the community that has them.

3. *Noncognitivism* holds that, strictly speaking, there are no such things as moral judgments. It seeks to bypass the problem of showing how we discover moral truth by saying that there is no such thing as moral truth to be discovered.

Noncognitivism arose historically because of its attraction to *logical positivists*. Logical positivists held that all meaningful sentences had to express either judgments that could be empirically verified (like the judgment that some wounds kill) or judgments that are tautological (like the judgment all *mortal* wounds kill). All the propositions of mathematics and logic were classified as being (disguised) tautologies. For example, the statement that $1 + 1 = 2$ was just a tautology, because "two" was defined as the number you got by adding one to one. More complicated judgments were held to be no different in principle. Scientific judgments were supposed to be known to be true by observing what is happening, or accepting or rejecting hypotheses by making experiments and observing the results. All other sentences were, strictly speaking, meaningless, although they might be poetic and moving.

This assertion had the *intended* consequence that all sentences about metaphysics and the deity became meaningless, because they fell neither into the category of tautologies nor into the category of empirically verifiable statements. The logical positivists view had, however, the *unintended* consequence that sentences expressing moral judgments also became meaningless. They, too, expressed neither tautologies nor empirically verifiable sentences. It did not seem that moral judgments could be empirically verified, for empirical verification tells only what the world is like (e.g., what people actually do approve of or what conventions they actually do have). It does not tell you what it ought to be like (e.g., what people ought to approve of or what conventions they ought to have).

But logical positivists thought they managed to avoid the extreme conclusion that ethical sentences were actually meaningless by saying that they did not express judgments at all. There is obviously a large class of sentences that do not express judgments. Judgments are by definition capable of being true or false; but "I name this ship the 'Margaret Thatcher,'" "Will no one rid me of this meddlesome priest?" "Oh to be in England, now that April's here," and "Give us this day our daily bread" are not capable of being either. They have some function other than that of stating truths or of saying that something is so or is the case.

The two main varieties of noncognitivism are *emotivism* and *imperativism*. According to emotivism, what we are doing when we seem to be making moral judgments is simply expressing feelings of approval. When we express our feelings (e.g., by saying "Alas, poor Yorick" or "Would that people were more honest than they are"), we are not saying anything that can be right or wrong, true or false. There is all the difference in the world between expressing one's approval and dispassionately stating the fact that one does feel approval.

Emotivism was once unkindly labeled the "Boo and Hurrah" theory. According to it, when we say that promise keeping is right or that killing people is wrong, we are not stating that either possesses a *characteristic* rightness or wrongness. If we were, what we said would be true if these actions did possess this characteristic and false if they did not. We are simply saying "Hurrah" for promise keeping or "Boo" to those who kill. We would also express such emotions (sincerely or otherwise) with a view to causing other people to share them.

Imperativism holds that moral sentences express imperatives or prescriptions. They can no more be true or false than can expressions of emotions. If I say that the door is shut, what I say is true if the door *is* shut and false if it is not. If I say "Shut the door," what I say cannot be true or false.

A ruler indoctrinationist could make use of emotivism or imperativism by holding some such thing as the reason we *have* the emotions that we *express* in moral language, or which cause us to issue imperatives forbidding people to perform the actions which arouse in us these feelings of disapprobation, is that these feelings have been inculcated into us by educators hired by the strong and the rich. An evolutionary skeptic could say that we have these emotions because our doing this has helped us to have a favorable attitude toward those actions the performance of which helps us to survive.

4. The *error theory* holds that *all* moral judgments are simply *false*. When we have moral sentiments, we falsely project these sentiments onto the action that produces them, much as when we think that the disgust that excrement arouses in us is somehow inherent in the excrement and essential to it. Hence, when we judge that an action is wrong, our judgment is mistaken. The sentiments lie in the spectator, and so we are wrong in ascribing them to the actions. Therefore, it is false that any actions are wrong (and also false that any are right).

All the theories we have outlined may threaten morality when combined with ruler indoctrinationism or evolutionary skepticism. If the deliverances of my conscience, or my approving of some things and disapproving of others, are only the result of indoctrination or the product of a blind process of random selection, why should I pay any attention to them? But there are reasons for thinking that all these theories threaten, or at least weaken, morality, even when *not* combined with either of these two beliefs.

In the case of naive subjectivism, there is no reason why we should regard judgments to the effect that we have certain feelings as a reason for performing the action which arouses them. Moral emotions, even our own, will be the feelings of fallible beings and the product of such things as a desire for conformity, ignorance, mistake, chance (if only because which society we happen to have been born into is a matter of chance), or what is happening to our brains. Because the state of our brains may be deliberately modified by taking drugs, we could in principle use drugs to cause ourselves to approve of adultery or murder before committing them, in which case, according to naive subjectivism, these things would become right.

Naive subjectivism must be rejected. The late A. C. Ewing has stated some of the most obvious objections to naive subjectivism with admirable clarity. "A number of incredibly paradoxical consequences," Ewing writes, "would follow from the adoption of this view. First, the judgments could not be false unless the person judging had made a mistake about his or her own psychology. Second, two different people would never mean the same thing when they made such a judgment, since each would mean 'This is approved by *me*.' Indeed, even the same person would not mean the same thing by it on two different occasions, because each time he or she would mean 'I *now* feel (or tend to feel) approval of this.' Third, if I judge something to be good and you judge it to be bad, our judgments would never be logically incompatible with each other."

There is a commonly held view to the effect that if we do something that we wrongly think to be right we *are* acting rightly, because it is right to follow even a misguided conscience. But what I think we think is that it is only *in a sense* right to do something we wrongly think is right. This must be a different sense of right from the sense in which what we thought was right was *not* right, to avoid the contradiction just mentioned. Philosophers have suggested that there is an objective and a subjective sense of "right", and that doing what is subjectively right is always doing what one thinks, mistakenly or otherwise, is objectively right. But this is an extreme view.

(2) *Conventionalism* also threatens morality, even when not combined with evolutionary skepticism or ruler indoctrination. The rules of one's society may demand that one send one's parents to the gas chamber, kill a casual acquaintance in a duel, burn to death someone who disagrees on an abstruse point of theology, or prohibit a marriage between a widower and his deceased wife's sister. Clearly it is necessary for society to have rules and for its members to obey them for the

most part, but if one were to suppose that *whatever* these rules enjoined was *necessarily* right, one might lead a very wicked kind of life.

Conventionalism, too, must be rejected. Whether imposed on us by rulers in their own interest or not, the rules are made by fallible and venal men and women and deserve little more reverence than the people who made them. As has already been suggested, there are some conventions which we would not have were it not for corruption, deception, ignorance, or mistake. The rules of one's society are the rules of one's society, not the laws of God.

For example, my society, if my position in it is sufficiently privileged, may expect me to kill and eat a virgin on the fourteenth day of every February, in order to make its members fertile (with the exception, of course, of the virgin I eat). If I believe that the medical opinions which give rise to this rule are erroneous, I am unlikely to regard it with great respect. I may then know that my society demands that I eat this unfortunate lady but think that cannibalism is wrong, which means that what I am thinking when I think that cannibalism is wrong cannot be that my society prohibits it; my society does not prohibit it.

Some philosophers and anthropologists think that it is an adequate reply to this difficulty to say that such rules are an integral and necessary part of the society which has them. There is some justice in what they say, but they are confused. It is true that missionaries trying to alter such rules may weaken the links which bind members of the society together, and (inadvertently) make them prey to demoralization by alcohol (as well, incidentally as to death from influenza). But this does not mean that the fact that it is my duty to eat people is just the fact that eating people is demanded by the conventions of my society. Nor does it mean that in complaining about the habit of eating people I am illegitimately judging actions performed in another's society by the conventions of my own. The reason it is sometimes right for me to eat virgins when the rules of my society demand it is not only that the rules demand it, but also that, given that they do demand it, the disruption caused if I were to disobey the rule ought to be avoided. Moreover, one would suppose that a visitor might not be too parochially wedded to the conventions of his or her own society if he or she were to explain tactfully to the natives that, in view of the shortage of virgins, there were cheaper and more reliable ways of increasing fertility than eating them, and that in any case, in view of overpopulation, increasing fertility might not be such a very good idea. (There are those who think they know that eating virgins is wrong, however bad the consequences, but a moderately good utilitarian like myself cannot share this opinion.)

(3) *Noncognitivism*, including *emotivism* and *imperativism*, also challenges morality, whether it is linked with ruler indoctrinationism or evolutionary skepticism or not. If there is no moral truth to be ob-

tained, then the whole object of moral thinking, which is to arrive at the correct (i.e., the true) answer to a moral question, is pointless. If there is no correct answer to moral questions, it does not matter morally what one does. (Strictly speaking, there would, according to this view, not even be, in the appropriate sense, any moral questions to answer.)

Emotivism and imperativism, however, must also be rejected. They must be rejected, for one thing, for the very reason that one of the things they both imply, which would challenge morality if it *were* true, is *not* true. They imply that there is no correct or incorrect answer to moral questions, and one intuitively feels that there *is*. For another thing, it makes sense to say of moral judgments, as it does of judgments of other sorts, some such thing as "Smith thinks that promises ought to be kept, and she is right, because promises *ought* to be kept." It does not make sense to say of an expression of emotion "Smith says 'Hurrah for marital fidelity,' and she is right, because hurrah for marital infidelity." Nor does it make sense to say of an imperative "Smith says 'Do not kill,' and she is right, because do not kill." Expressions of emotion and imperatives cannot be assessed as being right or wrong, because they do not assert anything for us to be right or wrong about.

Imperativism must be rejected for the further reason that the logic of imperatives fails to resemble the logic of moral judgments in a large number of different ways, of which it is possible here to give only a selection. If someone were to issue the imperative "Keep your promises," it would be linguistically appropriate to reply "I won't." It would not be appropriate to say "I won't" to someone who makes the moral judgment "It is your *duty* to keep your promises." The appropriate way of disagreeing with that person would be to say "It isn't." For another thing, it is quite sensible for a cat to say politely to a king, "It is wrong to overtax your subjects, your majesty." It is not sensible for the cat to *order* the king not to tax his subjects, as both the cat and the king know that the cat has neither the authority to issue nor the power to enforce such a command. It would be silly to order the whole human race not to kill, if only because they are not all within earshot. But it is not silly to say that every member of the human race *ought not* to kill. And, to repeat, it is possible to think that one may be mistaken in thinking that something is right, but it is not possible for an imperative to be mistaken.

Neither imperativism nor emotivism square with the fact that it is correct usage to speak of *knowing* or believing that certain things are right, or of the fact that moral judgments can occur as the antecedents of hypothetical propositions. Neither imperatives nor expressions of emotion can do either.

In addition, neither imperativism nor emotivism can give an account of the fact that imperatives have to be issued and emotions expressed out loud. It is, however, perfectly possible to think that something is wrong quietly to oneself, without *saying* anything at all, and so without issuing imperatives or expressing emotions. If all we were doing when we said that someone was wrong to visit South Africa was to express emotions unfavorable to the visit, it is difficult to see how we could be, or regard ourselves as perhaps being, mistaken about this. But according to imperativism and emotivism, there is no such characteristic as wrongness. When we say that an action is wrong, we are not, according to both imperativism and emotivism, saying that it has a characteristic of wrongness. We are only expressing the feeling that it arouses in us. Since we are not saying that it has a characteristic, there can be no possibility of our being mistaken in saying that it has it. Nor can there be any possibility of our being right. However, we all think that we can be mistaken when we think that something is wrong. Hence emotivism must be rejected.

One reason why we rejected emotivism and imperativism was that it was possible for moral judgments to be right or, on the other hand, wrong. There is nothing in this to say, however, that moral judgments are not *all wrong* (or false). This brings us to the error theory, according to which moral judgments *are* all wrong, because they hold that the characteristics we attempt to attribute to actions by making these moral judgments are bogus ones.

The error theory challenges morality because if, for example, it is false that I ought not to kill, then that I ought not to kill people cannot be a reason for *not* killing people. The only reason the error theory is not a very serious challenge to morality, indeed, is that people are sufficiently sensible not always to take the results of even their own philosophical reasoning seriously in practice. Moreover, nature, for reasons of evolutionary biology, has given most people no alternative than to behave quite well up to a point in normal circumstances, whatever academic doubts about the truth of moral judgments they may think they have. Mackie wants to maintain (because he holds an error theory) both that it is false, for example, that capital punishment is wrong, and at the same time (because he is an enlightened person) that capital punishment is wrong.

Of course, there are other theories. But this part ends by reemphasizing an argument stated earlier, which may show that *no* moral theory can satisfy our natural inclination to think that we have rational beliefs about what is morally right to do. David Hume ended the *Enquiry Concerning Human Understanding* by saying

> When we run over libraries, persuaded of these principles [the ones he adumbrated in *A Treatise of Human Nature*], what havoc must we make? If we take in our hand a volume; of divinity or school metaphysics, for instance; let us ask, Does it contain any abstract reasoning concerning quantity or number? No. Does it contain any experimental reasoning concerning matter of fact and existence? No. Commit it then to the flames, for it can contain nothing but sophistry and illusion.

This piece of advice (which I believe to be roughly sound), together with the added premises that moral judgments can be established neither by experimental reasoning nor by abstract reasoning (showing that to deny them would involve asserting a logical contradiction), leads to the conclusion that books on ethics ought to be confined to the flames.

It has been held that moral judgments *can* be rational, although they can be put into neither of Hume's categories (propositions established by experimental reasoning and propositions established by abstract reasoning). This attempt is called *intuitionism*, the view that we have a rational faculty for seeing a priori (i.e., without experimental reasoning) that certain moral truths must be so, although there is *no* logical contradiction involved in denying them. Although intuitionism accords more closely with the deliverances of the ordinary moral consciousness than any other theory, it is not credible that there should be a faculty of moral intuition. It is true that nature has given us no choice but to moralize, and morality, however irrational, does more good than harm. One sometimes feels, however, that the writing of long books on this somewhat problematic subject ought to be discouraged. Books on the second-order question of how we solve moral problems are permitted by Hume's principles but have been singularly unsuccessful.

SUMMARY

The following is a summary of the results of the previous parts.

1. Ethical hedonism is not a very fundamental challenge to morality, because it is itself a moral belief. It must be rejected because one reason for having moral rules (or the reason for their having evolved) is to *stop* people from seeking their own interest. For example, it is in each person's interest to break promises when he or she can get away with it. Each does him- or herself some good, and without the cooperation of others he or she can do the institution of promise keeping, which everybody needs, little or no harm. But if all people broke promises when they could get away with it, promises would be less heeded or not heeded at all, and an essential institution would be lost to everybody, including the promise-breakers. Hence all people's keeping their promises out of duty when it is not in their interest to keep them will achieve, even for those who from duty *sacrifice* their interest, something that self-interest cannot achieve. A large number of breaches of rules, in which each individual breach does the person who breaks it some good, in fact do the community (and so indirectly the individual rule breaker) harm.

Similarly, one straw does the camel no harm, but a large number of straws breaks its back. It is to misrepresent the situation to say that it is the *last* straw that breaks the camel's back. However overburdened the camel is, the addition of just one more straw never by itself does the camel any harm.

2. Psychological egoism challenges the factual belief that human beings are capable of unselfish or dutiful action and the moral beliefs (e.g., that some people are better than others) presupposed by this belief. But a hard-headed application of evolutionary biology would lead one to expect people to have desires that aimed at and/or produced the welfare of others. One way of almost everybody's having something they need but cannot get for themselves is for people to have evolved with a desire to get it for others. (That birds can pick ticks off the heads of other birds is a good illustration [p. 231].) The person performing the altruistic act in question may lose by that individual act, but he or she will usually (although not necessarily always) gain by other people's performing similar acts. Human beings collectively gain more than they lose by altruism, or altruism would not have survived.

People have evolved so that it is good for individual men and women that they satisfy desires that are not aimed at their own good. For example, a mother's satisfying her desire for the welfare of her children will usually be conducive to her own welfare. It is unwise to go against one's congenital nature beyond a certain point. (Because one has evolved to be a moral animal, it is also unwise to go too much against one's moral nature, however irrational one may suppose one's moral nature to be.)

Adam Smith thought that providence had made human beings so that one person's seeking his or her own interest automatically brought about the good of everybody. This is an exaggeration, but to the not inconsiderable extent to which it is true, there is a good biological explanation of the fact.

3. Having freedom of will, in the sense that people perform actions they want to do, is the way in which humans have evolved to meet a certain kind of need. There would be no point in an animal having evolved with the capacity to think rationally (which is not the same as acting rationally), if they did not have the capacity to put their rational conclusions into practice. We can conceive (as did Kant) of a race of people who, like ants, do by instinct what humans do freely and deliberately. This would have advantages and disadvantages. The advantage is that instinct is more reliable than freedom of choice as a way of producing the desired action. The disadvantage is that instinct is less flexible. Creatures governed by instinct will go through their routines in response to the stimulus that triggers them, like moths instinctively flying into a candle flame, however inappropriate the circumstances.

Because human beings have free will, they need a sense of duty to make them do the things that instinct or inclination does not make them do. A worker bee stings intruders to the hive instinctively, although it loses its life as a result. A person, on the other hand, has to be born with, or with the disposition to acquire, a love of honor or duty to make him or her do the same thing. Duty does not always work, but it has an advantage that instinct would not have, which is that people, not being as much as the slave of duty as bees are of instinct, can sometimes, although not always, see when their sense of duty is leading them to their (collective) destruction and *not* do what they feel to be their duty. It is a disadvantage of very rigid moralizing that it deprives people of this means of escape. The story, doubtless apocryphal, of the soldiers who marched over a precipice because no one gave them the order to halt is illustrative.

Hence it cannot be denied that the sense of duty has a disadvantage similar to that of instinct, although less acute. Humans fight because this is demanded by an outmoded morality that grew up to protect small groups of unarmed or ill-armed hunter-gatherers. Some of our moralists refuse to sanction the killing of those dying in agony because they cannot see that a rule that has evolved for a useful purpose does not apply when the rule is not useful. Some philosophers have, indeed, like moths who would argue that it was their duty to fly into the candle flame, simply failed to transcend their conditioning when they think that we have duties which demand actions in circumstances in which their performance does much harm.

4. Because people need morality for various human purposes, they will need it whether there is a God or not. It is possible, however, that the belief, whether true or not, that there is a God who rewards the good and punishes the wicked has some tendency to survive in those communities that have it because it gives their members support, binds them into a firmer unity, and makes them more likely to observe their community's rules. (It does not follow from this that belief in God is true).

5. The view that moral beliefs have been inculcated in us by the strong in their own interest is not very convincing. I think it *is* in the interest of our rulers (the strong) that their subjects observe their community's moral code and that the strong *do* in fact try to indoctrinate their subjects in this code. But to say that the code is in the interest of the strong only is to forget that many, perhaps most, moral rules are in almost everyone's interest, although perhaps more in the interest of the strong than of the weak. There are some moral rules — those protecting property and enforcing a hierarchy — that are more in the interest of the strong and rich than others, as there are some that are more in the interest of the weak.

We are all, consciously or otherwise, inclined to use moral weapons to get others to do what is in our interest or in the interests of our friends and allies. Rulers are better than most people at doing this, which is one reason they succeeded in becoming rulers.

That our moral rules favor the strong is not by itself a very good reason for ignoring or trying to overthrow one's rulers, unless they prey on the ruled beyond the point where obedience has even worse consequences than rebellion. Society does need rulers, despite the fact that acquiring an excessive love of power is an occupational disease of ruling.

6. The view that moral beliefs are the irrational products of selection must also be suspect. (I have no doubt that our moral beliefs are the product of natural selection, but they are not all its *irrational* products, although some of them are.) Moral codes have survived by enabling their possessors to survive, but it is a point in their favor that they have enabled us to survive, not a point against them. Many of our moral beliefs are certainly irrational and are prevalent because the communities having rival moral beliefs have perished or dispersed, not because we see the reasons for having these beliefs. But it is difficult to believe that some people have not seen the advantages of enforcing certain ways of behaving (not eating pork in hot countries, for example) and encouraging the beliefs that such ways of behaving were right, in order to further the welfare of their communities, which habit would itself have a survival value.

There is a self-correcting tendency in our moral beliefs, in that the very circumstances that, perhaps irrationally, produce them also tend to make having them useful and therefore right. For example, if one supposes that shortage of protein among the Aztecs was the cause of their having institutions demanding cannibalism, cannibalism was, in those circumstances, useful, and one could argue that it was right in consequence. Indeed, if protein were absolutely essential to the human race and could be obtained only by cannibalism, all humans would have evolved with a moral code permitting it, if they had evolved at all, and cannibalism would then *be* right. If protein could be obtained only from meat, there would not be many vegetarians, partly because if there were any vegetarians, they would be dead ones, and partly because if there were any vegetarians, it should in those circumstances be possible to persuade them of the imprudence of vegetarianism.

Bishop Butler thought that virtue accorded with human nature. But whereas Butler thought that certain dispositions accorded with our natures because we had been created that way by God, it is more likely that certain things accord with our natures because of natural selection. It is possible to combine the two hypotheses and hold that God made us as we are by *means* of natural selection; but that makes the second hypothesis, that there is a God, redundant.

7. I myself do not know what the academic justification of moral beliefs is. The strength of every epistemological theory about their justification seems to lie mainly in the weakness of its alternatives. Moral beliefs resemble neither factual statements about the world nor the truths of mathematics and logic. They do not seem to fit into any known pigeon hole of justification. It is fortunate that it is more important that they should be strong than that they should be rational. In this respect they are like our belief that the future will resemble the past, the truth of which is necessary to the success of all our enterprises. Philosophers have been trying for centuries to justify this belief without any great success. Faith in morality, like faith in induction, may be an irrational tendency that humans need.

But if one turns one's attention from the academic problem of justifying moral *beliefs* to that of finding reasons for having moral *rules*, it is not difficult to justify morality—up to a point, at any rate. We have morality because we need it. Having its members keep their promises; pay their debts; bring up their children; cooperate with one another; be honest, kind, moderately nonaggressive, truthful, and reliable are qualities that for rather obvious reasons benefit a community. They get the community what it wants or needs. Hence there are reasons for a community to reinforce these practices, and the belief that they are obligations or duties does reinforce them.

PART I

THE IMPOSSIBILITY OF ALTRUISM

1

FRANÇOIS, DUC DE LA ROCHEFOUCAULD

The Disguised Selfishness of Man

Introduction

François, Duc de la Rochefoucauld (1613–1680), was a daring soldier and politician, as well as a prominent literary figure. He was both sent to the Bastille and exiled and seriously wounded during the Fronde, the civil war that took place in France from 1648–1652. He became a leading figure in salon society in Paris. He had, surprisingly, no fewer than seven children.

The remarks included in this reading are not primarily philosophical. They record the results of acute observation of human nature and of sensitive introspection. As a result, La Rochefoucauld comes to roughly the same conclusions that many philosophers have reached on a priori grounds, but one difference is all important. That people are in fact very selfish and delude themselves into thinking that they are more altruistic than they are is for the most part true, although perhaps truer of La Rochefoucauld's contemporaries than of some other societies. That they are *necessarily* selfish and can be known to be selfish without the need for examining their behavior can be the result only of the kind of confusion discussed in the Introduction. It could be that La Rochefoucauld expects too much of human nature. (Bishop Butler thought that it was a good thing that human beings were actuated by self-love, which is not the same thing as selfishness. Butler thought that stronger self-love would prevent all or almost all wrongdoing, for wrongdoing is as much contrary to the interest of the wrongdoer as to that of the persons who are wronged. After all, we call behavior *selfish* if it is *contrary* to the interests of others, rather than because it is in our own interest.)

Reading

Self-love is more artful than the most artful man in the world.

· · · · ·

The clemency of princes is often only a stroke of policy to gain the affections of their people.

· · · · ·

We have all of us sufficient fortitude to bear the misfortunes of others.

· · · · ·

Pride has a greater share than goodness of heart in the remonstrances we make to those who are guilty of faults; we reprove not so much with a view to correct them as to persuade them that we are exempt from those faults ourselves.

· · · · ·

The contempt of riches among the philosophers was a hidden desire to revenge their merit for the injustice of fortune, by contempt of the very advantages of which she deprived them. It was a secret to secure themselves from the degradation of poverty: it was a by-road to arrive at that consideration which they could not obtain by riches.

· · · · ·

Sincerity is an opening of the heart: we find it in very few people; and that which we generally see is nothing but a subtle dissimulation to attract the confidence of others.

Aversion to lying is often an imperceptible desire to render our testimony important, and to give a religious respect to our words.

· · · · ·

Love of justice in the generality of men is only the fear of suffering from injustice.

· · · · ·

We can love nothing except with reference to ourselves; and we are merely following our own taste and pleasure when we prefer our friends to ourselves. It is, neverthe-

From *Maxims* By François, Duc De La Rochefoucauld. Arthur Humphreys, 1911.

less, by this preference alone that friendship can be true and perfect.

· · · · ·

What men have given the name of friendship to is nothing but an alliance, a reciprocal accommodation of interests, an exchange of good offices; in fact, it is nothing but a system of traffic, in which self-love always proposes to itself some advantage.

· · · · ·

We are so much accustomed to disguise ourselves to others, that at length we disguise ourselves to ourselves.

· · · · ·

We often do good, in order that we may do evil with impunity.

· · · · ·

The cleverest men affect all their lives to censure all artifice, in order that they may make use of it themselves on some great occasion, and for some great interest.

· · · · ·

We are not fond of praising, and never praise any one except from interested motives. Praise is a clever, concealed, and delicate flattery, which gratifies in different ways the giver and the receiver. The one takes it as a recompense of his merit, and the other bestows it to display his equity and discernment.

· · · · ·

Our repentance is not so much regret for the evil we have done, as fear of its consequences to us.

· · · · ·

Love of glory, fear of shame, the design of making a fortune, the desire of rendering our lives easy and agreeable, and the envious wish to lowering the fame of others are often the causes of that valour so celebrated among men.

· · · · ·

Perfect valour is to do unwitnessed what we should be capable of doing before all the world.

· · · · ·

Vanity, shame, and above all temperament, are often the causes of courage in men, and of virtue in women.

· · · · ·

It may seem that self-love is the dupe of good-nature, and that it forgets itself whenever we are labouring for the advantage of others. Nevertheless, it is taking the surest road to reach our objects; it is lending on usury under pretence of giving; it is in fact gaining over every one by a subtle and delicate method.

· · · · ·

What appears to be generosity is often nothing but a disguised ambition, which despises petty interests in order to reach greater ones.

The fidelity shown by the generality of men is only an invention of self-love to attract confidence — it is a means of raising ourselves above others, and of becoming depositaries of the most important affairs.

· · · · ·

Humility is often only a feigned submission, of which we make use to render others submissive. It is an artifice of pride which abases in order to exalt itself; and though it transforms itself in a thousand different ways, it is never better disguised and more capable of deceiving than when it conceals itself under the garb of humility.

· · · · ·

Civility is a desire to receive it in turn, and to be accounted well bred.

What is called liberality is most often only the vanity of giving, which we like better than the thing we give.

Pity is often a perception of our own misfortunes in those of others; it is a clever foresight of the evils into which we may fall. We succour others in order to engage them to succour us in similar circumstances; and the services we render them are, to speak properly, a good which we do to ourselves by anticipation.

2

JOSEPH BUTLER

Men Made for One Another

Introduction

Joseph Butler (1692–1752) was Bishop first of Bristol and then of Durham. He is, as one might expect, the author of numerous sermons that are incomparably better than most and of *The Analogy of Religion*, one of the most important books on the philosophy of religion ever written.

No comment will be made on the arguments Butler uses here. They are used as a basis of the Introduction, and Butler's refutation of *psychological hedonism* has never been improved on.

Butler points out, correctly, that human beings are mentally, as well as physically, adapted for certain ends. He thought that humans had the following "mental parts": (a) the particular passions (i.e., desires for particular things like food, shelter, clothing, sex, power, affection, approval, the welfare of one's children or friends, or even a large collection of postage stamps); (b) benevolence, which was a desire for the happiness of people in general; (c) self-love, which was a desire for one's own overall happiness; and (d) conscience, which both told one what one ought to do and provided one with an impulse to do it, and presided over the other parts of human nature.

Butler thought that satisfying the particular passions—hunger or parental affection, for example—tended both to the good of their owners and to the good of others. He thought that one's own happiness and that of others coincided. Hence benevolence in fact prompted one to perform actions which brought about one's own good, and self-love to perform actions which were for the good of others, even though this was not the *object* of either. Human conscience pointed one in the same direction as the other parts of human nature, for it disapproved both of conduct that was imprudent (lacking in self-love) and of conduct that was egoistical (lacking in benevolence).

Butler thought that people were this way because they had been created by a God who was concerned with their welfare. A modern biologist
might think that human beings had grown up over a long period of time
to be as they were because people whose natures approximated Butler's
ideal constitution were more likely to survive and have offspring than
others. People whose particular passions were (a) not dovetailed with one
another and the particular passions of others, (b) which frequently
prompted them to actions that resulted in their destruction, (c) who were
insufficiently benevolent to promote the welfare of others on whose
survival they themselves depended, (d) who were insufficiently prudent
not to take dangerous risks, or (e) whose consciences impelled them to
absurd acts of antisocial fanaticism or self-sacrifice, would tend to be
weeded out by natural selection. We approve of the result of natural
selection, but perhaps this is because natural selection would have eliminated our ancestors had they not felt approval of the result, and they have
handed on their feelings to us.

Reading

THE RELATION WHICH the several parts or members of the natural body
have to each other and to the whole body, is here compared to the
relation which each particular person in society has to other particular
persons and to the whole society; and the latter is intended to be
illustrated by the former. And if there be a likeness between these two
relations, the consequence is obvious: that the latter shews us we were
intended to do good to others, as the former shews us that the several
members of the natural body were intended to be instruments of good
to each other and to the whole body. But as there is scarce any ground
for a comparison between society and the mere material body, this
without the mind being a dead unactive thing; much less can the
comparison be carried to any length. And since the apostle speaks of
the several members as having distinct offices, which implies the mind;
it cannot be thought an unallowable liberty; instead of the *body* and *its
members*, to substitute the *whole nature of man*, and *all the variety of
internal principles which belong to it*. And then the comparison will be
between the nature of man as respecting self, and tending to private
good, his own preservation and happiness; and the nature of man as
having respect to society, and tending to promote public good, the
happiness of that society. These ends do indeed perfectly coincide; and
to aim at public and private good are so far from being inconsistent,
that they mutually promote each other: yet in the following discourse
they must be considered as entirely distinct; otherwise the nature of
man as tending to one, or as tending to the other cannot be compared.

From *Fifteen Sermons Upon Human Nature, or Man Considered As a Moral Agent.*
Sermon I, "On the Social Nature of Man," Ed. W. E. Gladstone. Oxford University Press,
1887.

There can no comparison be made, without considering the things compared as distinct and different.

From this review and comparison of the nature of man as respecting self, and as respecting society, it will plainly appear, that *there are as real and the same kind of indications in human nature, that we were made for society and to do good to our fellow-creatures; as that we were intended to take care of our own life and health and private good: and that the same objections lie against one of these assertions, as against the other.* For,

First, there is a natural principle of *benevolence* in man; which is in some degree to *society*, what *self-love* is to the *individual*. And if there be in mankind any disposition to friendship; if there be any such thing as compassion, for compassion is momentary love; if there be any such thing as the paternal or filial affections; if there be any affection in human nature, the object and end of which is the good of another, this is itself benevolence, or the love of another. Be it ever so short, be it in ever so low a degree, or ever so unhappily confined; it proves the assertion, and points out what we were designed for, as really as though it were in a higher degree and more extensive. I must, however, remind you that though benevolence and self-love are different; though the former tends most directly to public good, and the latter to private: yet they are so perfectly coincident that the greatest satisfactions to ourselves depend upon our having benevolence in a due degree; and that self-love is one chief security of our right behaviour towards society. It may be added, that their mutual coinciding, so that we can scarce promote one without the other, is equally a proof that we were made for both.

Secondly, This will further appear, from observing that the *several passions* and *affections*, which are distinct both from benevolence and self-love, do in general contribute and lead us to *public* good as really as to *private*. It might be thought too minute and particular, and would carry us too great a length, to distinguish between and compare together the several passions or appetites distinct from benevolence, whose primary use and intention is the security and good of society; and the passions distinct from self-love, whose primary intention and design is the security and good of the individual. It is enough to the present argument, that desire of esteem from others, contempt and esteem of them, love of society as distinct from affection to the good of it, indignation against successful vice, that these are public affections or passions; have an immediate respect to others, naturally lead us to regulate our behaviour in such a manner as will be of service to our fellow creatures. If any or all of these may be considered likewise as private affections, as tending to private good; this does not hinder them from being public affections too, or destroy the good influence of them upon society, and their tendency to public good. It may be added, that as persons without any conviction from reason of the desirableness of life, would yet of course preserve it merely from the appetite of hunger; so by acting merely from regard (suppose) to reputation, without any consideration of the good of others, men often contribute to public good. In both these instances they are plainly instruments in the hands of another, in the hands of Providence, to carry on ends, the preservation of the individual and good of society, which they themselves have not in their view or intention. The sum is, men have various appetites, passions, and particular affections, quite distinct both from self-love and from benevolence: all of these have a tendency to promote both public and private good, and may be considered as respecting others and ourselves equally and in common: but some of them seem most immediately to respect others, or tend to public good; others of them most immediately to respect self, or tend to private good: as the former are not benevolence, so the latter are not self-love: neither sort are instances of our love either to ourselves or others; but only instances of our Maker's care and love both of the individual and the species, and proofs that he intended we should be instruments of good to each other, as well as that we should be so to ourselves.

Thirdly, There is a principle of reflection in men, by which they distinguish between, approve and disapprove their own actions. We are plainly constituted such sort of creatures as to reflect upon our own nature. The mind can take a view of what passes within itself, its propensions, aversions, passions, affections, as respecting such objects, and in such degrees; and of the several actions consequent thereupon. In this survey it approves of one, disapproves of another, and towards a third is affected in neither of these ways, but is quite indifferent. This principle in man, by which he approves or disapproves his heart, temper, and actions, is conscience; for this is the strict sense of the word, though sometimes it is used so as to take in more. And that this faculty tends to restrain men from doing mischief to each other, and leads them to do good, is too manifest to need being insisted upon. Thus a parent has the affection of love to his children: this leads him to take care of, to educate, to make due provision for them; the natural affection leads to this: but the reflection that it is his proper business, what belongs to him, that it is right and commendable so to do; this added to the affection becomes a much more settled principle, and carries him on through more labour and difficulties for the sake of his children, than he would undergo from that affection alone, if he thought it, and the course of action it led to, either indifferent or criminal. This indeed is impossible, to do that which is good and not to approve of it; for which reason they are frequently not considered as distinct, though they really are: for men often approve of the actions of others, which they will not imitate, and likewise do that which they approve not. It cannot possibly be denied, that there is this principle of reflection or conscience in human nature. Suppose a man to relieve an innocent person in great distress; suppose the same man afterwards, in the fury of anger, to do the greatest mischief to a person who had given no just cause of offence; to aggravate the injury, add the circumstances of former friendship, and obligation from the injured person; let the man who is supposed to have done these two different actions, coolly reflect upon them afterwards, without regard to their consequences to himself: to assert that any common man would be affected in the same way towards these different actions, that he would make no distinction between them, but approve or disapprove them equally, is too glaring a falsity to need being confuted. There is therefore this principle of reflection or conscience in mankind. It is needless to compare the respect it has to private good, with the respect it has to public; since it plainly tends as much to the latter as to the former, and is commonly thought to tend chiefly to the latter. This faculty is now mentioned merely as another part in the inward frame of man, pointing out to us in some degree what we are intended for, and as what will naturally and of course have some influence. The particular place assigned to it by nature, what authority it has, and how great influence it ought to have, shall be hereafter considered.

From this comparison of benevolence and self-love, of our public and private affections, of the courses of life they lead to, and of the principle of reflection or conscience as respecting each of them, it is as manifest, that *we were made for society, and to promote the happiness of it; as that we were intended to take care of our own life, and health, and private good*.

And from this whole review must be given a different draught of human nature from what we are often presented with. Mankind are by nature so closely united, there is such a correspondence between the inward sensations of one man and those of another, that disgrace is as much avoided as bodily pain, and to be the object of esteem and love as much desired as any external goods: and in many particular cases persons are carried on to do good to others, as the end their affection tends to and rests in; and manifest that they find real satisfaction and enjoyment in this course of behaviour. There is such a natural principle of attraction in man towards man, that having trod the same tract of land, having breathed in the same climate, barely having been born in the same artificial district or division, becomes the occasion of contracting acquaintances and familiarities many years after: for any thing may serve the purpose. Thus relations merely nominal are sought and invented, not by governors, but by the lowest of the people; which are found sufficient to hold mankind together in little fraternities and copartnerships: weak ties indeed, and what may afford fund enough for ridicule, if they are absurdly considered as the real principles of that union: but they are in truth merely the occasions, as any thing may be of any thing, upon which our nature carries us on according to its own previous bent and bias; which occasions therefore would be nothing at all, were there not this prior disposition and bias of nature. Men are so much one body, that in a peculiar manner they feel for each other, shame, sudden danger, resentment, honour, prosperity, distress; one or another, or all of these, from the social nature in general, from benevolence, upon the occasion of natural relation, acquaintance, protection, dependence; each of these being distinct cements of society. And therefore to have no restraint from, no regard to others in our behaviour, is the speculative absurdity of considering ourselves as single and independent, as having nothing in our nature which has respect to our fellow-creatures, reduced to action and practice. And this is the same absurdity, as to suppose a hand, or any part to have no natural respect to any other, or to the whole body.

But allowing all this, it may be asked, "Has not man dispositions and principles within, which lead him to do evil to others, as well as to do good? Whence come the many miseries else, which men are the authors and instruments of to each other?" These questions, so far as they relate to the foregoing discourse, may be answered by asking, Has not man also dispositions and principles within, which lead him to do evil to himself, as well as good? Whence come the many miseries else, sickness, pain, and death, which men are instruments and authors of to themselves?

It may be thought more easy to answer one of these questions than the other, but the answer to both is really the same; that mankind have ungoverned passions which they will gratify at any rate, as well to the injury of others, as in contradiction to known private interest: but that as there is no such thing as self-hatred, so neither is there any such thing as ill-will in one man towards another, emulation and resentment being away; whereas there is plainly benevolence or good-will: there is no such thing as love of injustice, oppression, treachery, ingratitude; but only eager desires after such and such external goods; which, according to a very ancient observation, the most abandoned would choose to obtain by innocent means if they were as easy, and as effectual to their end: that even emulation and resentment, by any one who will consider what these passions really are in nature, will be found nothing to the purpose of this objection: and that the principles and passions in the mind of man, which are distinct both from self-love and benevolence, primarily and most directly lead to right behaviour with regard to others as well as himself, and only secondarily and accidentally to what is evil. Thus, though men, to avoid the shame of one villany, are sometimes guilty of a greater, yet it is easy to see, that the original tendency of shame is to prevent the doing of shameful actions;

and its leading men to conceal such actions when done, is only in consequence of their being done; i.e. of the passion's not having answered its first end.

If it be said, that there are persons in the world, who are in great measure without the natural affections towards their fellow-creatures: there are likewise instances of persons without the common natural affections to themselves: but the nature of man is not to be judged of by either of these, but by what appears in the common world, in the bulk of mankind.

I am afraid it would be thought very strange, if to confirm the truth of this account of human nature, and make out the justness of the foregoing comparison, it should be added, that, from what appears, men in fact as much and as often contradict that *part* of their nature which respects *self*, and which leads them to their *own private* good and happiness; as they contradict that *part* of it which respects *society*, and tends to *public* good: that there are as few persons, who attain the greatest satisfaction and enjoyment which they might attain in the present world; as who do the greatest good to others which they might do; nay, that there are as few who can be said really and in earnest to aim at one, as at the other. Take a survey of mankind: the world in general, the good and bad, almost without exception, equally are agreed, that were religion out of the case, the happiness of the present life would consist in a manner wholly in riches, honours, sensual gratifications; insomuch that one scarce hears a reflection made upon prudence, life, conduct, but upon this supposition. Yet on the contrary, that persons in the greatest affluence of fortune are no happier than such as have only a competency; that the cares and disappointments of ambition for the most part far exceed the satisfactions of it; as also the miserable intervals of intemperance and excess, and the many untimely deaths occasioned by a dissolute course of life: these things are all seen, acknowledged, by every one acknowledged; but are thought no objections against, though they expressly contradict, this universal principle, that the happiness of the present life consists in one or other of them. Whence is all this absurdity and contradiction? Is not the middle way obvious? Can any thing be more manifest, than that the happiness of life consists in these possessed and enjoyed only to a certain degree; that to pursue them beyond this degree, is always attended with more inconvenience than advantage to a man's self, and often with extreme misery and unhappiness. Whence then, I say, is all this absurdity and contradiction? Is it really the result of consideration in mankind, how they may become most easy to themselves, most free from care, and enjoy the chief happiness attainable in this world? Or is it not manifestly owing either to this, that they have not cool and reasonable concern enough for themselves to consider wherein their chief happiness in the present life consists; or else, if they do consider it, that they will not act conformably to what is the result of that consideration: i.e. reasonable concern for themselves, or cool self-love is prevailed over by passion and appetite. So that from what appears, there is no ground to assert that those principles in the nature of man, which most directly lead to promote the good of our fellow-creatures, are more generally or in a greater degree violated, than those, which most directly lead us to promote our own private good and happiness.

The sum of the whole is plainly this. The nature of man considered in his single capacity, and with respect only to the present world, is adapted and leads him to attain the greatest happiness he can for himself in the present world. The nature of man considered in his public or social capacity leads him to a right behaviour in society, to that course of life which we call virtue. Men follow or obey their nature in both these capacities and respects to a certain degree, but not entirely: their actions do not come up to the whole of what their nature leads them to in either of these capacities or respects: and they often violate their nature in both, i.e. as they neglect the duties they owe to their fellow-creatures, to which their nature leads them; and are injurious, to which their nature is abhorrent; so there is a manifest negligence in men of their real happiness or interest in the present world, when that interest is inconsistent with a present gratification; for the sake of which they negligently, nay, even knowingly, are the authors and instruments of their own misery and ruin. Thus they are as often unjust to themselves as to others, and for the most part are equally so to both by the same actions.

PART II

VIRTUE DOES NOT PAY

3

PLATO

Whether It Is Better to Be or Seem Just

Introduction

Plato (about 430 B.C. to about 350 B.C.) was the author of what are called the Socratic dialogues, so called because Socrates, of whom Plato might have been a pupil, was their main protagonist. These show both great philosophical acumen and high literary merit. Socrates used a profession of ignorance to enable him to ask awkward questions without giving offense and to lull his antagonists into a false sense of security. It also enabled him to use his opponents' own words to convict them. The effect on the reader whenever one of the protagonists agrees with everything Socrates says is hypnotic and needs to be resisted. Plato has been enormously influential.

In this reading Plato considers one of the most fundamental questions in moral philosophy, that is, whether it is better to be just without seeming to be so or better to seem just without being so. If one were given the ring of Gyges, which would enable one to make oneself invisible, would there be any need to continue to be just now that one could be unjust without being detected?

He answers this question later in the "Republic" by saying that a man is just to the extent that reason presides in his soul. It is the function of reason to control the passions. If the passions usurp the place of reason, he will be their slave. They will become insatiable, force him to commit the most heinous crimes and to make enemies of men and gods, and give him no peace. Hence it would be absurd to suppose that it would be better for reason to seem to preside in one's soul without doing so than to preside in one's soul without seeming to.

David Hume, in the eighteenth century, argued that it was impossible for reason to preside in one's soul. Reason was the slave of the passions.

By this he meant that the only function of reason was to point out the means to satisfying our wants (passions). To the example that Plato uses to prove that reason presides in the soul, that of a thirsty man who does not drink because reason warns him that the water is poisoned, Hume would have replied that this man's passion for water was not overcome by reason. It was overcome by another passion (i.e., desire for life).

People could be bad and still control their passions. They would, indeed, pursue a life of crime more successfully if reason presided in their souls. Such people could live by crime as others live by running a successful business. They are kind to their employees, eliminate police officers or rivals only when absolutely necessary, and retire early to a leisure they are well able to afford. You and I (and presumably Plato) might be made constantly miserable by remorse and fear of discovery if we were to live such a life. But not everybody is like you and me (and still less like Plato). Some people do not feel much remorse, and the risk of discovery adds zest to their lives.

Bishop Butler, writing early in the eighteenth century, argued that although it was not necessarily the case that a good man would be happier than a bad one, because the bad man might be lucky or healthy and the good man not, a man would *tend* to be happier *to the extent that* he was good.

I think Butler was right, for the most part, about the moderately virtuous man. The moderately virtuous man will obey those of a society's rules which will help him in his profession and enable him to support his wife and bring up his family, activities which are themselves forms of virtuous activity. But the immoderately virtuous man will give all his goods to the poor and denounce the rich and powerful for their selfishness and hypocrisy. Such a man may be outstandingly good, but it is not obvious that he is adopting a recipe that will make him outstandingly happy. It is possible that he may have such a sensitive conscience that he will be even more unhappy if he does *not* give all his goods to the poor and denounce the rich. But he is then likely to be unhappy, whether he follows his conscience or not.

Reading

I THOUGHT, AS I said this, that there would be no more argument; but in fact we had little more than begun. For Glaucon, who never lacked initiative, would not let Thrasymachus' withdrawal pass unchallenged, but asked: "Do you really want to convince us that right is in all circumstances better than wrong or not?"

"If I were given the choice," I replied, "I should want to convince you."

"Well then, you are not making much progress," he returned. "Tell me, do you agree that there is one kind of good which we want to have

Reprinted from Plato's *Republic*. Book II. Translated by B. Jowett, Oxford University Press, 1931. By permission of Oxford University Press.

simply for its own sake and without regard for its consequences? For example, happiness or pleasure, so long as pleasure brings no harm and its results don't make us unhappy."

"Yes, that is one kind of good."

"And is there not another kind of good which we desire both for itself and its consequences? Wisdom and sight and health, for example, we welcome on both grounds."

"We do," I said.

"And there is a third category of good which includes exercise and medical treatment and earning one's living as a doctor or otherwise. All these we should regard as painful but good for us; we should not choose them for their own sakes but for what we get out of them, wages or what not."

"There is this third category. But what is your point?"

"In which category do you place justice and right?"

"In the highest category, which anyone who is to be happy welcomes both for its own sake and for its consequences."

"That is not the common opinion," Glaucon replied. "It is normally put into the painful category, of goods which we pursue for the rewards they bring and in the hope of a good reputation, but which in themselves are to be avoided as unpleasant."

"I know that is the common opinion," I answered; "which is why Thrasymachus has been criticizing it and praising injustice. But I'm not easy to convince."

"Listen to me then, and see if I can change your mind," he said. "For you seem to have fascinated Thrasymachus into a premature submission, like a snake charmer; but I am not satisfied yet about justice and injustice. I want to be told what exactly each of them is and what its effects are on the mind of its possessor, quite apart from any question of rewards or consequences. So what I propose to do, if you agree, is this. I shall re-state Thrasymachus' argument under three heads: first, I shall state the common opinion on the nature and origin of justice; second, I shall show that those who practise it do so under compulsion and not because they think it good in itself; third, I shall argue that this conduct is reasonable because the unjust man has, by common reckoning, a better time than the just man. I don't believe all this myself, Socrates, but Thrasymachus and hundreds of others have dinned it into my ears till I don't know what to think; and I've never heard the case in favour of justice as against injustice argued to my satisfaction, that is, I've never heard justice recommended on its own merits apart from its consequences. That is what I want to hear you do. I therefore propose to state, forcibly, the argument in favour of injustice, and thus give you a model which I want you to follow when your turn comes to argue in favour of justice. Do you agree to this suggestion?"

"Nothing could please me better," I replied, "for it's a subject which all sensible men should be glad to discuss."

"Splendid," said Glaucon. "And now for my first heading, the nature and origin of justice. What they say is that our natural instinct is to inflict wrong or injury, and to avoid suffering it, but that the disadvantages of suffering it exceed the advantages of inflicting it; after a taste of both, therefore, men decide that, as they can't have the ha'pence without the kicks, they had better make a compact with each other and avoid both. They accordingly proceed to make laws and mutual agreements, and what the law lays down they call lawful and right. This is the origin and nature of justice. It lies between what is most desirable, to do wrong and avoid punishment, and what is most undesirable, to suffer wrong without redress; justice and right lie between these two and are accepted not as being good in themselves, but as having a relative value due to our inability to do wrong. For anyone who had the power to do wrong and called himself a man would never make any such agreement with anyone — he would be mad if he did.

"This then is the account they give of the nature and the origins of justice; the next point is that men practise it against their will and only because they are unable to do wrong. This we can most easily see if we imagine that a just man and an unjust man have each been given liberty to do what they like, and then follow their subsequent careers. We shall catch the just man in exactly the same pursuits as the unjust, led by self-interest, the motive which all men naturally follow if they are not forcibly restrained by the law and made to respect each other's claims.

"The best illustration of the liberty I am talking about would be if we supposed them to be possessed of the power which Gyges, the ancestor of the famous Lydian, had in the story. He was a shepherd in the service of the then king of Lydia, and one day there was a great storm and an earthquake in the district where he was pasturing his flock and a chasm opened in the earth. He was much amazed, and descended into the chasm and saw many astonishing things there, among them, so the story goes, a bronze horse, which was hollow and fitted with doors, through which he peeped and saw a corpse of more than human size. He took nothing from it save a gold ring it had on its finger, and then made his way out. He was wearing this ring when he attended the usual meeting of shepherds which reported monthly to the king on the state of his flocks; and as he was sitting there with the others he happened to twist the bezel of the ring towards the inside of his hand. Thereupon he became invisible to his companions, and they began to refer to him as if he had left them. He was astonished, and began fingering the ring again, and turned the bezel outwards; whereupon he became visible again. When he saw this he started experimenting with the ring to see if it really had this power, and found that every time he turned the bezel inwards he became invisible, and when he turned it outwards he became visible. Having made his discovery he managed to get himself included in the party that was to report to the king, and when he arrived seduced the queen and with her help attacked and murdered the king and seized the throne.

"Let us now imagine there to be two such rings, one for the just man and one for the unjust. There is no one, it would commonly be supposed, who would have such iron strength of will as to stick to what is right and keep his hands off other people's property. For he would be able to steal from the shops whatever he wanted without fear of detection, to go into any man's house and seduce his wife, to murder or to release from prison anyone he felt inclined, and generally behave as if he had supernatural powers. And in all this the just man would differ in no way from the unjust, but both would follow the same course. This, it would be claimed, is strong evidence that no man is just save under compulsion, and that no man thinks justice pays him personally, since he will always do wrong when he gets the chance. Indeed, the supporter of this view will continue, men are right in thinking that injustice pays the individual better than justice; and if anyone who had the liberty of which we have been speaking neither wronged nor robbed his neighbour, men would think him a most miserable idiot, though of course they would pretend to admire him in public because of their own fear of being wronged.

"So much for that. Finally, we come to the decision between the two lives, and we shall best be able to make this decision if we contrast extreme examples of just and unjust men. By that I mean if we make each of them perfect in his own line, and do not in any way mitigate the injustice of the one or the justice of the other. To begin with the unjust man. He must have a professional skill like that of the most capable pilot or doctor, for example, who know just what they can or can't do, never attempt the impossible, and are able to retrieve any errors they make. The unjust man must, similarly, if he is to be thoroughly unjust, be able to avoid detection in his wrong-doing; for the man who is found out is a poor specimen, and the most accomplished form of injustice is to seem just when you are not. So our completely unjust man must be perfect in his wickedness; he must be able to commit the greatest crimes and at the same time get himself an unblemished reputation, while, if he makes a mistake he must be able to retrieve it, and, if any of his wrong-doing comes to light, be ready with a convincing defence, or when force is needed be prepared to use force, relying on his own courage and energy or making use of his friends or his wealth.

"Beside our picture of the unjust man let us set one of the just man, the man of true simplicity of character who, as Aeschylus says, wants 'to be and not to seem good'. We must, indeed, not allow him to seem good, for if he does he will have all the rewards and honours paid to the man who has a reputation for justice, and we shall not be able to tell whether his motive is love of justice or love of the rewards and honours. No, we must strip him of everything except his justice, and our picture of him must be drawn in the opposite way to our picture of the unjust man; for our just man must have the worst of reputations even though he has done no wrong. So we shall be able to test his justice and see if it can stand up to unpopularity and all that goes with it; we shall give him an undeserved and lifelong reputation for wickedness, and make him stick to his chosen course until death. In this way, when we have pushed the life of justice and of injustice each to its extreme, we shall be able to judge which of the two is the happier."

4

NICCOLÒ MACHIAVELLI

It Is Better for Princes to Seem Just

Introduction

Niccolò Machiavelli (1469–1527) was secretary to The Ten, a group of
magistrates who in Florence were responsible for diplomacy and the
conduct of military operations. This position gave him an unrivaled experience, among philosophical writers, of actual government. Even Plato,
whose view Machiavelli's diametrically opposed, did not have such a
position. However, Machiavelli's most famous book, *The Prince*, from
which this reading is taken and which contains advice for success in
politics, was written when he was dismissed from office as a result of
having backed the losing side.

The Prince is a book of practical recipes on how to govern successfully.
These recipes are supported with numerous examples of successful rulers
who applied Machiavelli's precepts and of unsuccessful rulers who did
not. The frankness of the author shines through his work in a way that is
exceedingly rare, which must make one wonder whether in writing a
book that has brought him very considerable obloquy, he could have
been practicing the Machiavellism that he himself preached.

Machiavelli's problem is simple. There were a large number of virtues
and moral rules, which it is clear Machiavelli himself approved of. However, a prince who universally applied them in a world in which other
princes and would-be princes did not would be deposed or killed, and
probably bring trouble on his subjects.

Machiavelli's solution to this conflict is to advise a prince to be good
when he can afford to be, but to be ruthless and dishonest when necessary. At all times, however, he should give the *appearance* of being a good
(and devout) man. His advice to princes is therefore almost the opposite
of Plato's. Plato advised men to be good rather than to seem good,

62

because otherwise they would not be happy. Machiavelli advises *princes* to seem to be good rather than to be good, because otherwise they would lose their positions and their lives.

Machiavelli's work raises two problems. First, it raises the problem of "dirty hands": are the rules which apply to rulers different from those that apply to ordinary people? Mandeville, for example, suggests that it would be right for a government, but not for private individuals, to shoot a group of foreigners landed on English soil if they were suspected of carrying smallpox.

Second, it raises the question whether I myself ought to obey the moral law when my rivals are not obeying it. In Machiavelli's time other princes and would-be princes would certainly have taken advantage of a ruler who showed clemency or forbearance or who did not eliminate his rivals by ruthless or treacherous means. Many philosophers have argued that one would not be under any obligation to obey the moral law in what Hobbes called a state of nature, that is, a state in which no one else was obeying the moral law. Machiavelli's prince would be in a state of nature with regard to other princes.

It can be argued in favor of obeying the moral law in a state of nature that if no one were to obey the moral law in such a state, we would never get out of it. It can be argued against obeying it that if only one person (or prince) obeyed the moral law in a state of nature we would also never get out of it.

Reading

A PRINCE, THEREFORE, need not necessarily have all the good qualities I mentioned above, but he should certainly appear to have them. I would even go so far as to say that if he has these qualities and always behaves accordingly he will find them ruinous; if he only appears to have them they will render him service. He should appear to be compassionate, faithful to his word, guileless, and devout. And indeed he should be so. But his disposition should be such that, if he needs to be the opposite, he knows how. You must realize this: that a prince, and especially a new prince, cannot observe all those things which give men a reputation for virtue, because in order to maintain his state he is often forced to act in defiance of good faith, of charity, of kindness, of religion. And so he should have a flexible disposition, varying as fortune and circumstances dictate. As I said above, he should not deviate from what is good, if that is possible, but he should know how to do evil, if that is necessary.

A prince, then, should be very careful not to say a word which does not seem inspired by the five qualities I mentioned earlier. To those seeing and hearing him, he should appear a man of compassion, a man of good faith, a man of integrity, a kind and a religious man. And there is nothing so important as to seem to have this last quality. Men in general judge by their eyes rather than by their hands; because everyone is in a position to watch, few are in a position to come in close touch with you. Everyone sees what you appear to be, few experience what you really are. And those few dare not gainsay the many who are backed by the majesty of the state. In the actions of all men, and especially of princes, where there is no court of appeal, one judges by the result. So let a prince set about the task of conquering and maintaining his state; his methods will always be judged honourable and will be universally praised. The common people are always impressed by appearances and results. In this context, there are only common people, and there is no room for the few when the many are supported by the state. A certain contemporary ruler, whom it is better not to name, never preaches anything except peace and good faith; and he is an enemy of both one and the other, and if he had ever honoured either of them he would have lost either his standing or his state many times over.

XV. The things for which men, and especially princes, are praised or blamed

It now remains for us to see how a prince should govern his conduct towards his subjects or his friends. I know that this has often been written about before, and so I hope it will not be thought presumptuous for me to do so, as, especially in discussing this subject, I draw up an original set of rules. But since my intention is to say something that will prove of practical use to the inquirer, I have thought it proper to represent things as they are in real truth, rather than as they are imagined. Many have dreamed up republics and principalities which have never in truth been known to exist; the gulf between how one should live and how one does live is so wide that a man who neglects what is actually done for what should be done learns the way to self-destruction rather than self-preservation. The fact is that a man who wants to act virtuously in every way necessarily comes to grief among so many who are not virtuous. Therefore if a prince wants to maintain his rule he must learn how not to be virtuous, and to make use of this or not according to need.

So leaving aside imaginary things, and referring only to those which truly exist, I say that whenever men are discussed (and especially princes, who are more exposed to view), they are noted for various qualities which earn them either praise or condemnation. Some, for example, are held to be generous, and others miserly (I use the Tuscan word rather than the word avaricious: we call a man who is mean with what he possesses, miserly, and a man who wants to plunder others, avaricious).[1] Some are held to be benefactors, others are called grasping; some cruel, some compassionate; one man faithless, another faithful; one man effeminate and cowardly, another fierce and courageous; one man courteous, another proud; one man lascivious, another pure; one guileless, another crafty; one stubborn, another flexible; one grave, another frivolous; one religious, another sceptical; and so forth. I know everyone will agree that it would be most laudable if a prince possessed all the qualities deemed to be good among those I have enumerated. But, because of conditions in the world, princes cannot possess those qualities, or rather they cannot always exhibit them. So a prince should be so prudent that he knows how to escape the evil reputation attached to those vices which could lose him his state, and how to avoid those vices which are not so dangerous, if he possibly can; but, if he cannot, he need not worry so much about the latter. And then, he must not flinch from being blamed for vices which are necessary for safeguarding the state. This is because, taking everything into account, he will find that some of the things that appear to be virtues will, if he practises them, ruin him, and some of the things that appear to be wicked will bring him security and prosperity.

---

[1] The two words Machiavelli uses are *misero* and *avaro*.

5

PAUL W. TAYLOR

The Choice Between Duty and Interest Must be an Irrational One

Introduction

Paul Taylor recently retired from the chair of philosophy at Brooklyn College, New York. He is author of *Principles of Ethics: An Introduction.*

This reading is an attempt to answer what Taylor calls "the Ultimate Question." When faced with a choice between duty and interest, can any reasons be given for doing the one or the other, or is the choice between the two an arbitrary one? Taylor thinks that *no* reasons can be given for choosing duty rather than interest (or vice versa). When one says that something is a duty, one has already provided a conclusive reason for doing it, and one can no more give a conclusive reason for doing what one already has a conclusive reason for doing than one can provide a logical proof that logical proofs ought to be accepted (my comparison). Or, since all good reasons for doing something are either reasons of interest or reasons of duty, there can be no reason for choosing reasons of interest rather than reasons of duty. Hence we cannot answer the ultimate question in words but only by *doing* something, that is, by doing one's duty or not doing it, as the case may be. In so doing, one is both "defining oneself" as a person and answering the "ultimate question" in practice. Taylor deduces from his contention that the choice between virtue and interest is an ultimate choice, the resounding conclusion that it is absolutely wrong to interfere with the ultimate choices of others.

However, Taylor does seem to be overcome by his own very considerable rhetoric and had not considered very carefully just how one *would* interfere with the choice other people have to make between duty and interest. Offering them money to choose duty presumably could not make them choose duty (for the sake of duty) rather than interest, so much as make their interest coincide with duty. Threatening to send them to prison for doing what is wrong would be open to the same difficulty, together with the further difficulty that sending people to prison for acting wrongly, although it might well interfere with their ultimate choice, is not always wrong. In any case, being in prison does not prevent one from choosing between duty and interest, although the *importance* of one's choices may be circumscribed. Finally, it is not obvious that it would necessarily be wrong to deprive someone who was going to die in pain and degradation of the opportunity to make the ultimate choice between what he supposes to be his duty (to live) and interest (to die).

For, pace Taylor, however, one is not faced with one grand choice between duty on the one hand and interest on the other. One is rather faced with many little choices between duty and interest on quite specific occasions, which means that one might sometimes choose duty and at other times choose interest. One reason for thinking that there is some sense in doing the latter is that duties can be arranged in an order of decreasing importance. For example, a doctor's duty to attend a critically ill patient is much more important than his or her duty to attend one who has only a minor ailment. Duties can also be arranged in an order of *increasing difficulty*.

It is an interesting coincidence that some very unimportant duties are also very difficult to do. Perhaps in that case it really would not matter very much if one were to omit them. One would be a morally better person if one did not omit them, but then one would be a more tired and so a more boring person as well. There are probably many people who are quite properly not very interested in being better people but who want to be better philosophers, artists, or writers. Devoting themselves to duty more than necessary could interfere. Of course, one might try to persuade oneself that it was one's *duty* to devote oneself to art, but this would seem to be a rationalization. Moral philosophers who devote themselves to the study of duty, do sometimes exaggerate its importance.

Reading

THE ULTIMATE QUESTION

The Demand for a Justification of Morality THERE IS ONE problem of ethics that perhaps deserves, more than any other, to be called the Ultimate Question. It is the question of the rationality of the moral life itself. It may be expressed thus: Is the commitment to live by moral principles a commitment grounded on reason or is it, in the final analysis, an arbitrary decision?

The Ultimate Question is not itself a moral question. That is to say it does not ask what we morally ought to do or even how we can discover our moral duty. It is, instead, a question about the justification of

morality as a whole. Why, it asks, should we be concerned with morality at all? If living by moral principles can at times be so difficult, if our
moral integrity may, in some circumstances, require the sacrifice of our
happiness or even of our life, why not simply reject the whole moral
"game" and live amorally? In short, why be moral?

It is important to see exactly why this is not a moral question or a
question about what actions are morally right. When a person asks why
he should be moral, he assumes he already knows what "being moral"
means. He could not understand his own question when he asked,
"Why should I do what is morally right, especially when it conflicts
with my self-interest?" unless he understood the meaning of doing
what is morally right. Moreover, if his question concerns a *particular*
case of conflict between moral duty and self-interest, then it is assumed
that the questioner accepts the fact that, in the specific circumstances
referred to, a certain action *is* his duty. He recognizes it as an action
which, from the moral point of view, he ought to perform. But he also
recognizes it as conduct which, from the standpoint of his self-interest,
would be irrational. He then asks, Why, after all, should I do it? In
effect he is asking, Why should moral duty *outweigh* or *override* self-
interest when there is a conflict between them?

The demand for an ultimate justification of morality was first stated
in its classic form in Plato's *Republic*. Glaucon and Adeimantus, two of
the figures participating in the dialogue, challenge Socrates, the protagonist, to justify the living of a morally upright life. Their challenge is
presented in the form of the . . . story, which is known as The Myth of
Gyges.

Here is a classic statement of the case against morality. Socrates'
attempt to reply to it, which forms the main argument of Plato's *Republic*, consists in trying to show that moral virtue is its own reward and
that only the just (morally upright) man is truly happy. Thus, in effect,
Socrates claims that in the long run there is no real conflict between
duty and self-interest. Philosophers have been disputing about this ever
since.

In order to see exactly what is at stake in trying to answer the
question, Why be moral? we must recognize how it differs from a
question about the nature of moral reasoning. For the question, Why
be moral? arises the moment when someone realizes that, if he commits
himself to the principles of moral reasoning, he may find himself in
circumstances where his reasoning leads to the conclusion that he
ought to do an act which entails some inconvenience, unpleasantness,
or frustration for himself. It might even lead to the conclusion that in
the given situation confronting him he must give up his life. He then
wants to know why he should follow the rules of moral reasoning.

It should be noted that this problem does not arise for the ethical egoist, who *identifies* moral reasoning with prudential reasoning. As we saw, . . . ethical egoism is the view that each person ought to do whatever will most further his self-interest in the long run. If this is taken as an ultimate moral principle then the question, Why be moral? becomes the question, Why seek the furtherance of my self-interest in the long run? Such a question would only be asked by someone who did not want to give up his pleasures or who was satisfied with pursuing short-range goals in life, and who realized at the same time that his long-range interests might not be furthered by his continuing to live in the way he had been living. The answer to his question, of course, would be that, if he is not willing to put up with inconveniences and discomforts and if he is not able to discipline himself to sacrifice his short-range goals when his pursuit of them prevents him from achieving lasting satisfactions in life, then he will not in fact be happy. But for the ethical egoist, no sacrifice of his self-interest *as a whole* would ever be justified and no such sacrifice would ever be morally required of him.

Since the Ultimate Question arises only when it is logically possible for there to be a conflict between the demands of morality and the pursuit of self-interest, we shall be concerned from this point on with nonegoist moral principles only. We are not assuming that morality is superior to self-interest, but only that it is possible for them to be in conflict. Under this assumption, then, the next point to realize is that the Ultimate Question lies outside the framework of the logic of moral reasoning itself. For the logic of moral reasoning tells us what a good reason in ethics is. It defines the method of reasoning a person should use *if* he were to commit himself to trying to find out what he morally ought to do. In asking, Why be moral? on the other hand, one is challenging the reasonableness of being committed to trying to find out what one morally ought to do. It is a challenge to the whole enterprise of moral reasoning and moral conduct. The challenge can be put this way: Suppose there is a valid method of moral reasoning and suppose, by following it, I do find out what I morally ought to do. Why should I bother to act in accordance with this knowledge? Why shouldn't I follow my self-interest instead? In other words, granted that there is a logic of moral reasoning, why should I choose to let this logic outweigh the logic of self-interest or prudence when there is a conflict between them? In making this challenge the person is not questioning the validity of moral reasoning. Rather, he is asking why such reasoning should guide his conduct when he could just as well choose to have his conduct guided by another set of rules of reasoning, namely, the furtherance of his own self-interest. Thus, he is demanding a justification for morality (the commitment to use moral reasoning as a guide to conduct) *as a whole*.

Is the Ultimate Question an Absurdity?

One view that has been taken by philosophers regarding the Ultimate Question is that it cannot be answered because it is absurd. It has been seen that a person who asks why he should do what is morally right already presupposes that he knows, or at least believes, that certain acts *are* right. In asking his question, therefore, he is not asking what he morally ought to do. He already has an answer to this. What, then, does he want to know? It seems that he wants to know why he should do what he knows to be right. It is as if he is saying, "I know what my moral duty is — now tell me why I ought to act in accordance with this knowledge." This, however, is absurd. For if the person knows that something is his duty, then he already knows why he ought to do it, namely, *just because it is his duty.*

When it is understood in this way, the Ultimate Question cannot be answered. But the reason it cannot is that no real question is being asked. For suppose we try to answer it by showing the person why he ought to do a certain action. We are then giving him moral reasons for doing that particular action. This, however, will not be accepted by him as an answer to the question he is asking. *His* question is, Why should I do what is right?, not, Why is this action the right thing to do? So if we show him that it is the right thing to do, he will not be satisfied. He will still ask for reasons for being *committed to doing* what he *acknowledges* to be something he ethically ought to do. Therefore it is no answer to give him moral reasons for doing the action in question. One cannot cite moral reasons for being moral (that is, for being committed to do what one believes to be right). Someone who wants to justify being moral is asking why he ought to use moral reasons as actual guides in his practical life. To give him such reasons is to assume that he will accept them as reasons for action. But this is the very thing he is questioning.

Once we become aware of this, however, we can see that there is a deep confusion behind the question "Why be moral?" when it is interpreted as a demand for reasons for doing what one acknowledges to be morally right. A moral reason is, by its very nature, a *"reason for acting."* It is not merely a "reason for believing," that is, a reason for accepting or acknowledging the truth of a proposition such as, Act X is morally right. To show why act X is morally right is to give moral reasons why a person should actually perform it. At the same time, it justifies accepting the statement "Act X is morally right" as true. It has been pointed out that the person who asks, Why be moral? is asking (under the present interpretation), Why should I *do* what I *believe* to be morally right? It can now be seen that he is confused in asking this. For he is assuming a separation between moral belief and moral action that isn't possible. To *believe* that an action is morally right is to have a reason for *doing* it, namely, that it is morally right. It is this confusion that explains why his question cannot be answered by giving him moral reasons for being moral. The point is that, once a person accepts moral reasons for *believing* that some action ought to be done, he has all the basis he needs for *doing* it, to wit, those very reasons for believing it ought to be done.

Given this interpretation of the Ultimate Question, it can be dismissed as resting on a mistake. It is not worth trying to answer, since a clear-thinking person would never ask it.

THE MEANING OF THE ULTIMATE QUESTION

Does the foregoing argument successfully dispose of the Ultimate Question? Some philosophers are convinced that it does not. They claim that there is a genuine question behind the apparent oddity of asking why one ought to do something while acknowledging that a moral person would have good reason to do it. The true significance of the question, they say, has to do with a choice or decision to be made between two sorts of reasons: moral reasons and reasons of self-interest. To hold that a person who asks why he ought to do what is morally right already knows why (namely, because it *is* morally right), is to miss the real point of the Ultimate Question. It is true that one cannot give moral arguments for being moral, just as one cannot give prudential arguments for being prudent. Nevertheless there may be moral reasons *for*, and prudential reasons *against*, a certain action, and there may be moral reasons *against* and prudential reasons *for* another action. In situations of that sort, one must act either morally or in one's self-interest; one cannot do both. How is one to decide?

It is here that the question, Why be moral? does not seem at all absurd. This was why Socrates took seriously the challenge to morality expressed in the Myth of Gyges. He realized that, in normal circumstances of life, we do not ask for a justification of morality because society sees to it that it is generally in a person's self-interest to be moral. It pays to avoid social disapproval and to maintain a good reputation. But the philosopher cannot be satisfied with this, since it is possible to imagine a case where a person has the power (as described in the Myth of Gyges) to act immorally and escape social sanctions. Why, then, should he not act immorally? Unless there is a *reason* for his not doing so, morality reduces to the self-interested avoidance of social disapproval. Conformity to the actual moral code of one's own society would then be one's highest duty. This entails, of course, normative ethical relativism. The norms of each society would determine what is right and wrong in it, and no society's code as a whole could be shown to be unjust or evil. But to take the Ultimate Question seriously is to seek a reason for being moral even when it doesn't pay, and even when being moral involves a clash with what is socially approved.

So let us now interpret the Ultimate Question as asking, When moral reasons and reasons of self-interest are in conflict, why should one follow the first rather than the second (assuming that one had the power to do either)?

One possible response to the question so understood might be to try to strengthen in the questioner the desire to be moral, so that he will in fact act morally even when it is contrary to his self-interest. The Ultimate Question is then being taken as a demand for *motivating* reasons (reasons that will actually move a person to act) rather than as a demand for *justifying* reasons (reasons that show why an act ought to be done). Now it may sometimes be true that a person who asks, Why be moral? in real life does want to be motivated to such conduct. We then answer him, not by presenting him with a sound philosophical argument, but by trying to persuade or influence him so that he will feel inspired to do what is right. We try to reinforce his moral motives and strengthen his sense of duty. If he is a child we give him a moral upbringing. We not only try to instill in him a desire to abide by moral rules (of honesty, fairness, nonmaleficence, et cetera), we also try to develop his capacity and inclination to reason morally for himself. If we are successful in this, he will not feel the need to ask the question, Why be moral? in later life. He will have been motivated to be moral and thus not find it psychologically necessary to ask to be motivated.

The philosopher, however, is not interested in engaging in this kind of response. For him the Ultimate Question is a demand for a justification for being moral, not a request to be motivated to be moral. The difference is not always easy to grasp. (Indeed, there is a whole theory in psychology — the behaviorism of Professor B. F. Skinner — which overlooks the difference!) A person's motivation, we have seen, has to do with his desires, his actual tendencies to aim at certain ends or goals. Here the relevant questions are, Does this individual have a desire to be moral, and if so, how strong is that desire? In particular, is it strong enough to overcome the motive to pursue his self-interest in cases of conflict between what he believes to be morally right and what he believes will serve his own interests? Justification, on the other hand, has to do with reasons, not with desires. To justify being moral is to vindicate the belief that moral reasons outweigh or override reasons of self-interest when they conflict. It is to show why moral reasons take priority over, and hence are superior to, prudential reasons. Now the idea of one sort of reasons taking priority over, or being superior to, another sort is not to be confused with the idea of one sort of reasons having greater motivational strength than another sort. A person's believing that moral reasons are better or weightier grounds for an action than prudential ones does not imply that he will always be more strongly motivated to do what is moral than what is prudent. If there is such a discrepancy in a person between justifying reasons and their motivational effectiveness, the person is said to have "weakness of will," and he may even recognize this in himself as a flaw in his character. It is then possible for him to consider an action *unjustified* (because it is morally wrong though prudentially expedient) and still actually do it. In that case his desires and actions are simply not consistent with his moral beliefs.

To justify anyone's being moral, as distinct from motivating some particular individual to be moral, is to give a sound argument in support of the claim that moral reasons take priority over reasons of self-interest whenever they conflict. If we were able to discover, or construct, such an argument, it would follow that everyone ought to be motivated by moral reasons for acting rather than by prudential reasons for acting in cases of conflict. Whether any given individual will in fact be so motivated depends on the strength of his desires, not on the soundness of an argument. Even if a person's desire to be moral were indeed strengthened by his reading or hearing such an argument, thus motivating him to be moral, this is irrelevant to the question of whether the argument actually showed the moral reasons to be superior to those of self-interest. Similarly, the argument might not convince someone intellectually, nor persuade him to act morally, nor reinforce his moral motivation. But the failure of the argument to bring about such results in any given individual is strictly irrelevant to the philosophical acceptability of the argument's content.

Suppose, then, that the Ultimate Question is understood to mean, Why do moral reasons outweigh prudential reasons in cases of conflict, rather than the other way around? Now it will not do to reply, Because morality *by definition* is that set of principles which outweigh all other principles that might conflict with them. This is not an acceptable answer because a person might decide to make reasons of self-interest *his* highest overriding principles. Then, by the given definition, self-interest would become morality in his case, and there could be no conflict between moral reasons and prudential reasons. In short, he would be an ethical egoist, and we saw earlier that the Ultimate Question presupposes that ethical egoism is false. (If ethical egoism were true, the whole issue would cease to be a meaningful problem.)

It has now become clear where the crux of the matter lies. The Ultimate Question places before us a challenge that concerns our *ultimate normative commitments*. It asks: Are there any reasons that would justify our commitment to moral principles as being the supreme overriding norms of our practical life (where "moral principles" are not by definition supreme and where it is logically possible for them to be in conflict with prudential principles)? We shall take this as our final formulation of the Ultimate Question. What answers might be proposed for it when it is understood this way?

Two Proposed Answers to the Ultimate Question

(1) The first answer is that there are reasons that justify *everyone's* commitment to the priority of moral principles over self-interest. For

suppose *everyone* took the opposite position and made a commitment such that, whenever self-interest and morality conflict, considerations of self-interest are to override moral considerations. The consequence would be the total collapse of any social order. Each person would be out for himself and would know that every other person was out for himself. Thus, each could have no confidence that others would refrain from harming him. Everyone would live in continual fear of everyone else, since all would realize that no constraints upon self-interest would be operative (even when such constraints were required by moral principles of fairness and respect for life). A world where the priority rule, "Self-interest is to take precedence over morality," was generally accepted would be a world where no one could attain his goals. Each would lack the basic security of being able to count on others not to interfere with his pursuit of his own ends.

The conclusion is evident. The whole point of any individual's committing himself to the supremacy of self-interest over morality is to promote his own welfare. But if this commitment were made by everyone, each would be unable to promote his self-interest to as great a degree as he would when everyone made the opposite commitment. This is the paradox of universal selfishness. No one would be as well off as he would be under universal conformity to moral rules. The very purpose of universal selfishness, in other words, is undermined by its practice. The priority of self-interest over morality is therefore a self-defeating commitment. It frustrates its own purpose and is consequently irrational. Commitment to the priority of morality over self-interest, on the contrary, is self-fulfilling. Its purpose is to create a social order where everyone benefits from mutual trust. This trust is only possible under the condition that everyone makes a firm commitment to the supremacy of such moral principles as justice and nonmaleficence. For only under that condition can each person count on others not to harm him or interfere with his pursuit of his own goals.

Is this an acceptable answer to the Ultimate Question? Does it provide a sound argument to justify being moral? It seems not, for it is open to the following objection. The answer that has been proposed overlooks an important distinction, which can be brought out by comparing these two questions: (a) Why should I be moral? (b) Why should people in general be moral? The argument given above is an adequate answer to (b), but not to (a). And it is (a) that is the Ultimate Question. The person who asks, Why be moral? is asking why he, *as an individual*, should commit himself to the priority of moral principles over his self-interest. If such a person were given the argument stated above, he would reply, Yes, I agree that if *everyone* were to commit himself to the supremacy of self-interest, it would lead to the frustration of my own as well as everyone else's self-interest. So I agree that it would be irrational for everyone to do this. However, this does not show that it would

be irrational for *me* to make such a commitment. For in the world as it is
(where others are at least sometimes committed to being moral), by
making the commitment to self-interest over morality I would thereby
gain a major advantage for myself. This would be especially true if I
kept my commitment a secret from others. My self-interest would be
promoted by such a commitment on my part, and hence it would not
be self-defeating, but quite the contrary. So how can it be shown to be
irrational?

When the person who asks the Ultimate Question takes this stand, it
is true that the answer to (b) will not provide him with an answer to *his*
question, which is (a). But a new aspect of the situation has now come
to light; we see that such a person is assuming that his case is an
exception to a general rule. The argument against everyone's making a
commitment to self-interest, he claims, does not hold for him. Why
not? Because his commitment to self-interest can be self-fulfilling only
when others do not make a similar commitment. We can then ask him,
Why should your case be considered an exception? What is so special
about you that makes your commitment justifiable when those of,
others in circumstances similar to yours, are not? Indeed, by your own
argument you can be justified in making your commitment only on the
condition that others do *not* make the same commitment. Now unless
you can show that you deserve to be treated as a special case, you have
provided no justification for considering yourself an exception.

There is, however, a reply that can be made to this objection—a
reply available to the person who asks question (a). He can say, Since I
am asking for reasons that support an *ultimate* normative commitment,
I am seeking to justify commitment to *any* principle as a supreme one,
including the principle that I am not to make my case an exception to a
general rule. After all, I can always point to some property that I have
and that no one else has as the basis for claiming that my own case is to
be treated differently from theirs. That is, I can commit myself to the
principle (as a supreme one) that having the attribute in question is a
relevant difference between one person and another, as far as the
promotion of self-interest is concerned. The Ultimate Question can
now simply be restated to include this principle, thus: Why ought a
person—*any* person—having that property not be considered an exception to the general rule that moral reasons override reasons of
self-interest?

To see how such a position is perfectly consistent, consider the
property of having six toes on each foot with a wart on each toe.
Suppose someone endowed by nature with that property states that he
adopts, as an ultimate normative commitment, the principle that *anyone* with such feet is to be permitted to further his interests whenever
they conflict with the interest of others. It is not possible, then, to claim
that he is making an unjustifiable exception in his own favor (knowing

that he alone has the property in question). For he is quite willing to universalize that principle, letting *everyone* commit himself to it and letting it be applied to *all* cases where the property in question is exemplified. Thus he is not claiming that his own case is to be treated differently from others' *merely because it is his own*. Instead, he is committing himself to the principle (as a supreme one) that having the property in question is a relevant difference between persons.

Given this commitment, the Ultimate Question can be rephrased as follows. Instead of asking "Why should I be moral?" the individual now can ask, "Why should I not adopt the principle that anyone having six toes on each foot with a wart on each toe is an exception to the general rule that moral reasons override reasons of self-interest?" This question cannot be answered by asserting that there is no relevant difference between the questioner's case and that of others, for this would simply mean that the one who asserts this does not subscribe to the principle adopted by the questioner. To make such a statement is not to show why the questioner is mistaken, illogical, or unjustified in adopting his principle. It is merely to indicate that one has not made the same ultimate normative commitment that the questioner has. So an adequate answer has not yet been given to question (a): Why should I (as an individual) be moral?

(2) A second way to respond to the Ultimate Question can be seen as emerging from the foregoing considerations. When the Ultimate Question is interpreted as question (a), — Why should I be moral? — what is being asked for are reasons that would justify an individual's making an ultimate choice of the priority of morality over self-interest. But an *ultimate* choice, by its very nature, cannot be based on reasons, since any arguments given to justify it will themselves presuppose a principle that has already been chosen, from which it follows that the choice being justified is not an ultimate one. Let us set out this argument fully and explicitly.

To give "reasons for choosing" is to show that a person is justified in choosing one thing rather than another when he can do one or the other but not both. Giving such reasons is possible only within the framework of some principle according to which the reasons given do indeed warrant the choice based on them. (That doing X will satisfy a desire is a reason for choosing to do X only because one accepts the *principle*, What satisfies a desire is a good thing to do.) Thus giving reasons for choosing already presupposes commitment to a principle. Now suppose one were to give reasons for choosing one principle rather than another — that is, justification for a commitment to follow one as a guide to conduct rather than another. Then to give reasons for choosing *that* principle would presuppose commitment to some higher principle. And if reasons for choosing this higher principle were offered, commitment to still another at a higher level would be presupposed. And so on, for any higher principle. Therefore, with regard to any choice, if reasons for choosing are given to justify it, it cannot be an *ultimate* choice — the choice of a *highest* principle. Now the Ultimate Question is precisely the demand for reasons for making an ultimate choice. Such a demand is incoherent, as can be seen from the fact that it asks for what is impossible. No reasons can be given for an ultimate choice, for an ultimate choice rules out the possibility of reasons for choosing.

We are now in a position to understand how the challenge expressed in the Ultimate Question is to be met. We simply say to the person who poses the question, "We cannot give you reasons that will show what choice you must make. You must decide for yourself. You cannot avoid this final responsibility. The choice of how you are to live, of the supreme normative axioms of your conduct, is a choice that no one can make but yourself. Even your own reason cannot do this job for you. As we have seen, your acceptance of any reasons for choosing will presuppose some principle that has already been chosen by you. Thus it is a matter, not of your reason, but of your will. You must *decide* what shall be your ultimate commitment, and this requires an exercise of your capacity to make an autonomous, self-directed choice about the kind of life you are to live. In this sort of situation to ask for reasons is actually an unconscious attempt to evade the burden of an ultimate choice. Such an attempt is futile, however, for it is an attempt to deny what cannot be denied: that each individual must finally answer for himself the question of what principles he is to live by."

This line of thought has led some philosophers to the following conclusion. To make an ultimate commitment is nothing less than *to define oneself.* It is to decide to be a certain kind of person. There is no way to escape this choice, the reason being that we *are* at every moment what we choose to *make* ourselves, and we can always choose to create a different self and so define our nature in a new way. Most of our decisions and choices, it is true, are not consciously directed to alternatives of this ultimate kind. But that is because we make most decisions and choices within the framework of a way of life. Our way of life is our mode or "style" of carrying on human existence. It is the expression of our own conception of what it means to be human, and it includes our commitment to the very principles that determine what we accept as reasons for acting and reasons for choosing. Hence, though we make decisions and choices in daily life that are not themselves ultimate, we do so only in terms of the conceptual system embodied in the ultimate principles of our way of life.

Since our way of life is our way of defining ourselves, it is not imposed on us from the outside. Nor is it merely a reflection of the kind of person we already are. For our being a certain kind of person is due to our having chosen to live in a certain way, not the other way around. (This is a logical point about the concepts of a way of life and of personhood, not a psychological account of the origins of our "personality." To exist as a person by choosing to define oneself in a certain way is logically prior to having a "personality" as that is empirically explained and described by the science of psychology.) At every moment, whether we realize it or not, we are choosing our way of life, since at each instant there is some way of life that may be correctly ascribed to us. The fact that we do not change our mode of living from one moment to the next does not show that no choice is being made. For if we do not change, we are choosing to continue to be what we have been. And so we are still creating ourselves, making ourselves in a certain image of man, defining our own nature by living as we do. Thus, whether our way of life is one in which morality outweighs self-interest (in cases of conflict between them) or one in which self-interest overrides morality, it is *our* way of life because we have *made* it so. It is we who determine which shall be supreme, ethics or ego. As an ultimate choice, it is a matter of how we decide to live and to define ourselves. And whether our past decisions continue to mold our way of life in the present is something only we have the power to determine. The decision to change or not to change is forever inescapable. We cannot free ourselves from the responsibility to define our selfhood at every moment. At the same time, at every moment we have the "existential" freedom to define our selfhood as we will.

The Commitment to Be Moral

Do these considerations necessarily imply that a person's commitment to the supremacy of moral principles over self-interest is an *arbitrary* decision, like the tossing of a coin? As an ultimate choice it can be called extrarational, beyond reason, neither rational nor irrational. But one can say the same of the contrary choice, by which a person commits himself to the priority of self-interest over morality. Is this all there is to be said?

Something further can indeed be said, but this something further is not the giving of a reason that would justify the choice of one alternative rather than the other. It is, instead, a matter of bringing clearly before one's mind a full recognition of the *nature* of the choice, an ultimate one. Now if it is true that in some sense ultimate choices cannot be avoided — that everyone must make them, and at every moment of life — then making such choices is simply a necessary aspect of one's autonomy as an individual. Thus suppose someone said, "I refuse to make an ultimate choice between morality and self-interest." He would actually be making an ultimate choice, namely, not to commit himself in advance but to wait until he finds himself in a situation of conflict between morality and self-interest and then commit himself on the spur of the moment. His supreme commitment is to whatever principles he chooses to follow as an immediate reaction to particular situations confronting him with the necessity to choose. This is the way he is defining *his* nature. And his decision to refuse to commit himself in advance is itself an exercise of his autonomy as an individual! It seems, then, that there can be no genuine counter-instance to the generalizations that ultimate choices must be made at every moment by each person, and that such choices realize or express the autonomy of each individual.

Now this is of great significance. For if every person, as a person, must bear the responsibility of making his own ultimate choices at every moment of his life, anything that took away or diminished the possibility of someone's exercise of this autonomy would be a violation of the very foundation of rational action and choice in that person's life. In not allowing the person to define himself, it would deny him existence as a person. What is more, to interfere with or destroy someone's capacity for making ultimate choices would be to negate that person's responsibility to answer the Ultimate Question for himself. So if the Ultimate Question is not an absurdity and if one individual can never answer it for another but each must find his own answer, then, as far as solving the Ultimate Question is concerned, each person must be unhindered in the exercise of his autonomy as a maker of ultimate choices.

The necessary conditions for each person's asking and answering the Ultimate Question are now seen to impose a restriction upon human conduct: that no one shall deprive another of his capacity to make ultimate choices, nor interfere with his exercise of that capacity. To put it another way, each person must respect every other person's autonomy. If, in any particular set of circumstances, one person's acting from self-interest would transgress this primary rule of respect for everyone's autonomy, then his action must not be permitted. To allow him to do it would be to deny the principle which lies at the very foundation of all rational action and choice. For the freedom to make ultimate choices is necessarily presupposed by anyone's having *any* reasons for acting and reasons for choosing, whether they be moral or prudential reasons.

It seems plausible to hold that respect for the autonomy of persons is itself a moral principle. If this is so, then the choice between *this* principle and the pursuit of self-interest, even when it is an ultimate choice, is not arbitrary. Although one cannot give reasons for choosing this moral principle, one can examine fully the true nature of the choice and recognize that commitment to the principle in question is a precondition for all ultimate choices made by anyone, and hence a precondition for anyone's being able to carry on practical reasoning.

Let us then suppose, as our final consideration, that a person who has followed the foregoing argument still wants to know why he should be moral to the extent of respecting the autonomy of others. He admits that he can meaningfully ask this question only because others are respecting *his* autonomy and that, if he were not to respect *their* autonomy, they would be unable to find an answer, or even seek an answer, to the Ultimate Question. But he says, "Why should I care whether they seek an answer, or find one?"

There are no reasons that can be given which provide an answer to his question. He must decide for himself what he is to care about in his life. The only thing that can be done is to point out to him that this is a decision of a fundamental kind. It is the decision to be a certain sort of person. Can he face himself openly and unevasively and still decide not to respect the autonomy of others, having clearly before his mind the full meaning of such a choice? If he can, then he has determined what conception of being human shall be exemplified in his life and this is all one can say about his decision. No argument can be given to show that his decision is irrational or that it is based on false assumptions.

This, after all, is in keeping with the idea emphasized above: that each person must take upon himself the responsibility for his ultimate normative commitment. In subscribing to the basic principles of his way of life, a person chooses to define himself in a certain way. If he decides to be the kind of person who deprives another of the capacity for an autonomous choice of a way of life, he cannot be said to be inconsistent. One can only ask, Can he make such a decision *authentically*, that is, sincerely acknowledging it as his own and at the same time making the decision, as it were, with his whole being? If he can, he knows what sort of conception of man he chooses to exemplify. And if he is willing to choose to be that sort of person — one who denies the personhood of another in the very act of defining his own personhood — nothing more can be said.

Commitment to moral principles, then, is finally a matter of one's will, not of one's reason. Reason can make clear to us the nature of the commitment and can lead us to a full awareness of the alternatives among which we must choose. But reason alone cannot tell us what choice to make. We must not expect, therefore, that someone might provide us with an argument showing which alternative *ought* to be chosen. There is simply no way to evade the responsibility — a responsibility that rests upon each of us alone — for defining our own selves. It is up to us to answer, each in his own way, that haunting question, Who am I? We give our answer to it by deciding whether our lives shall exemplify, to whatever extent is in our power, the principles of morality, or some other principles. Even to say, "Let each one decide for himself," is to express a doctrine that imposes a restraint upon action. And it is possible for a person to commit himself to some other principle contrary to this one, without being inconsistent. As long as he understands and acknowledges the nature of his choice and does not try to evade the fact that it is *his* choice, such a person cannot be shown to have chosen against the dictates of reason.

It is simply that he decides to be a certain kind of human being. Whether we also decide to be that kind of human being ourselves is a question only we can answer. For no one can escape the necessity to determine for himself what the answer, in his own life, shall be.

PART III

VIRTUE NOT WITHIN MAN'S POWER

6

DAVID HUME

Of Liberty and Necessity

Introduction

David Hume (1711–1776) was a diplomat, librarian, historian, and economist as well as a philosopher. He was never an academic and was indeed turned down from the chairs of philosophy at Edinburgh and Glasgow. He was the author of *A Treatise of Human Nature, An Enquiry Concerning the Principles of Morals, An Enquiry Concerning Human Understanding, Dialogues on Natural Religion*, numerous essays, and a history of England. The latter makes excellent reading, although it is inaccurate. St. David's Street, in the Edinburgh New Town, was named after him. By almost common consent, he was one of the greatest philosophers who has ever lived.

In order to understand this reading, it is necessary to know something about Hume's views on causation. According to Hume, one event causes another if the two events are contiguous in space and time (which rules out action at a distance) and if events *like* the cause are uniformly followed by events *like* the effect. For example, taking arsenic causes death on this occasion only if taking arsenic is uniformly followed by death on other occasions. The necessitation of an effect by its cause—Hume is not wholly consistent about this—consists simply in the fact that, because the cause is uniformly followed by the effect, knowledge of this uniformity tends to make the spectator infer the effect from the cause. Because of this, it is difficult for the spectator not to expect the effect after having witnessed a cause whose results are known. Since all that can be *observed* is the uniformity, and our ideas come to us only from observation, any other kind of necessity is unintelligible, and we have no idea of it. Because the actions of human beings are just as regular and predictable as the behavior of inanimate objects, they are just as much necessitated as the latter.

It is usual to point out, in criticism of Hume, that not just any constant conjunction is a necessary connection. For example, the constant conjunction between what is happening to the cogwheels in your watch and what is happening to its hands is a necessary connection, because if the wheels stop, the hands will stop. But the constant conjunction between what is happening to the cogwheels in your watch and what is happening to the hands in mine is *not* a necessary connection, because the wheels in your watch can stop without anything happening to the hands of mine. Two uniformities may differ, in that *if* one were to attempt to separate the events conjoined in one uniformity, one *would* succeed, but *if* one were to attempt to separate the events conjoined in the other, one *would* fail. Hence one can force apart the second pair of uniformly connected events but not the first.

Hume can allow that some constant conjunctions, but not all, are necessary connections. He can say that attempts to separate the moving of the cogwheels and the hands in your watch fail, whereas attempts to separate the moving of the cogwheels in your watch and the hands of mine succeed. We know that this is so by observation, because in the case of other watches, such attempts did succeed (when the hands and the cogwheels belonged to different watches) or fail (when the watches were the same). (Hume can hold this view without inconsistency, provided he does not maintain that they cannot be separated *because* they are necessarily connected, which might presuppose the kind of necessity that he himself has declared to be unintelligible. That two events—taking arsenic and death, for example—are necessarily connected consists only in the fact that once arsenic has been ingested, attempts to prevent death, if made, will fail.)

Hume admits—indeed, he maintains—that happenings both to inanimate objects and to human actions are necessitated in this way. For example, the behavior of my jailer is just as much governed by necessity as the behavior of the iron bars that confine me to my cell. The former prevents me from escaping just as much as the latter. All attempts to modify the behavior of the iron bars that do not include using a file (which I do not have) fail, as much as do all attempts to modify the behavior of the jailer that do not include offering a bribe (which I also do not have).

In this reading (Section 2) Hume discusses some objections to the view that the actions of human beings are as much necessitated as is the behavior of material objects:

1. Those who suppose it is incompatible with commonsense beliefs about freedom confuse the freedom of *spontaneity* with the freedom of *indifference*. We *have* freedom of spontaneity, that is, we feel that we can do things like move our arms this way or that without impediment, and we *can* do this. What is not the case is that our moving our hands spontaneously in one way rather than another is *not caused*. It is caused by the internal propensities (the desires and beliefs) of the agent, for example, a desire to show that I have freedom of spontaneity by moving my hand this way rather than that. Hence we do *not* have freedom of indifference.

2. We confuse the aforementioned liberty of spontaneity, which is something experienced by the *agent*, with chance, which happens when the spectator is not determined by past experience to expect the agent to perform one action rather than another. The agent's experiencing (and, indeed, possessing) the mere liberty of spontaneity, however, does not prevent the spectator from feeling an absolute *necessitation* to infer the agent's action from knowledge of its causes. For example, Smith may be exercising freedom of spontaneity when he accepts the drink we offer him, because he feels nothing impedes his refusal. But we (the spectators) have no freedom of indifference because, owing to past experience of Smith, we cannot help expecting him to accept.

3. It is a mistake to suppose that the doctrine that all action is necessitated conflicts with religion (and, Hume adds later, with morality). Even if it did, this would not be a reason for rejecting it. If people's behavior were not uniform, there would be no point in threatening to punish them for acting wrongly, for it is only because of the uniform way in which a threat of punishment deters crime that punishment is effective. Different circumstances (the presence or absence of a threat of punishment) regularly produce different outcomes (the presence or absence of a crime). Indeed, people would *not* have been to blame for their actions, were the actions a matter of chance (and so possessing the freedom of indifference). Unless the external action of a person whose fingers have pulled the trigger were *caused* by an internal intention, the action would not be capable of moral assessment at all.

Reading

OF LIBERTY AND NECESSITY

Section 1

WE COME NOW to explain the *direct* passions, or the impressions, which arise immediately from good or evil, from pain or pleasure. Of this kind are, *desire and aversion, grief and joy, hope and fear.*

Of all the immediate effects of pain and pleasure, there is none more remarkable than the WILL; and tho', properly speaking, it be not comprehended among the passions, yet as the full understanding of its nature and properties, is necessary to the explanation of them, we shall here make it the subject of our enquiry. I desire it may be observ'd, that by the *will*, I mean nothing but *the internal impression we feel and are conscious of, when we knowingly give rise to any new motion of our body, or new perception of our mind.* This impression, like the preceding ones of pride and humility, love and hatred, 'tis impossible to define, and needless to describe any farther; for which reason we shall cut off all those definitions and distinctions, with which philosophers are wont to perplex rather than clear up this question; and entering at

Reprinted from Hume's *Treatise of Human Nature*, edited by L. A. Selby-Bigge, 2nd edition revised by P. H. Nidditch (1978) by permission of Oxford University Press.

first upon the subject, shall examine that long disputed question concerning *liberty and necessity*; which occurs so naturally in treating of
the will.

'Tis universally acknowledg'd, that the operations of external bodies
are necessary, and that in the communication of their motion, in their
attraction, and mutual cohesion, there are not the least traces of indifference or liberty. Every object is determin'd by an absolute fate to a
certain degree and direction of its motion, and can no more depart from
that precise line, in which it moves, than it can convert itself into an
angel, or spirit, or any superior substance. The actions, therefore, of
matter are to be regarded as instances of necessary actions; and whatever is in this respect on the same footing with matter, must be acknowledg'd to be necessary. That we may know whether this be the case
with the actions of the mind, we shall begin with examining matter, and
considering on what the idea of a necessity in its operations are
founded, and why we conclude one body or action to be the infallible
cause of another.

It has been observ'd already, that in no single instance the ultimate
connexion of any objects is discoverable, either by our senses or reason,
and that we can never penetrate so far into the essence and construction of bodies, as to perceive the principle, on which their mutual
influence depends. 'Tis their constant union alone, with which we are
acquainted; and 'tis from the constant union the necessity arises. If
objects had not an uniform and regular conjunction with each other, we
shou'd never arrive at any idea of cause and effect; and even after all,
the necessity, which enters into that idea, is nothing but a determination of the mind to pass from one object to its usual attendant, and infer
the existence of one from that of the other. Here then are two particulars, which we are to consider as essential to necessity, *viz.* the constant
union and the *inference* of the mind; and wherever we discover these
we must acknowledge a necessity. As the actions of matter have no
necessity, but what is deriv'd from these circumstances, and it is not by
any insight into the essence of bodies we discover their connexion, the
absence of this insight, while the union and inference remain, will
never, in any case, remove the necessity. 'Tis the observation of the
union, which produces the inference; for which reason it might be
thought sufficient, if we prove a constant union in the actions of the
mind, in order to establish the inference, along with the necessity of
these actions. But that I may bestow a greater force on my reasoning, I
shall examine these particulars apart, and shall first prove from experience, that our actions have a constant union with our motives, tempers,
and circumstances, before I consider the inferences we draw from it.

To this end a very slight and general view of the common course of
human affairs will be sufficient. There is no light, in which we can take
them, that does not confirm this principle. Whether we consider mankind according to the difference of sexes, ages, governments, condi-

tions, or methods of education; the same uniformity and regular operation of natural principles are discernible. Like causes still produce like effects; in the same manner as in the mutual action of the elements and powers of nature.

There are different trees, which regularly produce fruit, whose relish is different from each other; and this regularity will be admitted as an instance of necessity and causes in external bodies. But are the products of *Guienne* and of *Champagne* more regularly different than the sentiments, actions, and passions of the two sexes, of which the one are distinguish'd by their force and maturity, the other by their delicacy and softness?

Are the changes of our body from infancy to old age more regular and certain than those of our mind and conduct? And wou'd a man be more ridiculous, who wou'd expect that an infant of four years old will raise a weight of three hundred pound, than one, who from a person of the same age, wou'd look for a philosophical reasoning, or a prudent and well-concerted action?

We must certainly allow, that the cohesion of the parts of matter arises from natural and necessary principles, whatever difficulty we may find in explaining them: And for a like reason we must allow, that human society is founded on like principles; and our reason in the latter case, is better than even that in the former; because we not only observe, that men *always* seek society, but can also explain the principles, on which this universal propensity is founded. For is it more certain, that two flat pieces of marble will unite together, than that two young savages of different sexes will copulate? Do the children arise from this copulation more uniformly, than does the parents care for their safety and preservation? And after they have arriv'd at years of discretion by the care of their parents, are the inconveniences attending their separation more certain than their foresight of these inconveniencies, and their care of avoiding them by a close union and confederacy?

The skin, pores, muscles, and nerves of a day-labourer are different from those of a man of quality: So are his sentiments, actions and manners. The different stations of life influence the whole fabric, external and internal; and these different stations arise necessarily, because uniformly, from the necessary and uniform principles of human nature. Men cannot live without society, and cannot be associated without government. Government makes a distinction of property, and establishes the different ranks of men. This produces industry, traffic, manufactures, law-suits, war, leagues, alliances, voyages, travels, cities, fleets, ports, and all those other actions and objects, which cause such a diversity, and at the same time maintain such an uniformity in human life.

Shou'd a traveller, returning from a far country, tell us, that he had seen a climate in the fiftieth degree of northern latitude, where all the fruits ripen and come to perfection in the winter, and decay in the summer, after the same manner as in *England* they are produc'd and decay in the contrary seasons, he wou'd find few so credulous as to believe him. I am apt to think a traveller wou'd meet with as little credit, who shou'd inform us of people exactly of the same character with those in *Plato's Republic* on the one hand, or those in *Hobbes's Leviathan* on the other. There is a general course of nature in human actions, as well as in the operations of the sun and the climate. There are also characters peculiar to different nations and particular persons, as well as common to mankind. The knowledge of these characters is founded on the observation of an uniformity in the actions, that flow from them; and this uniformity forms the very essence of necessity.

I can imagine only one way of eluding this argument, which is by denying that uniformity of human actions, on which it is founded. As long as actions have a constant union and connexion with the situation and temper of the agent, however we may in words refuse to acknowledge the necessity, we really allow the thing. Now some may, perhaps, find a pretext to deny this regular union and connexion. For what is more capricious than human actions? What more inconstant than the desires of man? And what creature departs more widely, not only from right reason, but from his own character and disposition? An hour, a moment is sufficient to make him change from one extreme to another, and overturn what cost the greatest pain and labour to establish. Necessity is regular and certain. Human conduct is irregular and uncertain. The one, therefore, proceeds not from the other.

To this I reply, that in judging of the actions of men we must proceed upon the same maxims, as when we reason concerning external objects. When any phænomena are constantly and invariably conjoin'd together, they acquire such a connexion in the imagination, that it passes from one to the other, without any doubt or hesitation. But below this there are many inferior degrees of evidence and probability, nor does one single contrariety of experiment entirely destroy all our reasoning. The mind ballances the contrary experiments, and deducting the inferior from the superior, proceeds with that degree of assurance or evidence, which remains. Even when these contrary experiments are entirely equal, we remove not the notion of causes and necessity; but supposing that the usual contrariety proceeds from the operation of contrary and conceal'd causes, we conclude, that the chance or indifference lies only in our judgment on account of our imperfect knowledge, not in the things themselves, which are in every case equally necessary, tho' to appearance not equally constant or certain. No union can be more constant and certain, than that of some actions with some motives and characters; and if in other cases the union is uncertain, 'tis no more than what happens in the operations of body, nor can we conclude any thing from the one irregularity, which will not follow equally from the other.

'Tis commonly allow'd that mad-men have no liberty. But were we to judge by their actions, these have less regularity and constancy than the actions of wise-men, and consequently are farther remov'd from necessity. Our way of thinking in this particular is, therefore, absolutely inconsistent; but is a natural consequence of these confus'd ideas and undefin'd terms, which we so commonly make use of in our reasonings, especially on the present subject.

We must now shew, that as the *union* betwixt motives and actions has the same constancy, as that in any natural operations, so its influence on the understanding is also the same, in *determining* us to infer the existence of one from that of another. If this shall appear, there is no known circumstance, that enters into the connexion and production of the actions of matter, that is not to be found in all the operations of the mind; and consequently we cannot, without a manifest absurdity, attribute necessity to the one, and refuse it to the other.

There is no philosopher, whose judgment is so riveted to this fantastical system of liberty, as not to acknowledge the force of *moral evidence*, and both in speculation and practice proceed upon it, as upon a reasonable foundation. Now moral evidence is nothing but a conclusion concerning the actions of men, deriv'd from the consideration of their motives, temper and situation. Thus when we see certain characters or figures describ'd upon paper, we infer that the person, who produc'd them, would affirm such facts, the death of *Caesar*, the success of *Augustus*, the cruelty of *Nero*; and remembring many other concurrent testimonies we conclude, that those facts were once really existent, and that so many men, without any interest, wou'd never conspire to deceive us; especially since they must, in the attempt, expose themselves to the derision of all their contemporaries, when these facts were asserted to be recent and universally known. The same kind of reasoning runs thro' politics, war, commerce, oeconomy, and indeed mixes itself so entirely in human life, that 'tis impossible to act or subsist a moment without having recourse to it. A prince, who imposes a tax upon his subjects, expects their compliance. A general, who conducts an army, makes account of a certain degree of courage. A merchant looks for fidelity and skill in his factor or super-cargo. A man, who gives orders for his dinner, doubts not of the obedience of his servants. In short, as nothing more nearly interests us than our own actions and those of others, the greatest part of our reasonings is employ'd in judgments concerning them. Now I assert, that whoever reasons after this manner, does *ipso facto* believe the actions of the will to arise from necessity, and that he knows not what he means, when he denies it.

All those objects, of which we call the one *cause* and the other *effect*, consider'd in themselves, are as distinct and separate from each other, as any two things in nature, nor can we ever, by the most accurate survey of them, infer the existence of the one from that of the other. 'Tis only from experience and the observation of their constant union, that we are able to form this inference; and even after all, the inference is nothing but the effects of custom on the imagination. We must not here be content with saying, that the idea of cause and effect arises from objects constantly united; but must affirm, that 'tis the very same with the idea of these objects, and that the *necessary connexion* is not discover'd by a conclusion of the understanding, but is merely a perception of the mind. Wherever, therefore, we observe the same union, and wherever the union operates in the same manner upon the belief and opinion, we have the idea of causes and necessity, tho' perhaps we may avoid those expressions. Motion in one body in all past instances, that have fallen under our observation, is follow'd upon impulse by motion in another. 'Tis impossible for the mind to penetrate farther. From this constant union it *forms* the idea of cause and effect, and by its influence *feels* the necessity. As there is the same constancy, and the same influence in what we call moral evidence, I ask no more. What remains can only be a dispute of words.

And indeed, when we consider how aptly *natural* and *moral* evidence cement together, and form only one chain of argument betwixt them, we shall make no scruple to allow, that they are of the same nature, and deriv'd from the same principles. A prisoner, who has neither money nor interest, discovers the impossibility of his escape, as well from the obstinacy of the goaler, as from the walls and bars with which he is surrounded; and in all attempts for his freedom chuses rather to work upon the stone and iron of the one, than upon the inflexible nature of the other. The same prisoner, when conducted to the scaffold, foresees his death as certainly from the constancy and fidelity of his guards as from the operation of the ax or wheel. His mind runs along a certain train of ideas: The refusal of the soldiers to consent to his escape, the action of the executioner; the separation of the head and body; bleeding, convulsive motions, and death. Here is a connected chain of natural causes and voluntary actions; but the mind feels no difference betwixt them in passing from one link to another; nor is less certain of the future event than if it were connected with the present impressions of the memory and senses by a train of causes cemented together by what we are pleas'd to call a *physical necessity*. The same experienc'd union has the same effect on the mind, whether the united objects be motives, volitions and actions; or figure and motion. We may change the names of things; but their nature and their operation on the understanding never change.

I dare be positive no one will ever endeavour to refute these reasonings otherwise than by altering my definitions, and assigning a different meaning to the terms of *cause, and effect, and necessity, and liberty, and chance*. According to my definitions, necessity makes an essential part of causation; and consequently liberty, by removing necessity, removes also causes, and is the very same thing with chance. As chance is commonly thought to imply a contradiction, and is at least directly contrary to experience, there are always the same arguments against liberty or free-will. If any one alters the definitions, I cannot pretend to argue with him, 'till I know the meaning he assigns to these terms.

Section 2

I believe we may assign the three following reasons for the prevalence of the doctrine of liberty, however absurd it may be in one sense, and unintelligible in any other. First, After we have perform'd any action; tho' we confess we were influenc'd by particular views and motives; 'tis difficult for us to perswade ourselves we were govern'd by necessity, and that 'twas utterly impossible for us to have acted otherwise; the idea of necessity seeming to imply something of force, and violence, and constraint, of which we are not sensible. Few are capable of distinguishing betwixt the liberty of *spontaniety*, as it is call'd in the schools, and the liberty of *indifference*; betwixt that which is oppos'd to violence, and that which means a negation of necessity and causes. The first is even the most common sense of the word; and as 'tis only that species of liberty, which it concerns us to preserve, our thoughts have been principally turn'd towards it, and have almost universally confounded it with the other.

Secondly, there is a *false sensation or experience* even of the liberty of indifference; which is regarded as an argument for its real existence. The necessity of any action, whether of matter or of the mind, is not properly a quality in the agent, but in any thinking or intelligent being, who may consider the action, and consists in the determination of his thought to infer its existence from some preceding objects: As liberty or chance, on the other hand, is nothing but the want of that determination, and a certain looseness, which we feel in passing or not passing from the idea of one to that of the other. Now we may observe, that tho' in reflecting on human actions we seldom feel such a looseness or indifference, yet it very commonly happens, that in performing the actions themselves we are sensible of something like it: And as all related or resembling objects are readily taken for each other, this has been employ'd as a demonstrative or even an intuitive proof of human liberty. We feel that our actions are subject to our will on most occasions, and imagine we feel that the will itself is subject to nothing; because when by a denial of it we are provok'd to try, we feel that it moves easily every way, and produces an image of itself even on that side, on which it did not settle. This image or faint motion, we perswade ourselves, cou'd have been compleated into the thing itself; because, shou'd that be deny'd, we find, upon a second trial, that it can. But these efforts are all in vain; and whatever capricious and irregular actions we may perform; as the desire of showing our liberty is the sole motive of our actions; we can never free ourselves from the bonds of necessity. We may imagine we feel a liberty within ourselves; but a spectator can commonly infer our actions from our motives and character; and even where he cannot, he concludes in general, that he might, were he perfectly acquainted with every circumstance of our situation and temper, and the most secret springs of our complexion and disposition. Now this is the very essence of necessity, according to the foregoing doctrine.

A third reason why the doctrine of liberty has generally been better receiv'd in the world, than its antagonist, proceeds from *religion*, which has been very unnecessarily interested in this question. There is no method of reasoning more common, and yet none more blameable, than in philosophical debates to endeavour to refute any hypothesis by a pretext of its dangerous consequences to religion and morality. When any opinion leads us into absurdities, 'tis certainly false; but 'tis not certain an opinion is false, because 'tis of dangerous consequence. Such topics, therefore, ought entirely to be foreborn, as serving nothing to the discovery of truth, but only to make the person of an antagonist odious. This I observe in general, without pretending to draw any advantage from it. I submit myself frankly to an examination of this kind, and dare venture to affirm, that the doctrine of necessity, according to my explication of it, is not only innocent, but even advantageous to religion and morality.

I define necessity two ways, conformable to the two definitions of *cause*, of which it makes an essential part. I place it either in the constant union and conjunction of like objects, or in the inference of the mind from the one to the other. Now necessity, in both these senses, has universally, tho' tacitely, in the schools, in the pulpit, and in common life, been allow'd to belong to the will of man, and no one has ever pretended to deny, that we can draw inferences concerning human actions, and that those inferences are founded on the experienc'd union of like actions with like motives and circumstances. The only particular in which any one can differ from me, is either, that perhaps he will refuse to call this necessity. But as long as the meaning is understood, I hope the word can do no harm. Or that he will maintain there is something else in the operations of matter. Now whether it be so or not is of no consequence to religion, whatever it may be to natural philosophy. I may be mistaken in asserting, that we have no idea of any other connexion in the actions of body, and shall be glad to be farther instructed on that head: But sure I am, I ascribe nothing to the actions of the mind, but what must readily be allow'd of. Let no one, therefore, put an invidious construction on my words, by saying simply, that I assert the necessity of human actions, and place them on the same footing with the operations of senseless matter. I do not ascribe to the will that unintelligible necessity, which is suppos'd to lie in matter. But I ascribe to matter, that intelligible quality, call it necessity or not, which the most rigorous orthodoxy does or must allow to belong to the will. I change, therefore, nothing in the receiv'd systems, with regard to the will, but only with regard to material objects.

Nay I shall go farther, and assert, that this kind of necessity is so essential to religion and morality, that without it there must ensue an absolute subversion of both, and that every other supposition is entirely destructive to all laws both *divine* and *human*. 'Tis indeed certain, that as all human laws are founded on rewards and punishments, 'tis suppos'd as a fundamental principle, that these motives have an influence on the mind, and both produce the good and prevent the evil actions. We may give to this influence what name we please; but as 'tis usually conjoin'd with the action, common sense requires it shou'd be esteem'd a cause, and be look'd upon as an instance of that necessity, which I wou'd establish.

This reasoning is equally solid, when apply'd to *divine* laws, so far as the deity is consider'd as a legislator, and is suppos'd to inflict punishment and bestow rewards with a design to produce obedience. But I also maintain, that even where he acts not in his magisterial capacity, but is regarded as the avenger of crimes merely on account of their odiousness and deformity, not only 'tis impossible, without the necessary connexion of cause and effect in human actions, that punishments cou'd be inflicted compatible with justice and moral equity; but also that it cou'd ever enter into the thoughts of any reasonable being to inflict them. The constant and universal object of hatred or anger is a person or creature endow'd with thought and consciousness; and when any criminal or injurious actions excite that passion, 'tis only by their relation to the person or connexion with him. But according to the doctrine of liberty or chance, this connexion is reduc'd to nothing, nor are men more accountable for those actions, which are design'd and premeditated, than for such as are the most casual and accidental. Actions are by their very nature temporary and perishing; and where they proceed not from some cause in the characters and disposition of the person, who perform'd them, they infix not themselves upon him, and can neither redound to his honour, if good, nor infamy, if evil. The action itself may be blameable; it may be contrary to all the rules of morality and religion: But the person is not responsible for it; and as it proceeded from nothing in him, that is durable or constant, and leaves nothing of that nature behind it, 'tis impossible he can, upon its account, become the object of punishment or vengeance. According to the hypothesis of liberty, therefore, a man is as pure and untainted, after having committed the most horrid crimes, as at the first moment of his birth, nor is his character any way concern'd in his actions; since they are not deriv'd from it, and the wickedness of the one can never be us'd as a proof of the depravity of the other. 'Tis only upon the principles of necessity, that a person acquires any merit or demerit from his actions, however the common opinion may incline to the contrary.

But so inconsistent are men with themselves, that tho' they often assert, that necessity utterly destroys all merit and demerit either towards mankind or superior powers, yet they continue still to reason upon these very principles of necessity in all their judgments concerning this matter. Men are not blam'd for such evil actions as they perform ignorantly and casually, whatever may be their consequences. Why? but because the causes of these actions are only momentary, and terminate in them alone. Men are less blam'd for such evil actions, as they perform hastily and unpremeditately, than for such as proceed from thought and deliberation. For what reason? but because a hasty temper, tho' a constant cause in the mind, operates only by intervals, and infects not the whole character. Again, repentance wipes off every crime, especially if attended with an evident reformation of life and manners. How is this to be accounted for? But by asserting that actions render a person criminal, merely as they are proofs of criminal passions or principles in the mind; and when by any alteration of these principles they cease to be just proofs, they likewise cease to be criminal. But according to the doctrine of *liberty* or *chance* they never were just proofs, and consequently never were criminal.

Here then I turn to my adversary, and desire him to free his own system from these odious consequences before he charge them upon others. Or if he rather chuses, that this question shou'd be decided by fair arguments before philosophers, than by declamations before the people, let him return to what I have advanc'd to prove that liberty and chance are synonymous; and concerning the nature of moral evidence and the regularity of human actions. Upon a review of these reasonings, I cannot doubt of an entire victory; and therefore having prov'd, that all actions of the will have particular causes, I proceed to explain what these causes are, and how they operate.

7

PAUL RÉE

We Are Not Responsible for What We Do

Introduction

Paul Rée (1849–1901) wrote books on the freedom of the will and the origin of conscience, and a larger work (including a defense of atheism) which was not published until after his death. In this reading, Rée produces arguments for determinism. He then adds that, although we cannot help believing that we are responsible for our actions, this belief must be false if determinism is true. The reason more people are not determinists is that the brain, which is the cause of human actions, is hidden inside the skull where we cannot see how actions are caused. (The fact that automobile engines are hidden under car hoods, however, does not produce a similar belief in indeterminism in the behavior of the internal combustion engine, perhaps because it is easier to open a car hood than a skull.)

The Introduction of this text argues that freedom and determinism are compatible, whereas Rée is what William James called a "hard determinist" who thinks they are not compatible. Rée says that there are *senses* in which our actions *are* free. "A man free from passion [for example] is still subject to the law of causality. He is *necessarily free* [italics added] from passion. The word 'free' has different meanings." It may be that he thinks one of these meanings records the fact, which he himself insists on, that there are some things (e.g., walking) that we can do and other things (e.g., flying) that we cannot do.

Rée is not, however, similarly equivocal about *responsibility*. Determinism, he thinks, implies that we are *not responsible* for what we do. However, if determinism is true, I can do certain things in the sense that if my character leads me to want to do them, there is nothing to stop me from doing them; I cannot help the fact that I have the character that necessarily results in my wanting to do what I do. Hence it is not within my power to produce a state of affairs which results in the occurrence of anything other than my action. To do so, I would need to alter the causes of my having the character that results in my doing what I do, and these lie in the past and are in any case themselves necessitated. Hence, remorse and blame, and consequently the practice of punishing people, are alike irrational.

Rée states that people cannot *help* believing that they are responsible for what they do. (Kant, too, thought that rational beings could not act in any way except under the *idea* of freedom.) Here I suspect that both Kant and Rée are mistaken. What people cannot help believing is *not* that their actions do *not* have *causes*, but that their actions *do* have *effects*. For example, I cannot help believing that if I were to make the effort not to pull the trigger, the result would be Smith's not dying; that is, that my action had an effect. This belief is true whether determinism is true or not.

So far as the *causes* of our pulling the trigger are concerned, my belief is not that this action is *not* caused but that its causes are not *complete* until I have performed an "act of will" (which must itself have causes). This belief, too, is true. We have no difficulty in believing that *other people's* acts of will, as well as our own *past* ones, do have complete sets of causes.

Rée thinks that it is an illusion that I could have done anything other than what I did. Rée says (of the donkey into whose mental deliberations he shows such insight) "Having become a different animal since the time of the action, perhaps because of it, she thinks—by way of a kind of optical illusion—that she was that other animal already then." For example, we look back on some past action and assume that we had the knowledge which we have now, but did not have then. It is tempting to argue against Rée that this assumes, inconsistently, that we *can* do it *now*, when we *do* have the knowledge that we formerly lacked.

Reading

1. NOTHING HAPPENS WITHOUT A CAUSE

TO SAY THAT the will is not free means that it is subject to the law of causality. Every act of will is in fact preceded by a sufficient cause. Without such a cause the act of will cannot occur; and, if the sufficient cause is present, the act of will must occur.

To say that the will is free would mean that it is not subject to the law of causality. In that case every act of will would be an absolute beginning [a first cause] and not a link [in a chain of events]: it would not be the effect of preceding causes.

The reflections that follow may serve to clarify what is meant by saying that the will is not free. . . . Every object—a stone, an animal,

From the *Concise Encyclopaedia of Western Philosophy*, edited by J. O. Urmson and J. Rée. Reprinted by permission of Routledge, Chapman, and Hall, Ltd.

a human being — can pass from its present state to another one. The stone that now lies in front of me may, in the next moment, fly through the air, or it may disintegrate into dust or roll along the ground. If, however, one of these *possible* states is to be *realized*, its sufficient cause must first be present. The stone will fly through the air if it is tossed. It will roll if a force acts upon it. It will disintegrate into dust, given that some object hits and crushes it.

It is helpful to use the terms "potential" and "actual" in this connection. At any moment there are innumerably many potential states. At a given time, however, only *one* can become actual, namely, the one that is triggered by its sufficient cause.

The situation is no different in the case of an animal. The donkey that now stands motionless between two piles of hay may, in the next moment, turn to the left or to the right, or he may jump into the air or put his head between his legs. But here, too, the sufficient cause must first be present if of the *possible* modes of behavior one is to be *realized*.

Let us analyze one of these modes of behavior. We shall assume that the donkey has turned toward the bundle on his right. This turning presupposes that certain muscles were contracted. The cause of this muscular contraction is the excitation of the nerves that lead to them. The cause of this excitation of the nerves is a state of the brain. It was in a state of decision. But how did the brain come to be in that condition? Let us trace the states of the donkey back a little farther.

A few moments before he turned, his brain was not yet so constituted as to yield the sufficient cause for the excitation of the nerves in question and for the contraction of the muscles; for otherwise the movement would have occurred. The donkey had not yet "decided" to turn. If he then moved at some subsequent time, his brain must in the meantime have become so constituted as to bring about the excitation of the nerves and the movement of the muscles. Hence the brain underwent some change. To what causes is this change to be attributed? To the effectiveness of an impression that acts as an external stimulus, or to a sensation that arose internally; for example, the sensation of hunger and the idea of the bundle on the right, by jointly affecting the brain, change the way in which it is constituted so that it now yields the sufficient cause for the excitation of the nerves and the contraction of the muscles. The donkey now "wants" to turn to the right; he now turns to the right.

Hence, just as the position and constitution of the stone, on the one hand, and the strength and direction of the force that acts upon it, on the other, necessarily determine the kind and length of its flight, so the movement of the donkey — his turning to the bundle on the right — is no less necessarily the result of the way in which the donkey's brain and the stimulus are constituted at a given moment. That the donkey turned toward this particular bundle was determined by something trivial. If the bundle that the donkey did not choose had been positioned just a bit differently, or if it had smelled different, or if the subjective factor —the donkey's sense of smell or his visual organs—had developed in a somewhat different way, then, so we may assume, the donkey would have turned to the left. But the cause was not complete there, and that is why the effect could not occur, while with respect to the other side, where the cause was complete, the effect could not fail to appear.

For the donkey, consequently, just as for the stone, there are innumerably many *potential* states at any moment; he may walk or run or jump, or move to the left, to the right, or straight ahead. But only the one whose sufficient cause is present can ever become *actual*.

At the same time, there is a difference between the donkey and the stone in that the donkey moves because he wants to move, while the stone moves because it is moved. We do not deny this difference. There are, after all, a good many other differences between the donkey and the stone. We do not by any means intend to prove that this dissimilarity does not exist. We do not assert that the donkey is a stone, but only that the donkey's every movement and act of will has causes just as the motion of the stone does. The donkey moves because he wants to move. But that he wants to move at a given moment, and in this particular direction, is causally determined.

Could it be that there was no sufficient cause for the donkey's wanting to turn around—that he simply wanted to turn around? His act of will would then be an absolute beginning. An assumption of that kind is contradicted by experience and the universal validity of the law of causality. By experience, since observation teaches us that for every act of will some causes were the determining factors. By the universal validity of the law of causality, since, after all, nothing happens anywhere in the world without a sufficient cause. Why, then, of all things should a donkey's act of will come into being without a cause? Besides, the state of willing, the one that immediately precedes the excitation of the motor nerves, is no different in principle from other states—that of indifference, of lassitude, or of weariness. Would anyone believe that all of these states exist without a cause? And if one does not believe that, why should just the state of willing be thought to occur without a sufficient cause?

It is easy to explain why it seems to us that the motion of the stone is necessary while the donkey's act of will is not. The causes that move the stone are, after all, external and visible. But the causes of the donkey's act of will are internal and invisible; between us and the locus of their effectiveness lies the skull of the donkey. Let us consider this difference somewhat more closely. The stone lies before us as it is constituted. We can also see the force acting upon it, and from these two factors, the constitution of the stone and the force, there results, likewise visible, the rolling of the stone. The case of the donkey is different. The state of his brain is hidden from our view. And, while the bundle of hay is visible, its effectiveness is not. It is an internal process. The bundle does not come into visible contact with the brain but acts at a distance. Hence the subjective and the objective factor — the brain and the impact that the bundle has upon it — are invisible.

Let us suppose that we could depict the donkey's soul in high relief, taking account of and making visible all those states, attitudes, and feelings that characterize it before the donkey turns. Suppose further that we could see how an image detaches itself from the bundle of hay and, describing a visible path through the air, intrudes upon the donkey's brain and how it produces a change there in consequence of which certain nerves and muscles move. Suppose, finally, that we could repeat this experiment arbitrarily often, that, if we returned the donkey's soul into the state preceding his turning and let exactly the same impression act upon it, we should always observe the very same result. Then we would regard the donkey's turning to the right as necessary. We would come to realize that the brain, constituted as it was at that moment, had to react to such an impression in precisely that way.

In the absence of this experiment it seems as though the donkey's act of will were not causally determined. We just do not see its being causally determined and consequently believe that no such determination takes place. The act of will, it is said, is the cause of the turning, but it is not itself determined; it is said to be an absolute beginning.

The opinion that the donkey's act of will is not causally determined is held not only by the outsider; the donkey himself, had he the gift of reflection, would share it. The causes of his act of will would elude him, too, since in part they do not become conscious at all and in part pass through consciousness fleetingly, with the speed of lightning. If, for example, what tipped the scales was that he was closer by a hair's breadth to the bundle on the right, or that it smelled a shade better, how should the donkey notice something so trivial, something that so totally fails to force itself upon his consciousness?

In *one* sense, of course, the donkey is right in thinking "I could have turned to the left." His state at the moment, his position relative to the bundle, or its constitution need merely have been somewhat different, and he really would have turned to the left. The statement "I could have acted otherwise" is, accordingly, true in this sense: turning to the left is one of the movements possible for me (in contrast, for example, to the movement of flying); it lies within the realm of my possibilities.

We arrive at the same result if we take the law of inertia as our point of departure. It reads: every object strives to remain in its present state. Expressed negatively this becomes: without a sufficient cause no object can pass from its present state to another one. The stone will lie forever just as it is lying now; it will not undergo the slightest change if no causes — such as the weather or a force — act upon it to bring about a change. The donkey's brain will remain in the same state unchanged for all eternity if no causes — the feeling of hunger or fatigue, say, or external impressions — bring about a change.

If we reflect upon the entire life of the donkey *sub specie necessitatis*, we arrive at the following result. The donkey came into the world with certain properties of mind and body, his genetic inheritance. Since the day of his birth, impressions — of the companions with whom he frolicked or worked, his feed, the climate — have acted upon these properties. These two factors, his inborn constitution and the way in which it was formed through the impressions of later life, are the cause of all of his sensations, ideas, and moods, and of all of his movements, even the most trivial ones. If, for example, he cocks his left ear and not the right one, that is determined by causes whose historical development could be traced back ad infinitum; and likewise when he stands, vacillating, between the two bundles. And when action, the act of feeding, takes the place of vacillation, that, too, is determined: the idea of the one bundle now acts upon the donkey's mind, when it has become receptive to the idea of that particular sheaf, in such a way as to produce actions.

2. Human Beings and the Law of Causality

Let us now leave the realm of animals and proceed to consider man. Everything is the same here. Man's every feeling is a necessary result. Suppose, for example, that I am stirred by a feeling of pity at this moment. To what causes is it to be attributed? Let us go back as far as possible. An infinite amount of time has elapsed up to this moment. Time was never empty; objects have filled it from all eternity. These objects . . . have continually undergone change. All of these changes were governed by the law of causality; not one of them took place without a sufficient cause.

We need not consider what else may have characterized these changes. Only their *formal* aspect, only this *one* point is of concern to us: no change occurred without a cause.

At some time in the course of this development, by virtue of some causes, organic matter was formed, and finally man. Perhaps the organic world developed as Darwin described it. Be that as it may, it was in any case due to causes that I was born on a particular day, with particular properties of body, of spirit, and of heart. Impressions then acted upon this constitution; I had particular governesses, teachers, and playmates. Teaching and example in part had an effect and in part were lost upon me; the former, when my inborn constitution made me receptive to them, when I had an affinity for them. And that is how it has come to be, through the operation of [a chain of] causes, that I am stirred by a feeling of pity at this moment. The course of the world would have had to be somewhat different if my feelings were to be different now.

It is of no consequence for the present investigation whether the inborn capacity for pity, for taking pleasure in another's pain, or for courage remains constant throughout life or whether teaching, example, and activity serve to change it. In any case the pity or pleasure in another's pain, the courage or cowardice, that a certain person feels or exhibits at a given moment is a necessary result, whether these traits are inborn — an inheritance from his ancestors — or were developed in the course of his own life.

Likewise every intention, indeed, every thought that ever passes through the brain, the silliest as well as the most brilliant, the true as well as the false, exists of necessity. In that sense there is no freedom of thought. It is necessary that I sit in this place at this moment, that I hold my pen in my hand in a particular way, and that I write that every thought is necessary; and if the reader should perchance be of the opinion that this is not the case, i.e., if he should believe that thoughts may not be viewed as effects, then he holds this false opinion of necessity also.

Just as sensations and thoughts are necessary, so, too, is action. It is, after all, nothing other than their externalization, their objective embodiment. Action is born of sensations and thoughts. So long as the sensations are not sufficiently strong, action cannot occur, and when the sensations and thoughts are constituted so as to yield the sufficient cause for it, then it must occur; then the appropriate nerves and muscles are set to work. Let us illustrate this by means of an action that is judged differently at different levels of civilization, namely, murder.[1] Munzinger, for example, says that among the Bogos the murderer, the terror of the neighborhood, who never tires of blood and murder, is a man of respect. Whoever has been raised with such views will not be deterred from murder either by external or by internal obstacles. Neither the police nor his conscience forbids him to commit it. On the contrary, it is his habit to praise murder; his parents and his gods stimulate him to commit it, and his companions encourage him by their example. And so it comes to be that, if there is a favorable opportunity, he does the deed. But is this not terribly trivial? After all, everyone knows that an act of murder is due to *motives*! True, but almost no one (except perhaps a philosopher) knows that an act of murder, and indeed every action, has a *cause*. Motives are a part of the cause. But to admit that there are motives for an action is not yet to recognize that it is causally determined, or to see clearly that the action is determined by

[1]The German here is *Raubmord*, a compound noun denoting a combination of murder and robbery (with overtones of pillage and rape). In his discussion Rée will focus now on the one aspect, now on the other. To avoid lengthy periphrasis in English, the action in question has been uniformly termed murder. The Bogos to whom Rée refers in the next sentence are a tribe occupying a district in the highlands north of Abyssinia. Werner Munzinger (1832–1875) was a Swiss explorer and linguist who spent many years in Eritrea, Abyssinia, and the Sudan. He described the customs of the Bogos in his book *Über die Sitten und das Recht der Bogos*, published in 1859.

thoughts and sensations — which in turn are effects — just as the rolling of a ball is determined by a force. But it is this point, and only this one, to which we must pay heed.

Let us now consider the act of murder from the same point of view in the case of civilized peoples. Someone raised at a higher level of civilization has learned from childhood on to disapprove of murder and to regard it as deserving punishment. God, his parents, and his teachers — in short, all who constitute an authority for him — condemn acts of this kind. It is, moreover, inconsistent with his character, which has been formed in an era of peace. Lastly, too, fear of punishment will deter him. Can murder prosper on such soil? Not easily. Fear, pity, the habit of condemning murder — all these are just so many bulwarks that block the path to such an action. Nevertheless need, passion, or various seductive influences will perhaps remove one after another of these bulwarks. Let us consider the cause of an act of murder more closely. First it is necessary to distinguish between two components, the subjective and the objective, in the total cause. The *subjective* part of the cause consists of the state of the murderer at the moment of the deed. To this we must assign all ideas that he had at the time, the conscious as well as the unconscious ones, his sensations, the temperature of his blood, the state of his stomach, of his liver — of each and every one of his bodily organs. The *objective* component consists of the appearance of the victim, the locality in which the deed took place, and the way it was illuminated. The act of murder was necessarily consummated at that moment because these impressions acted upon a human being constituted in that particular way at the time. "Necessarily" means just that the act of murder is an effect; the state of the murderer and the impressions acting upon it are its cause. If the cause had not been complete, the effect could not have occurred. If, for example, the murderer had felt even a trifle more pity at that moment, if his idea of God or of the consequences that his deed would have here on earth had been somewhat more distinct, or if the moon had been a little brighter, so that more light would have fallen upon the victim's face and his pleading eyes — then, perhaps, the cause of the act of murder would not have become complete, and in consequence the act would not have taken place.

Thus for man, as for animal and stone, there are at any moment innumerably many *potential* states. The murderer might, at the moment when he committed the murder, have climbed a tree instead or stood on his head. If, however, instead of the murder one of these actions were to have become *actual*, then its sufficient cause would have had to be present. He would have climbed a tree if he had had the intention of hiding, or of acting as a lookout, that is to say, if at that moment he had had other ideas and sensations. But this could have been the case only if the events that took place in the world had been somewhat different [stretching back in time] ad infinitum.

3. Determinism and Will-Power

But I can, after all, break through the network of thoughts, sensations, and impressions that surrounds me by resolutely saying "I will not commit murder!" No doubt. We must, however, not lose sight of the fact that a resolute "I will" or "I will not" is also, wherever it appears, a necessary result; it does not by any means exist without a cause. Let us return to our examples. Although the Bogo really has reasons only to commit murder, it is nevertheless possible for a resolute "I will not commit murder" to assert itself. But is it conceivable that this "I will not" should occur without a sufficient cause? Fear, pity, or some other feeling, which in turn is an effect, overcomes him and gives rise to this "I will not" before the cause of the murder has yet become complete. Perhaps Christian missionaries have had an influence upon him; hence the idea of a deity that will visit retribution on him for murder comes before his soul, and that is how the "I will not" comes to be. It is easier to detect the causes of the resolute "I will not commit murder" in someone raised at a higher level of civilization; fear, principles, or the thought of God in most cases produce it in time.

A resolute will can be characteristic of a man. No matter how violently jealousy, greed, or some other passion rages within him, he does not want to succumb to it; he does not succumb to it. The analogue of this constitution is a ball that, no matter how violent a force acts upon it, does not budge from its place. A billiard cue will labor in vain to shake the earth. The earth victoriously resists the cue's thrusts with its mass. Likewise man resists the thrusts of greed and jealousy with the mass of his principles. A man of that kind, accordingly, is free — from being dominated by his drives. Does this contradict determinism? By no means. A man free from passion is still subject to the law of causality. He is necessarily free. It is just that the word "free" has different meanings. It may be correctly predicated of man in every sense except a single one: he is not free from the law of causality. Let us trace the causes of his freedom from the tyranny of the passions.

Let us suppose that his steadfastness of will was not inherited, or, if so, merely as a disposition. Teaching, example, and, above all, the force of circumstances developed it in him. From early childhood on he found himself in situations in which he had to control himself if he did not want to perish. Just as someone standing at the edge of an abyss can banish dizziness by thinking "If I become dizzy, then I will plunge," so thinking "If I yield to my excitation — indeed, if I so much as betray it — I will perish" has led him to control of his drives.

It is often thought that those who deny that the will is free want to deny that man has the ability to free himself from being dominated by his drives. However, one can imagine man's power to resist passions to be as great as one wants, even infinitely great; that is to say, a man may possibly resist even the most violent passion: his love of God or his principles have still more power over him than the passion. The question whether even the most resolute act of will is an effect is entirely independent of this.

But is being subject to the law of causality not the weak side of the strong? By no means. Is a lion weak if he can tear a tiger apart? Is a hurricane weak if it can uproot trees? And yet the power by means of which the lion dismembers and the storm uproots is an effect, and not an absolute beginning. By having causes, by being an effect, strength is not diminished.

Just as resolute willing is to be considered an effect, so is irresolute willing. A vacillating man is characterized by the fact that he alternately wants something and then doesn't want it. To say that someone contemplating murder is still vacillating means that at one time the desire for possessions, greed, and jealousy predominate — then he wants to commit murder; at another time fear of the consequences, the thought of God, or pity overcomes him, and then he does not want to commit murder. In the decisive moment, when his victim is before him, everything depends upon which feeling has the upper hand. If at that moment passion predominates, then he wants to commit murder; and then he commits murder.

We see that, from whatever point of view we look at willing, it always appears as a necessary result, as a link [in a chain of events], and never as an absolute beginning.

But can we not prove by means of an experiment that willing is an absolute beginning? I lift my arm because I *want* to lift it. . . . Here my *wanting* to lift my arm is the cause of the lifting, but this wanting, we are told, is not itself causally determined; rather, it is an absolute beginning. I simply want to lift my arm, and that is that. We are deceiving ourselves. This act of will, too, has causes; my intention to demonstrate by means of an experiment that my will is free gives rise to my wanting to lift my arm. But how did this intention come to be? Through a conversation, or through reflecting on the freedom of the will. Thus the thought "I want to demonstrate my freedom" has the effect that I want to lift my arm. There is a gap in this chain. Granted that my intention to demonstrate that my will is free stands in some relation to my wanting to lift my arm, why do I not demonstrate my freedom by means of some other movement? Why is it *just my arm* that I want to lift? This specific act of will on my part has not yet been causally explained. Does it perhaps not have causes? Is it an uncaused act of will? Let us note first that someone who wishes to demonstrate that his will is free will usually really extend or lift his arm, and in particular his right arm. He neither tears his hair nor wiggles his belly. This can be explained as follows. Of all of the parts of the body that are subject to our voluntary control, there is none that we move more frequently than the right arm. If, now, we wish to demonstrate our freedom by means of some movement, we will automatically make that one to which we are most accustomed. . . . Thus we first have a conversation about or reflection on the freedom of the will; this leads to the intention of demonstrating our freedom; this intention arises in an organism with certain [physiological] habits [such as that of readily lifting the right arm], and as a result we want to lift (and then lift) the right arm.

I remember once discussing the freedom of the will with a left-handed man. He asserted "My will is free; I can do what I want." In order to demonstrate this he extended his *left* arm.

It is easy to see, now, what the situation is with regard to the assertion "I can do what I want." In one sense it is indeed correct; in another, however, it is wrong. The *correct* sense is to regard willing as a cause and action as an effect. For example, I can kill my rival if I want to kill him. I can walk to the left if I want to walk to the left. The causes are *wanting* to kill and *wanting* to walk; the effects are killing and walking. In some way every action must be preceded by the act of willing it, whether we are aware of it or not. According to this view, in fact, I can do *only* what I want to do, and only if I want to do it. The *wrong* sense is to regard willing *merely* as a cause, and not at the same time as the effect of something else. But, like everything else, it is cause *as well as effect.* An absolutely initial act of will does not exist. Willing stands in the middle: it brings about killing and walking to the left; it is the effect of thoughts and sensations (which in turn are effects).

4. IGNORANCE OF THE CAUSATION OF OUR ACTIONS

Hence our volition (with respect to some action) is always causally determined. But it seems to be free (of causes); it seems to be an absolute beginning. To what is this appearance due?

We do not perceive the causes by which our volition is determined, and that is why we believe that it is not causally determined at all.

How often do we do something while "lost in thought"! We pay no attention to what we are doing, let alone to the causes from which it springs. While we are thinking, we support our head with our hand. While we are conversing, we twist a piece of paper in our hand. If we then reflect on our behavior — stimulated perhaps by a conversation about the freedom of the will — and if we are quite incapable of finding a sufficient cause for it, then we believe that there was no sufficient cause for it at all, that, consequently, we could have proceeded differently at that moment, e.g., supporting our head with the left hand instead of the right.

To adduce yet another example: suppose that there are two eggs on the table. I take one of them. Why not the other one? Perhaps the one I took was a bit closer to me, or some other trivial matter, which would be very difficult to discover and is of the kind that almost never enters our consciousness, tipped the scales. If I now look back but do not see why I took *that* particular egg, then I come to think that I could just as well have taken the other.

Let us replace "I could have taken the other egg" by other statements containing the expression "I could have." For example, I could, when I took the egg, have chopped off my fingers instead, or I could have jumped at my neighbor's throat. Why do we never adduce such statements . . . but always those contemplating an action close to the one that we really carried out? Because at the moment when I took the egg, chopping off my fingers and murder were far from my mind. From this point of view the two aspects of our subject matter—the fact that acts of will are necessary and that they appear not to be necessary —can be perceived especially clearly. *In fact* taking the other egg was at that moment just as impossible as chopping off a finger. For, whether a nuance of a sensation or a whole army of sensations and thoughts is lacking in the complete cause obviously does not matter; the effect cannot occur so long as the cause is incomplete. But it *seems* as though it would have been possible to take the other egg at that moment; if something almost happened, we think that it could have happened.

While in the case of unimportant matters we perhaps do not notice the causes of our act of will and therefore think that it has no causes, the situation is quite different—it will be objected—in the case of important matters. We did not, after all, marry one girl rather than another while "lost in thought." We did not close the sale of our house while "lost in thought." Rather, everyone sees that motives determined such decisions. In spite of this, however, we think "I could have acted differently." What is the source of this error?

In the case of unimportant matters we do not notice the cause of our action at all; in the case of important ones we perceive it, but not adequately. We do, to be sure, see the separate parts of the cause, but the special relation in which they stood to one another at the moment of the action eludes us.

Let us first consider another example from the realm of animals. A vixen vacillated whether to sneak into the chicken coop, to hunt for mice, or to return to her young in her den. At last she sneaked into the chicken coop. Why? Because she wanted to. But why did she want to? Because this act of will on her part resulted from the relation in which her hunger, her fear of the watchdog, her maternal instinct, and her other thoughts, sensations, and impressions stood to one another at that time. But a vixen with the gift of reflection would, were she to look back upon her action, say "I could have willed differently." For, although she realizes that hunger influenced her act of will, the *degree* of hunger on the one hand, and of fear and maternal instinct on the other, present at the moment of the action elude her. Having become a different animal since the time of the action, perhaps because of it, she thinks — by way of a kind of optical illusion — that she was that other animal already then. It is the same in the case of man. Suppose, for example, that someone has slain his rival out of jealousy. What does he himself, and what do others, perceive with respect to this action? We see that on the one hand jealousy, the desire for possessions, hatred, and rage were present in him, and on the other fear of punishment, pity, and the thought of God. We do not, however, see the particular relation in which hatred and pity, and rage and fear of punishment, stood to one another at the moment of the deed. If we could see this, keep it fixed, and recreate it experimentally, then everyone would regard this action as an effect, as a necessary result.

Let us now, with the aid of our imagination, suppose that the sensations and thoughts of the murderer at the moment of the deed were spread out before us, clearly visible as if on a map. From this reflection we shall learn that *in fact* we are lacking such an overview, and that this lack is the reason why we do not ascribe a cause (or "necessity") to the action.

The kaleidoscopically changing sensations, thoughts, and impressions would, in order for their relation to one another to become apparent, have to be returned to the state in which they were at the moment of the deed, and then made rigid, as if they were being nailed to their place. But beyond that, the thoughts and sensations would have to be spatially extended and endowed with a colored surface; a stronger sensation would have to be represented by a bigger lump. A clearer thought would have to wear, say, a bright red color, a less clear one a gray coloration. Jealousy and rage, as well as pity and the thought of God, would have to be plastically exhibited for us in this way. We would, further, have to see how the sight of the victim acts upon these structures of thoughts and sensations, and how there arises from these two factors first the desire to commit murder and then the act of murder itself.

Moreover, we would have to be able to repeat the process, perhaps as follows: we return the murderer to the state of mind that he had some years before the act of murder; we equip his mind with precisely the same thoughts and sensations, and his body with the same constitution. Then we let the very same impressions act upon them; we bring him into contact with the same people, let him read the same books, nourish him with the same food, and, finally, we will place the murdered person, after having called him back to life, before the murderer with the very same facial expression, in the same illumination and at the same distance. Then, as soon as the parts of the cause have been completely assembled, we would always see that the very same effect occurs, namely, wanting to commit, and then committing, murder.

Finally, too, we would have to vary the experiment, in the manner of the chemists; we would have to be able now to weaken a sensation, now to strengthen it, and to observe the result that this produces.

If these conditions were fulfilled, if we could experimentally recreate the process and also vary it, if we were to see its components and, above all, their relation to one another with plastic clarity before us — on the one hand, the *degree* of jealousy and of rage present at the moment; on the other, the *degree* of fear of punishment and of pity — then we would acknowledge that wanting to commit murder and committing murder are necessary results. But as it is we merely see that, on the one hand, jealousy and related feelings, and, on the other, pity and the idea of God, were present in the murderer. But, since we do not see the particular relation in which the sensations and thoughts stood to one another at the moment of the deed, we simply think that the *one* side could have produced acts of will and actions as well as the *other*, that the murderer could, at the moment when he wanted to commit and did commit murder, just as well have willed and acted differently, say compassionately.

It is the same if we ourselves are the person who acts. We, too, think "I could have willed differently." Let us illustrate this by yet another example. Yesterday afternoon at 6:03 o'clock I sold my house. Why? Because I wished to do so. But why did I wish to do so? Because my intention to change my place of residence, and other circumstances, caused my act of will. But was I compelled to will? Could I not have postponed the sale or forgone it altogether? It seems so to me, because I do not see the particular relation in which my thoughts, sensations, and impressions stood to one another yesterday afternoon at 6:03 o'clock.

Thus: we do not see the sufficient cause (either not at all, in the case of unimportant matters; or inadequately, in the case of important ones); consequently it does not exist for us; consequently we think that our volition and our actions were not causally determined at all, that we could just as well have willed and acted differently. No one would say "I could have willed differently" if he could see his act of will and its causes displayed plastically before him, in an experiment permitting repetition.

But who are the mistaken "we" of whom we are speaking here? Patently the author does not consider himself to be one of them. Does he, then, set himself, along with a few fellow philosophers, apart from the rest of mankind, regarding them as ignorant of the truth? Well, it really is not the case that mankind has always concerned itself with the problem of the freedom of the will and only a small part arrived at the result that the will is not free; rather, in precivilized ages no one, and in civilized ages almost no one, concerned himself with this problem. But of the few who did address themselves to this question, as the history of philosophy teaches us, almost all recognized that there is no freedom of the will. The others became victims of the illusion described above, without ever coming to grips with the problem in its general form (is the will subject to the law of causality or not?).

5. Determinism Is Inconsistent with Judgments of Moral Responsibility

We hold ourselves and others responsible without taking into account the problem of the freedom of the will.

Experience shows that, if someone has lied or murdered, he is told that he has acted reprehensibly and deserves punishment. Whether his action is uncaused or whether, like the other processes in nature, it is subject to the law of causality — how would people come to raise such questions in the ordinary course of their lives? Or has anyone ever heard of a case in which people talking about an act of murder, a lie, or an act of self-sacrifice discussed these actions in terms of the freedom of the will? It is the same if we ourselves are the person who acted. We say to ourselves "Oh, if only I had not done this! Oh, if only I had acted differently!" or "I have acted laudably, as one should act." At best a philosopher here or there changes upon the question whether our actions are causally determined or not, certainly not the rest of mankind.

Suppose, however, that someone's attention is directed to the fact that the will is not free. At first it will be very difficult to make this plausible to him. His volition is suspended from threads that are too nearly invisible, and that is why he comes to think that it is not causally determined at all. At last, however — so we shall assume — he does come to recognize that actions are effects, that their causes are thoughts and impressions, that these must likewise be viewed as effects, and so on. How will he then judge these actions? Will he continue to maintain that murder is to be punished by *reprisal* and that benovolent actions are to be considered *meritorious*? By no means. Rather, the first conclusion that he will — validly — draw from his newly acquired insight is that we cannot hold anyone responsible. *"Tout comprendre c'est tout pardonner"*; no one can be made to answer for an *effect*.

In order to illustrate this important truth, that whoever considers intentions to be effects will cease to assign merit or blame for them, let us resume discussion of the examples above. From early childhood on the Bogo has learned to praise murder. The praiseworthiness of such an action already penetrated the consciousness of the child as a secondary meaning of the word "murder," and afterward it was confirmed by every impression: his gods and his fellow men praise murder. In consequence he involuntarily judges acts of murder to be praiseworthy, no matter whether it was he himself or someone else who committed them. Let us assume, now, that a philosopher had succeeded in persuading the Bogos that the act of murder and the intention to practice cruelty are causally determined. Then their judgment would undergo an essential modification.

To conceive of actions and intentions as causally determined, after all, means the following. We go back in the history of the individual, say to his birth, and investigate which of his characteristics are inborn and to what causes they are due.[2] Then, ever guided by the law of causality, we trace the development or transformation of these properties; we see how impressions, teachings, and examples come to him and, if his inborn constitution has an affinity for them, are taken up and transformed by it, otherwise passing by without leaving a trace. Finally we recognize that the keystone, the necessary result of this course of development, is the desire to commit murder and the act of murder.

A Bogo who looks upon murder and the intention to practice cruelty in this way — that is, as an effect — will say that it is impossible to regard them as meritorious.

But will he now look upon these actions with apathy, devoid of all feeling? By no means. He will still consider them to be pleasant or unpleasant, agreeable or disagreeable.

When the action is directed against himself, he will perceive it as pleasant or as unpleasant; the prospect of being murdered is unpleasant for everyone, whether he considers the action to be causally determined or uncaused.

Similarly our liking or dislike for the character of a human being will persist even if we regard it as the result of causes. To say that I find someone agreeable means that I am drawn to him; I like him. Of a landscape, too, one says that it is agreeable, and, just as this liking cannot be diminished even if we consider the trees, meadows, and hills to be the result of causes, so our liking for the character of a human being is not diminished if we regard it *sub specie necessitatis.* Hence to the Bogo who has come to see that murder is causally determined it is still agreeable or disagreeable. Usually he will consider it to be agreeable. He will say that it warms the cockles of his heart to observe such an action; it accords with his wild temperament, as yet untouched by civilization. Therefore he will, in view of the necessity, suspend only the specifically moral practice of regarding it as meritorious. But his liking may become love, and even esteem and reverence. It will be objected, however, that "I revere a mode of behavior" entails "I consider it meritorious for a person to behave in that way," and similarly for esteem. To be sure, the words "reverence" and "esteem" *frequently* have this meaning, and *to the extent that they do* a determinist would cease using them. But all words that denote human feelings have not only one, but several meanings. They have, if I may express it in that way, a harem of meanings, and they couple now with this one, now with that one. So, if I "revere" someone, it means also that I esteem him, that he impresses me, and that I wish to be like him. . . . Reverence and esteem in *this* sense can coexist with determinism.

Hence the Bogo who conceives of the intention to practice cruelty and the act of murder as effects can nevertheless consider them to be

[2] An investigation as detailed as that is, of course, never possible in practice.

agreeable or disagreeable, and in a certain sense he can also have esteem and reverence for them, but he will not regard them as meritorious.

Let us now consider the act of murder at high levels of civilization. Civilization, as it progressed, stigmatized murder and threatened penalties for it on earth and in heaven. This censure already penetrates the consciousness of the child as a secondary meaning of the word "murder" and afterward is confirmed through every impression. All the people whom one knows, all the books that one reads, the state with its institutions, pulpit and stage always use "murder" in a censorious sense. That is how it comes to be that we involuntarily declare an act of murder to be blameworthy, be it that others or that we ourselves, driven by passion, committed it. Whether the action was determined by causes or uncaused — that question is raised neither by the person who acted nor by the uninvolved observers. But *if* it is raised, if someone considers the act of murder *sub specie necessitatis*, then he ceases to regard it as blameworthy. He will then no longer want to see punishment in the proper sense — suffering as retribution — meted out for it, but merely punishment as a safety measure.[3] The feelings of liking and dislike, however, will continue to exist even then. On the whole, someone raised at a high level of civilization will have a feeling of dislike for acts of murder; he will not feel drawn to whoever commits it; he will not like him. For such an act does not accord with his temperament, which was formed as he was engaged in non-violent occupations. In spite of the recognition that the action was necessary, this dislike can at times grow to revulsion, and even to contempt — given that the latter notion is stripped of the specifically moral elements that it contains (the attribution of blame). It will then mean something like this: I do not want to be like that person.

The situation is the same in the case of benevolent actions and those performed out of a sense of duty; we cease to regard them as meritorious if we consider them to be effects. Let us look more closely at actions performed out of a sense of duty. To say that someone acts out of a sense of duty means that he performs an action, perhaps contrary to his inclinations, because his conscience commands him to do it. But how does conscience come to issue such commandments? As follows: with some actions (and intentions) there is linked for us from early childhood on a categorical "thou shalt do (or have) them"; for example, "you *should* help everyone as much as possible." If someone then makes this habitual judgment into the guiding principle of his behavior, if he helps a person because his conscience commands "thou *shalt* help thy fellow man," then he is acting "out of a sense of duty." . . . If we want to consider such an action from the point of view of eternity and

---

[3] Punishments are causes that prevent the repetition of the action punished.

necessity, we shall have to proceed as follows: we investigate (1) the constitution of the child who receives the teaching "thou shalt help," (2) the constitution of those who give it to him. The child absorbing this doctrine has some inborn constitution of nerves, of blood, of imagination, and of reason. The commandment "thou shalt help" is impressed upon this substance with some degree of insistence; the deity, heaven, hell, approval of his fellow men and of his own conscience — these ideas are presented to him, depending upon his teachers, as being more or less majestic and inspiring. And the child transforms them with greater or lesser intensity, depending upon his receptivity. The ultimate constitution of a man, the preponderance within him of the sense of duty over his own desires, is in any case a necessary result, a product of his inborn constitution and the impressions received. To someone who contemplates this, such a temperament may, to be sure, still seem agreeable (perhaps because he himself is or would like to be similarly constituted), but no one can regard as *meritorious* behavior that he conceives to be an *effect*.

But what if we ourselves are the person who acted? Then the circumstances are analogous; then, too, liking and dislike remain, while the attribution of merit or blame (the "pangs of conscience") disappears.

Our own action, too, can remain agreeable or become disagreeable for us after it has occurred. It is agreeable if the disposition from which we acted persists after the action; it will become disagreeable if we change our frame of mind. Suppose, for example, that we have acted vengefully and are still in the same mood; then the act of revenge is still agreeable, whether we conceive it to be an effect or not. If, however, a feeling of pity takes the place of our desire for revenge, then we come to dislike our action; we cannot stand our earlier self — the less so, the more pronounced our feeling of pity is. The reflection that the action is an effect in no way affects this feeling of dislike, perhaps of disgust, or even of revulsion for ourselves. We say to ourselves that the desire for revenge was, to be sure, necessarily stronger than the ideas and impressions that stood in its way, hence the action took place necessarily, too; but now it happens that pity is necessarily present, and, along with it, regrets that we acted as we did.

6. CAN WE ABANDON JUDGMENTS OF MORAL RESPONSIBILITY?

But is it really possible to shake off feelings of guilt so easily? Do they disappear, like a spook, when the magic word *effect* is pronounced? Is the situation with respect to this feeling not quite like that with regard to dislike? It was, to be sure, necessary that I took revenge, but now I necessarily feel dislike for my own action, along with guilt. I can no more prevent the onset of the one feeling than of the other. But if the feeling of guilt asserts itself in spite of the recognition that actions are effects, should we not suspect that our holding others responsible, too, will persist in spite of this insight? Did we commit an error somewhere? Is it that responsibility and necessity do not exclude each other? The situation is as follows. The reason why we assign moral praise to some actions and moral censure to others has already been mentioned repeatedly. Censure already penetrates the consciousness of the child as a secondary meaning of the words "murder," "theft," "vengefulness," and "pleasure in another's pain," and praise as a secondary meaning of the words "benevolence" and "mercy." That is why censure seems to him to be a constituent part of murder, and praise, of benevolence. At a later point in his life, perhaps in his twentieth year, the insight comes to him from somewhere that all actions are effects and therefore cannot earn merit or blame. What can this poor little insight accomplish against the accumulated habits of a lifetime of judging? The habit of mind of assigning blame for actions like murder makes it very difficult to think of them without this judgment. It is all very well for reason to tell us that we may not assign blame for such actions, since they are effects — our habit of judging, which has become a feeling, will see to it that it is done anyway. But — let habit confront habit! Suppose that, whenever someone involuntarily wants to assign blame or merit for an action, he ascends to the point of view of eternity and necessity. He then regards the action as the necessary result of [a chain of events stretching back into] the infinite past. Through that way of looking at things the *instinctive* association between the action and the judgment will be severed, if not the first time, then perhaps by the thousandth. Such a man will shed the habit of assigning blame or merit for any action whatsoever.

In fact, of course, human beings almost never behave like that; this way of looking at things is completely foreign to them. Furthermore, human beings determine their actions by considering whether they will make them happy or unhappy; but shedding the habit of making judgments [of moral responsibility] would hardly increase their happiness. . . .

The situation with respect to a person's character is no different from that with respect to his individual actions. *Customarily* one assigns blame or merit, whether to himself or to others, for a single action: a single act of cheating or of giving offense. But *sometimes* we go back from the action to its source, to a person's character. In reality, of course, character, in its broadest as well as its smallest traits, is just as necessary as an individual action; it is the product of [a chain of events stretching back into] the infinite past, be it that it was inherited in its entirety or that it was formed in part during the individual's lifetime. But with regard to character, too, hardly anyone adopts this point of view. Just as in the case of particular actions, character is regarded neither as free nor as necessary; that is to say, people do not raise the question at all whether the law of causality is applicable also to actions and character. Hence one assigns blame and merit for character as for actions, though they are effects; for one does not see that they are effects. If one sees this, if one regards character *sub specie necessitatis,* then he ceases to assign blame or merit for it. Liking and dislike, on the other hand, nevertheless persist even then: a character closely related to mine will garner my liking, my love, and perhaps even, in the sense mentioned above, my esteem and reverence — whether I conceive of it as an effect or not.

Hence we assign blame or merit for character and actions out of the habit of judging, without concerning ourselves with the question whether they are causally determined or not. We cease to assign blame or merit for character and actions as soon as we recognize that they are causally determined (if we ignore the remnants of our habits).

Let us recapitulate: the character, the intentions, and the actions of every human being are effects, and it is impossible to assign blame or merit for effects.

8

RICHARD TAYLOR

A Defense of Fatalism

Introduction

Richard Taylor holds the chair of philosophy at Union College and is well known for his work on Schopenhauer as well as on metaphysics. Professor Taylor claims to be a fatalist. He finds fatalism consoling, for, if it is up to him what happens in the future, he has all the worry of trying to bring about some things and avoid others. If it is not up to him, he will be freed from this anxiety. He forgets, however, that it might be better to worry in case one might not succeed in avoiding an unpleasant fate than not to have the ability to avoid it at all.

Taylor compares two arguments: (a) Because (*ex hypothesi*) there being a sea battle *yesterday* is a *necessary condition* of there being headlines in today's newspapers about a sea battle (presumably American journalists are more reliable than British), I will be unable to read such headlines if there has been no battle. (b) Because (*ex hypothesi*) the sea captain's issuing the order for a sea battle *tomorrow* is a *sufficient condition* of there being a sea battle, there being a sea battle will be a *necessary condition* of the sea captain's issuing the order for one. Hence the sea captain will be *unable* to issue the order for a battle if there is not going to be a battle. Hence it is no more up to the sea captain whether he issues the order than it is up to me whether I read the headlines. (This argument applies to all human actions.) The notions of necessary and sufficient conditions will be explained shortly.

The following is a selection from a large number of objections to Taylor's argument (which is more convincing, although not any sounder, when stated at greater length):

116

1. Issuing the order is not analogous to reading the headlines. I can choose to read what headlines there are; what I cannot do is choose what headlines there are to read. Where the order is concerned, the sea captain *can* choose what order to give. There is not an independently existing order (like the independently existing headlines) which will be there whether or not the sea captain chooses to give it (like signing one's name to an already existing petition). If there were, it might well be that he could not give such an order, if there were not such an order already existing to be given.

2. To say that one thing is a *sufficient condition* of another is to say that if the first thing occurs, then the second will occur. To say that a thing is a *necessary condition* of another is to say that, if the second thing does *not* occur, the first thing will *not* occur. Professor Taylor makes use of what is supposed to be a law of logic (the law of *contraposition*) to the effect that if one thing is a *sufficient* condition of a second, the second thing is a *necessary* condition of the first. For example, if it is true that if I have eaten too much I will get indigestion, then it must be true that if I am *not* going to get indigestion, I have *not* eaten too much.

Taylor argues that because issuing the order for a naval battle is, *ex hypothesi*, a *sufficient condition* of there being a naval battle, the occurrence of a naval battle must be a *necessary condition* of the issuing of the order. Hence if there is not going to be a naval battle, a necessary condition for the captain's order is absent. Hence, the sea captain will be *unable* to issue the order.

This argument rests on an abuse of the operation of contraposition. Contraposition can be used safely in *inferences*. For example, anyone knowing that the sea captain's issuing the order for a naval battle is a sufficient condition of there being a naval battle can argue that, since there was *not* a naval battle, the sea captain cannot have issued the order, for whatever reason. But that the captain *cannot* have issued the order does not show that he was *unable* to issue the order. He might have decided not to issue the order for a battle because he thought he would lose.

Taylor confuses the notion of being a necessary or sufficient condition of the *truth* of something with the different notion of what it is necessary or sufficient to *do* in order to achieve some end. But, although it is true that the statement that if the order had been issued there would be a battle entails that if there was no battle the order cannot have been issued, the absence of a battle is not the absence of something (like the absence of a megaphone) that the sea captain needs to have in order to bring about a battle. The notion of what it is necessary to do in order to achieve something does not contrapose. For example, from the fact (if it is a fact) that, in order to be saved it is *necessary* to believe the Athanasian creed, it does not at all follow that in order to believe the Athanasian creed it is *sufficient* to be saved. It may be sufficient to eat an apple a day in order to be healthy, but this does not at all entail that in order to eat an apple a day it is necessary to be healthy. Hence from the fact that in order to bring about a sea battle it is sufficient for the captain to give the order for one, it does not at all follow that it is necessary for there to be a battle if the captain is to be able to issue the order. The idea that tomorrow's sea battle is some kind of means to the issuing of an order, the absence of which prevents the sea captain from issuing it, is absurd.

3. Finally, Taylor is confused about what he ought to be proving. He starts this piece by saying that he is a fatalist. Fatalism, as we have seen, is the view that I do not need to worry about what I do, because the same fate will befall me regardless of what I do. For example, I do not need to take precautions against being shot, because if a bullet has my name on it, I will be killed by it whether I take precautions, say, by avoiding being the third person to light a cigarette with the same match, or not.

To prove that fatalism is true of everything, one would have to prove that no human actions ever have any effects (or, at any rate, any effects that are of concern to the agent). For example, one would need to prove such things as that if there is to be a naval battle, it will occur whether the sea captain issues the order for one or not. What Taylor's argument would prove, if it were valid, however, is not that the sea captain's issuing the order would make no difference to whether or not there was a sea battle. What it would prove would be the totally different proposition that the sea captain is *unable* to issue the order. From this it would *not* follow that his issuing the order, if he could issue it, would make no difference to whether or not there was one. Indeed, one of Taylor's own premises is, inconsistently, that his issuing the order *will* make a difference, because it is a sufficient condition of the battle.

Reading

WE ALL, AT certain dramatic moments of pain, threat, or bereavement, entertain the idea of fatalism, the thought that what is then happening just had to be, that we are powerless to prevent it. Sometimes we find ourselves in circumstances not of our own making, circumstances in which our destinies and our very being are thoroughly anchored, and then the thought of fatalism can be quite overwhelming and sometimes consoling. Whatever then happens, one feels, and however good or ill, will be what those circumstances yield, and we are helpless. There is nothing for you or me to do about it, hence nothing for us to think or deliberate about; we can only wait and see. Soldiers, it is said, are sometimes possessed by such thoughts. Perhaps all men would feel more inclined to such thoughts if they paused to think more often of how little they ever had to do with bringing themselves to wherever they have arrived in life, of how much their fortunes and destinies were decided for them by sheer circumstance, and how the entire course of their lives is often set, once for all, by the most trivial incidents, which they did not produce and could not even have foreseen. If we are free

From *Metaphysics* by Richard Taylor. Richard Taylor, *Metaphysics*, 3e, © 1983, pp. 51–62. Reprinted by permission of Prentice Hall, Inc., Englewood Cliffs, New Jersey.

to work out our destinies at all, which is doubtful, it is a freedom that is at best exercised within exceedingly narrow paths. The important things — when we are born, of what parents, into what culture, of what sex and temperament, of what intelligence or stupidity, indeed everything that makes for the bulk of our happiness and misery — is decided for us by the most casual and indifferent circumstances, by sheer coincidences, chance encounters, and seemingly insignificant fortuities. One can see this in retrospect if he searches, but few search to find it. The fate that has given us our very being and human natures has thereby made us so that, being human, we congratulate ourselves on our blessings, which we can deem our achievements, blame the world for our deficiencies, which we call our ill luck, and scarcely think of the fate which arbitrarily dispenses both.

A theory of fatalism is often distinguished academically from the theory of determinism by noting that, whereas determinism is a theory about all things and events, fatalism is a theory about some events only; the theory, namely, that these events could never have been otherwise, regardless of whatever else happened; or that certain events are such that they cannot fail to occur, no matter what else occurs. But this distinction is only academic. A determinist is simply, if he is consistent, a fatalist about everything; or at least, he should be. For the essential idea that a man would be expressing by saying that his attitude was one of fatalism with respect to this or that event — his own death, for instance — is that it is not up to him whether, or when or where, this event will occur, that it is not within his control. But the theory of determinism, as we have seen, once it is clearly spelled out and not hedged about with unresolved "ifs," entails that this is true of everything that ever happens, that it is never really up to any man what he does or what he becomes, and that nothing ever can happen, except what does in fact happen. One can indeed find verbal formulas for distinguishing the two theories, but if we think of a fatalist as one who has a certain attitude toward certain events, we find that it is the attitude that a thoroughgoing believer in determinism should, in consistency, assume toward all events.

A fatalist is best thought of, quite simply, as someone who thinks he cannot do anything about the future. He thinks it is not up to him what will happen next year, tomorrow, or the very next moment. He thinks that even his own behavior is not in the least within his power, any more than the motions of distant heavenly bodies, the events of remote history, or the political developments in faraway countries. He supposes, accordingly, that it is pointless for him to deliberate about anything, for a man deliberates only about those future things he believes to be within his power to do and forego. He does not pretend always to know what will happen. Hence, he might try sometimes to read signs and portents, or contemplate the effects upon him of the various things that might, for all he knows, be fated to occur. But he does not suppose that, whatever will happen, it will ever have been really avoidable.

A fatalist, then, thinks of the future in the manner in which we all think of the past, for all men are fatalists as they look *back* upon things. He thinks of both past and future "under the aspect of eternity," the way God is supposed to view them. We all think of the past in this way, as something once for all settled and fixed, to be taken for just what it is. We are never in the least tempted to modify it, or even to suppose that we ever can. We all believe that it is not in the least now up to us what happened last year, yesterday, or even a moment ago; that these things are no longer within our power, any more than the motions of the heavens or the political developments in China. And of course we are not ever tempted to deliberate about what we have done or left undone. At best we can speculate on these things, try to figure out what they were in case we do not know, or we can rejoice over them or repent. If we are not fatalists about the future, we can extract lessons from the past to apply in the future. But as for what has in fact happened, we do, and feel we certainly must, simply take it as given. The possibilities for action, if there are any at all, do not lie there. We might, indeed, believe that some past things *were* once within our power, to do or avoid, while they were still future — but this expresses our attitude toward the future, not the past.

Such is surely our conception of the whole past, whether near or remote. But the true fatalist thinks of the future in just the same way. We all think things past are no longer within our power; the fatalist thinks they never were. It is a consoling doctrine, as many contemplative minds have discovered; but it somehow seems to violate the common sense of the greater part of mankind.

There are various ways in which one might get thinking fatalistically about the future, but they are most apt to arise from certain theological ideas, or from the metaphysical theory of determinism. Thus, if God is really all-knowing and all-powerful, then it is not hard to suppose that he has already arranged for everything to happen just as it is going to happen, and there is nothing left for you and me to do about it, except to watch things unfold and see what is to become of us, in the here or hereafter. Religious systems have used this thought as a cornerstone, and it is a firm one indeed for those who have this kind of faith. But without bringing God into the picture, it is not hard to suppose, as we have seen, that everything that happens is wholly determined by what went before it, and hence that whatever happens at any future time is the only thing that can then happen, given that certain other things will happen just before then, and that these, in turn, are the only things that can happen then, given the state of the world just before that, and so on, through the infinite past. So again, there is no more left for us to do about what is to be than about what already has been. What we do in the meantime will, to be sure, determine how some things eventually turn out; but these things that we are going to do will, on this conception, be only the causal consequences of what will be happening just before we do them, and so on back to a not distant point at which it seems obvious that we have nothing to do with what happens then.

No man needs convincing that fatalism is the only proper attitude to hold toward things past, but we want to see whether we should think in the same way of the future. The consequences of doing so are obviously momentous. To say nothing of the consolation of fatalism — a consolation which enables one to view all things as they arise, with the same undisturbed mind with which he contemplates even the horrors of remote history — the attitude of fatalism relieves one's mind of all tendency toward both blame and approbation of others and of both guilt and conceit in himself. It promises one that a perfect understanding of everything is at least possible, even if never actually possessed. This thought alone, once firmly grasped, yields a sublime complacency toward everything that life offers, whether to oneself or to his fellows; and while it thereby reduces one's pride, it simultaneously enhances the feelings, opens the heart, and enormously broadens one's understanding.

Like any metaphysical theory, the theory of fatalism cannot be evaluated apart from one's presuppositions or data. Theological conceptions obviously cannot be invoked here, for they are far more doubtful than any metaphysical theory that one might try to erect on them. At best, they could only serve to convey the theory of fatalism more easily to an unphilosophical imagination. Similarly, the theory of determinism will be of no use to us, for it is not a datum but a theory, and a controversial one too.

For our data we shall use only six claims, each of which recommends itself to the ordinary understanding as soon as it is understood, and hardly any of which have very often been doubted even by the most critical philosophical minds, many of whom, however, have failed to see their implications. These six suppositions, with some explanation of each, are simply these.

First, we suppose that any proposition or statement whatever is either true or, if not true, then false. If anyone affirms anything whatever, as distinguished from merely uttering nonsense, then what he affirms is, if not false, true; and if not true, false. There is no middle ground. This is simply the standard interpretation (*tertium non datur*) of what is called in logic "the law of excluded middle." It has generally been thought to be a necessary truth, and an indisputable law of logical thought. It seems, in any case, quite unexceptionable.

Second, we suppose that if any change or state of affairs is *sufficient* for the occurrence of some other change or state of affairs at the same or any other time, then the former cannot occur without the latter occurring also, even though the two are logically unconnected. This is simply the standard way in which the concept of *sufficiency* is explained in philosophy. A perhaps clearer way of saying the same thing is that if one state of affairs *ensures* another, then the former cannot exist without the other occurring too. The ingestion of cyanide, for instance, ensures death under certain familiar circumstances, which only means that one cannot normally swallow cyanide without dying, even though it is not logically impossible to do so.

Third, we suppose that if any change or state of affairs is *necessary* for some other change or state of affairs at the same or any other time, then the latter cannot occur without the former occurring too, even though they are logically unconnected. This is simply the standard way in which the concept of a *necessary condition* is explained in philosophy. A perhaps clearer way of saying the same thing is that if one state of affairs is *essential* for another, then the latter cannot occur without it. Oxygen, for instance, is essential for life, which means that we cannot normally live without it, even though it is not logically impossible that we should.

Fourth, we suppose that if some change or state of affairs is sufficient for (ensures) another, then that other is necessary (essential) for it; and conversely, if some change or state of affairs is necessary (essential) for another, then that other is sufficient for (ensures) it. This is simply a logical consequence of our second and third data; it follows from the definitions themselves.

Fifth, we suppose that no agent can perform any given action if there is lacking, at the same or any other time, some condition or state of affairs necessary for the occurrence of that act. This follows simply from the idea of anything being necessary or essential for the accomplishment of something else. For example, I cannot live without oxygen, or swim five miles without ever having been in water, or win a certain election without having been nominated, or fly to the moon without some sort of rocket, and so on, for these are all conditions that are necessary, or essential, for doing the things in question. Something is always necessary for the accomplishment of anything at all, and without the thing that is needed, nothing can be done. This is no law of logic, and in fact cannot be expressed even in the contemporary modal logics, and it is nonetheless manifestly true.

And *sixth*, we suppose that time is not "efficacious," that is, that the mere passage of time does not augment or diminish the powers or capacities of anything and, in particular, that it does not enhance or decrease an agent's powers or abilities. This means that if any substance or agent gains or loses powers or abilities over the course of time, then such a gain or loss is always due to something other than the mere passage of time. For instance, if a substance loses or gains in its power to corrode things, or if a man loses or gains the power to do push-ups, or lift weights, or what not, then such gains and losses are always due to certain things that happen over the course of time. They are not due *merely* to the passage of time alone, which has no causal effect upon anything. This cannot be proved, but it is never doubted in physical science, and can hardly be doubted by anyone who thinks on it.

With these data before us, we are now going to compare two simple situations in turn. The relations involved in both situations will be identical except for certain relations of time, and we want to see whether an examination of each situation warrants similar inferences in both cases.

Let us assume that I am going to open my morning newspaper and glance over the headlines. There have for weeks been rumors of an impending naval battle, and I am intensely interested to learn from the paper whether any such battle has occurred. I have a son who is a sailor, we may suppose, and I am anxious for his safety. Assume further, then, that conditions are such that only if there was such a battle yesterday does my newspaper carry a certain kind of headline — i.e., that such a battle is, in the sense defined, necessary or essential for that kind of headline — whereas if it carries a certain different sort of headline, this will ensure that there was no such battle. Of course newspapers are not always that reliable, but we shall suppose that this one is, at least this time.

Now then, I am about to perform one or the other of two acts; namely, seeing a headline of the first kind or seeing one of the second kind. We shall call these alternative possible acts S and S' respectively. And let us call the two propositions; "A naval battle occurred yesterday" and "No naval battle occurred yesterday," P and P' respectively. We can now assert that if I perform act S, then my doing so will ensure that there was a naval battle yesterday (i.e., that P is true), whereas if I perform S' then my doing that will ensure that no such battle occurred (or, that P' is true). This logically follows from the description of the situation.

With reference to this example, then, let us now ask whether it is up to me which sort of headline I read as I open the newspaper. More precisely, let us consider whether the following statement is true:

(A) It is now within my power to do S, and it is also now within my power to do S'.

It seems quite obvious that this is not true. For if both these acts were equally within my power, that is, if it were up to me which one to do, then it would also be up to me whether or not a naval battle has taken place yesterday, giving me a power over the past which I plainly do not possess. It will be well, however, to express this point in the form of a proof, as follows:

Argument I:

1. If P is true, then it is not within my power to do S' (for in case P is true, then there is, or was, lacking a condition essential for my doing S', the condition, namely, of there being no naval battle yesterday).
2. But if P' is true, then it is not within my power to do S (for a similar reason).
3. But either P is true or P' is true.
4. Either it is not within my power to do S, or it is not within my power to do S';

and A is accordingly false. A common-sense way of expressing this is to say that what sort of headline I see depends, among other things, on whether a naval battle took place yesterday, and that in turn is not now up to me.

Now this conclusion is perfectly in accordance with common sense, for we all are, as noted, fatalists with respect to the past. We sometimes try to find out what has happened by reading newspapers and so on, but on one ever supposes that he can determine or in any way influence what has happened, or that the past is in any way within his power to control. We simply have to take past things as they have happened and make the best of them.

It is significant to note incidentally that in the hypothetical sense in which statements of human power or ability are often formulated by philosophers, one *does* have power over the past. For we can surely assert that *if* I do S, this will ensure that a naval battle occurred yesterday; whereas *if*, alternatively, I do S', this will equally ensure the nonoccurrence of such a battle, for these acts are, in the conditions assumed in our example, quite sufficient for the truth of P and P' respectively. Or we can say that I can ensure the occurrence of such a battle yesterday simply by doing S, and that I can ensure its nonoccurrence simply by doing S'. Indeed, if I should ask *how* I can go about ensuring that no naval battle occurred yesterday, perfectly straightforward instructions can be given; namely, the instruction to do S' and by all means to avoid doing S. But of course the hitch is that I cannot do S' *unless* P' is true, the occurrence of the battle in question rendering me quite powerless to do it.

Now let us imagine that I am a naval commander about to issue my order of the day to the fleet. We assume, further, that within the totality of other conditions prevailing, my issuing of a certain kind of order will ensure that a naval battle will occur tomorrow, whereas if I issue another kind of order this will ensure that no such battle occurs.

Now then, I am about to perform one or the other of these two acts; namely, one of issuing an order of the first sort or one of the second sort. We shall call these alternative possible acts O and O' respectively. And let us call the two propositions "A naval battle will occur tomorrow" and "No naval battle will occur tomorrow," Q and Q' respectively. We can now assert that if I do act O, then my doing such will ensure that there will be a naval battle (i.e., that Q is true), whereas if I do O' my doing that will ensure that no naval battle will occur (or, that Q' is true).

With reference to this example, then, let us now ask whether it is up to me which sort of order I issue. More precisely, let us consider whether the following statement is true:

(B) It is now within my power to do O, and it is also now within my power to do O'.

Anyone except a fatalist would surely want to say that, in the situation we have envisaged, this statement might well be true; that is, that each of these acts is quite within my power. In the circumstances we assume to prevail, it is, one would think, up to me as the commander whether the naval battle occurs tomorrow or not. It depends only on what kind of order I issue, given all the other conditions as they are; and what kind of order is issued is something for me to decide, something wholly within my power. It is precisely the denial that such statements are ever true that renders one a fatalist.

But we have, alas, exactly the same argument to show that B is false that we had for proving the falsity of A; namely:

Argument II:

1. If Q is true, then it is not within my power to do O' (for in case Q is true, then there is, or will be, lacking a condition essential for my doing O', the condition, namely, of there being no naval battle tomorrow).
2. But if Q' is true, then it is not within my power to do O (for a similar reason).
3. But either Q is true or Q' is true.
4. Either it is not within my power to do O, or it is not within my power to do O';

and B is accordingly false. Another way of expressing this is to say that what kind of order I issue depends, among other things, on whether a naval battle takes place tomorrow—for in this situation a naval battle tomorrow is a necessary condition of my doing O, whereas no naval battle tomorrow is equally essential for my doing O'.

In view of the fact that probably everything anyone does, and certainly everything of any significance that anyone ever does, has consequences for the future, so that, his act being sufficient for those consequences, they are in turn necessary conditions of his act, we can generalize upon this conclusion by saying that, for any such act A, either it is not within one's power to do A, or it is not within his power to refrain from doing it, depending of course on which consequences are in fact going to ensure.

At this point most persons are apt to feel most intensely that something has gone wrong, that a piece of sophistry has been concocted merely to puzzle and bewilder; but this is only because most persons are not fatalists about the future. No one feels the slightest suspicion about the first argument. Indeed, the logic of it seems so obvious that one might well wonder what can be the point of spelling it all out so exactly. But that is because everyone is already a fatalist about the past — no one supposes it is up to him what has happened, or that past things are still within his power.

The thing to note, however, is that these two arguments are formally identical, except only for tenses. If the occurrence of a naval battle yesterday is a necessary condition of my reading a certain kind of headline today, then it logically follows that my reading that headline today is a sufficient condition for the prior occurrence of that battle. This is obvious and indisputable. But, similarly, if my issuing a certain kind of order today is a sufficient condition for the occurrence of a naval battle tomorrow, then the occurrence of that naval battle tomorrow is a necessary condition of my issuing that order. This too is indisputable but somehow not so obvious. If, then, either argument is a good one — and surely the first one is — then the other is just as good no matter how anyone might feel about its conclusion.

People do nevertheless seem to have an almost deathless conviction that fatalism about the future has got to be false, though no one, it seems, has ever given a very good reason for thinking so. Men do, as we noted when considering the theory of determinism, have a conviction that future things are within their control, that what is going to happen is somehow up to them, at least sometimes. What they have failed to note, and what it in fact takes considerable sophistication to see, is that the very reasons that can be given for being a fatalist about the past can be given for being a fatalist about the future. Similarly, whatever arguments can be given for rejecting fatalism with respect to the future turn out to be just as conclusive for rejecting it with respect to the past. This is a consequence of the fact that the relations of necessity and sufficiency are perfectly timeless, and hold in exactly the same way, whether from past to future or from future to past, together with the fact that time, by itself, makes no difference to things.

Fatalism is nevertheless an odious philosophy to most persons. It is repellent only to the will, however, and not to the intellect, for men's wills do not normally crave the serenity to which a fatalist is rightly entitled upon his doctrine. Still, the question can only be settled by intelligence, and we shall therefore consider the arguments against this view that some persons are always eager to press.

It may be tempting, for example, to suggest that perhaps time makes a difference, so that no state of affairs can be necessary for any other *before* that state of affairs exists. But this escape from fatalism is closed by both our fifth and sixth data. Surely if some state of affairs at *any* given time, whether past, present, or future, is necessary for the occurrence of something else, and that state of affairs does not in fact exist *at the time it is needed*, then nothing anyone does can be of the slightest avail in bringing about that occurrence for which it is necessary. To deny this would be equivalent to saying that I can do something now which is sufficient for, or which ensures, the occurrence of something else in the future, *without* getting that future occurrence as a result. This is absurd in itself, and contrary to our second datum. If anyone were to suggest, in spite of this, that a state of affairs that exists *not yet* cannot, just because of that temporal removal, be a necessary condition of anything existing prior to it, this would be logically equivalent to saying that no present state of affairs can ensure another subsequent to it, which is manifestly absurd. We could with equal justice say that a state of affairs, such as yesterday's naval battle, which exists *no longer*, cannot be a necessary condition of anything existing subsequently, there being the same temporal interval here; and that would be arbitrary and false. All that is needed, to restrict the powers that I imagine myself to have to do this thing or that, is that some condition essential to my doing it *does* not, *did* not, or *will* not occur.

Nor can anyone wriggle out of fatalism by representing this sort of situation as one in which there is a simple loss of ability or power resulting from the passage of time. It is one of our data, and a fairly obvious one, that the mere passage of time does not enhance or diminish the powers or abilities of anything. It would be idle to say that I have the power to do O' until, say, tomorrow's naval battle occurs, or the power to do O until tomorrow arrives and we find no naval battle occurring, and so on. What restricts the range of my power to do this thing or that is not the mere *temporal* relations between my acts and certain other states of affairs, but the very existence of those states of affairs themselves. And according to our very first datum, the fact of tomorrow's containing or lacking a naval battle, as the case may be, is already no less a fact than yesterday's containing or lacking one. If at any time I lack the power to perform a certain act, it can only be the result of something, other than the passage of time, that has happened, is happening, or will happen. The fact that there is going to be a naval battle tomorrow, if it is a fact at all, just as surely suffices to render me unable to do O', as the fact that there has been one yesterday, if it is a fact, suffices to render me unable to do S'. The nonoccurrence of those things is, by our very descriptions of the two situations, essential for my doing those things.

It will not help in the least here to appeal to any particular analysis of causation, or to the fact, if indeed it is one, that causes only "work forward" and not backward. Our problem has been formulated without any reference whatever to causation. It may well be, for all we know, that causal relations have an unalterable direction in time, which is an unclear claim itself; but if so this is perfectly irrelevant, for it is very certain that the relations of necessity and sufficiency between changes and states of affairs do not, and it is in terms of these relations alone that our data and our examples have been described.

The most philosophically sophisticated criticism of fatalistic arguments of the kind here presented, and one which is centuries old, amounts essentially to denying our fifth datum, to the effect that no agent is able to perform any given act in the absence of some condition necessary for its accomplishment. It is often claimed that all this means, really, is that it is impossible, as a simple matter of logic, *both* that an agent should perform a certain act, *and* that there should be lacking some condition necessary for his doing that act. From this it does not follow, it is claimed, that the agent is *unable* to do that act, but only, that he *does not* do it—and this is perfectly consistent with his still having the ability to do it.

Thus, a gymnast does not lift a weight if he has no weight to lift, but the absence of this necessary condition for lifting a weight does not diminish his strength or his ability to lift weights. Indeed, if the presence of a weight were a necessary condition, not merely of his lifting it, but of his *ability* to lift it, then it would logically follow that his mere ability to lift it would be a sufficient condition for a weight's being present, that his strength would by itself guarantee the perpetual presence of a weight! Gymnasts are sometimes able to lift weights even when none are present, just as musicians are able to make music even when they are not doing so, and horsemen are able to ride horses even when they are walking. The argument for fatalism is, then, it is suggested, a simple *non sequitur*.

Now all this is true in the usual sense of ability, which consists in having the skill, strength, equipment, or knowing how. But to make that point is really to miss the point. If there is lacking some condition C, necessary for my doing a certain act A, or which is such that A cannot occur without it, then not only do I not do A, I *cannot* do it, no matter what my natural or acquired abilities might be. This is perfectly obvious when one considers necessary conditions which are lacking in the past. It should be no less obvious when one considers necessary conditions which are lacking in the future.

For example, we noted that if conditions are such that a naval battle yesterday is a necessary condition for there being a certain kind of headline today, then, given that no such battle occurred, we can conclude not only that I *do not* read such a headline, but that I *cannot*, that it is not within my power, for there is just no such headline for me to read. This is perfectly consistent with my *knowing how* to read it, having the requisite skill and vision, and so on, and thus being able in *that* sense. But if it were within my power to read such a headline, then it logically follows that it would be within my power to make a naval battle occur yesterday which, we are supposing, did not occur; and this is manifestly absurd.

If, accordingly, we were to take the present criticism as a good refutation of fatalism with respect to the future, then it would be just as good a refutation of fatalism about the past, which would be a most extraordinary outcome. For in the sense of ability that this criticism rests upon — namely, the sense of having a certain skill, strength, equipment, or knowing how — we *do* have the ability to change the past. I have the *ability* to read a certain kind of headline — my vision is all right, I know how to read, and so on — and hence am able to do something sufficient for the occurrence of a naval battle yesterday, even though there was no such battle, and therefore some condition is lacking, necessary for there being any such headline for me to read.

Now this observation plainly does not refute fatalism with respect to the past. Sometimes one is prevented from doing what he has the ability to do. Similarly, one cannot, by exploiting this sense of ability, refute fatalism with respect to the future. Just as my knowing how to read does not give me the power to make a battle occur yesterday which did not then occur, so also a man's knowing how to issue an order does not give him the power to make a battle occur tomorrow which will not then occur. The argument for fatalism about the future is just as good as the argument for fatalism about the past; and the argument against either is no better than the argument against the other, the arguments being, in fact, in both cases the same.

9

JONATHAN HARRISON

God, The Arch-Hypnotist

Introduction

Jonathan Harrison is the author of *Our Knowledge of Right and Wrong*, two books on Hume, two collections of stories with philosophical morals, and numerous articles. The theme of this story is taken from the novel *Trilby*, by George Du Maurier.

When Harrison wrote this story, he supposed that the actions of Mrs. O'Farrell, which were produced by Dr. Svengali's setting the dial on his machine to the appropriate place, were nevertheless free actions which Mrs. O'Farrell was capable of not performing. Harrison was assuming the truth of the compatibilist view (see the Introduction) that an action is free if, among its causes are desires or beliefs of the agent. Dr. Svengali's machine operated not by *compelling* Mrs. O'Farrell to do the things she did, but by making her *desire* to do them, or causing her to *believe* that there was some good reason for doing them. According to compatibilism, as long as the agent's wants and beliefs are among the causes of his or her actions, it does not matter that the desires and beliefs that cause the actions are themselves produced by circumstances over which the agent has no control. Hence Mrs. O'Farrell's actions are still free, if compatibilism is true, even though the wants and beliefs that produced them are caused by Dr. Svengali's setting the indicator to the appropriate place on the dial of his machine. Some may think this a conclusive objection to compatibilism.

This story is subtitled "What Price Pelagius?" because the Irish heretic Pelagius held that God would be acting unjustly if He damned us for performing actions He had predestined us to perform. Pelagius thought that, if God predestined us to sin, we were not free not to sin.

However, if God, like Dr. Svengali, predestines us to do things by giving us the motives and beliefs which result in our performing them, perhaps the actions God predestines us to perform are nevertheless free. Indeed, they *will* be free if compatibilism is true.

It follows from this compatibilist view that God is not acting unjustly in damning me for sinning, even if He does predestine me to sin. I am responsible for my sins, even if they are predestined. What God is doing is damning me for actions for which He, as well as I, am responsible. *He* gave us the wants and beliefs that caused them and the type of brain that resulted in our having these wants and beliefs. He is therefore like some omniscient and omnipotent examiner, who gives marks only to students who merit them, but who himself gives students the capacities which result in some students but not others getting good marks. (In theological language, He gives some people, but not all, grace not to sin.)

Harrison is less sure that Mrs. O'Farrell's actions are free than he was at the time he wrote this story.

Reading

ONCE UPON A time Dr. Thomas Svengali was walking by the side of a lake when he saw some children playing with their boats. They were model boats of course, but it was possible to control them by short-wave radio. In this way they could be made to go through all the manoeuvres which life-sized boats could execute, but in an unrealistically jerky way, like mice pretending to be elephants.

This gave Dr. Svengali an idea. It was not an original one. Even some twentieth-century philosophers had had it before him. Had he not spent so much of his life immersed in his study of the human brain he would probably have had it before. He had recently been experiencing a great deal of trouble with his housekeeper, a Mrs. Geraldine O'Farrell. He had never liked the new-fangled practice of having his house run by a computer, but being as unversed in the ways of the opposite sex as he was knowledgeable about brain physiology and electronics, he had not the faintest idea how to manage a woman. And the fact that Mrs. O'Farrell considered that she would not have been compelled to occupy her present poorly paid position had it not been for the deplorably inequitable way in which her sex was treated made her quite exceptionally and often quite deliberately incompetent.

It occurred to Dr. Svengali that if he could not make her perform her household duties in any other way he might insert a device into her skull which would enable her to be controlled by a short-wave radio transmitter, which Dr. Svengali prudently kept locked in a cupboard when not in use, out of Mrs. O'Farrell's reach. Though this transmitter could, if necessary, be worked manually, doing so would save Dr.

Reprinted from Jonathan Harrison, "Tom and Jerry, or What Price Pelagius?", *Religious Studies*, Vol. 17, 1981. From *Religious Studies*, © 1986, Cambridge University Press. "God, the Arch-hypnotist" by Jonathan Harrison.

Svengali only labour, but no time. Hence, when familiarity caused him no longer to regard it as a plaything, he built into it a programmer which, at the appointed hours, caused Mrs. O'Farrell to cook, shop and clean, without any further intervention on his part. When these things were not necessary the transmitter automatically switched itself off, and left Mrs. O'Farrell to do what she thought she pleased.

Dr. Svengali found, however, that this way of solving the problem presented by Mrs. O'Farrell's intransigence had a drawback. Though her limbs went through the movements of polishing and bed-making in a highly efficient and satisfactory way, the expression on her face was disturbingly resentful, and her language so appalling as to be quite unacceptable to someone as gently nurtured as Dr. Svengali. It was also extremely embarrassing to him when he had visitors.

To a man of Dr. Svengali's ability the task of modifying the controlling device in Mrs. O'Farrell's brain in such a way as to produce a more pleasing facial expression and a less colourful vocabulary was easily accomplished. Dr. Svengali, however, was a sensitive man, and he found the mere knowledge of the resentment that Mrs. O'Farrell felt, but could not express, extremely disturbing to him. And though a very poor housekeeper, she had been a good companion, and resentment at being forced to do her work in such a humiliating manner made her extremely disagreeable to Dr. Svengali in the evenings. Most of these she spent in reproaching him bitterly for the way in which he treated her, and in trying to bring home to him how dreadful it was to find one's limbs manipulated from without—just as if, as Mrs. O'Farrell herself strikingly and originally put it, she was possessed.

Dr. Svengali took longer to solve this second problem. He reasoned that just as he could move Mrs. O'Farrell's limbs, so he could produce or eradicate the desires which normally made her move them. Hence he thought he might make her a better housekeeper without at the same time making her a worse companion if he built a modified device, which would make her *want* to cook, shop and clean at the required times.

Promising though this idea seemed to Dr. Svengali when it first occurred to him, it in fact turned out to be a complete failure. Mrs. O'Farrell did, at the times the controlling device decided that she should, want to cook, clean and shop. But by now she had become so incensed that no such inducement would make her perform these duties well. However intensely Dr. Svengali's machine made her want to do things, she regarded the desires so produced as akin to temptations from the devil. A calvinistic upbringing and a naturally obdurate disposition aided her in her determination to resist, and she very rarely succumbed. When the strength of her wants became overwhelming and, for a short while she did her work in a satisfactory way, she was subsequently so overcome with exasperation and remorse that she treated Dr. Svengali in the evenings in a way which he found nearly unendurable.

Clearly, Dr. Svengali thought, he must modify his device a second time. He decided that the easiest thing to do was simply to combine the first two versions of it, and insert in Mrs. O'Farrell's brain a dual instrument which both made her limbs adequately perform her external tasks, and which also made her want to do, and enjoy doing, them, though it was in fact the instrument, and not the wants, which produced the movements. But Mrs. O'Farrell's fanaticism was so implacable that even the knowledge that in caring for Dr. Svengali, she was simply doing what she herself wanted to do, did little, if anything, to diminish the hostility with which she treated him when the transmitter was switched off.

Since a remote ancestor of hers had once read philosophy in a twentieth-century British university, her mother had inherited some books and journals. One of them, she had been told, contained an article by someone called Harrison,[1] arguing that a man was free so long as he was doing what he wanted to do. In a rare philosophical moment, Mrs. O'Farrell reasoned that, in cooking, shopping and cleaning she was doing what she wanted to do. Nevertheless, so far from being free, she was even more helpless than when she had been controlled by Dr. Svengali's first device, which had made her look after him, even when she did not want to. She at first thought that the reason why she could not be free, although she both wanted to keep house and did, was that she would still be keeping house even though she did not want to. A little reflection, however, made her realise that this was not so. For Dr. Svengali had so constructed his radio control that the only dial setting which made Mrs. O'Farrell *want* to make the beds, for example, also caused the control to direct her to move her limbs to go through the external motions of making them. Hence had she not wanted to make the beds, she would not have. Mrs. O'Farrell failed to find consolation in philosophy and efficiently though his household was run, Dr. Svengali's evenings were as miserable as before.

The intractable nature of his problem caused Dr. Svengali also to engage in unwonted philosophical reflection. After all, he thought, Geraldine (he was not a man to insist in superficial ways upon the superiority of his position) must want not to be made to do the housework, for whatever absurd reason, or she would not resist my attempts to make her do it. So if I can make her want to do the housework, why cannot I eradicate those more central and recalcitrant impulses which make her want not to want to do the housework, and which motivate her prolonged and determined resistance to all my efforts to manage

[1] A careful scrutiny of the surviving remains of twentieth-century philosophers reveals no record of there having been a philosopher of this name. [Ed]

her? Perhaps if I could learn to control those impulses which lie at the very core of her being, I might be able so to manipulate her that I can get my house looked after and some agreeable conversation and pleasant companionship in the evenings.

Trial and error showed that he was right in his surmise. The correct dial setting on his radio control blotted out Mrs. O'Farrell's sense of her duty to the community of women, and she happily did everything Dr. Svengali wished to his entire satisfaction. But success had whetted Dr. Svengali's appetite, and Faustus-like he looked about for more worlds to conquer.[2] In the days when Mrs. O'Farrell was controlled by Mark I of his device, he had made her steal the notes of some experiments from a colleague, to whose study she, but not he, had access. A man naturally prone to make other people bear the guilt which he incurred by his own actions, Dr. Svengali had tried to put the blame upon her, but without success. She had not, she always insisted, stolen the papers. Her feet had gone to the study and her hands taken them against her will. She had even threatened to inform the police of what she considered Dr. Svengali had done, and at one time only doubts about the possibility of convicting him had prevented her from doing so. Now, however, Dr. Svengali saw the chance of having her a willing accomplice to his schemes. He did not consider that Mrs. O'Farrell would make a very effective criminal, but at least, if she were found out, his machine could eradicate any inclination she might have to turn informer.

After a surprisingly successful criminal career, Mrs. O'Farrell was eventually apprehended, tried, convicted and sentenced to a long term of imprisonment. The sentence proved not to be nearly as onerous as intended. She died a week after entering prison from a brain tumour caused by Dr. Svengali's insertion of the control. She herself felt, as was only to be expected, no inclination to blame him, or to feel anything other than that she was herself responsible for what she had apparently done. No-one, she now argued, had compelled her to do it. She had simply done what she herself pleased, and had she not wanted to steal it was by no means outside her power to refrain. She had simply not tried. The remote causes of her want to steal, she thought, were irrelevant. For her wanting to steal must have been caused by something, and the fact that it was actually caused by Dr. Svengali, though highly relevant to what moral judgements ought to be passed upon him, were quite beside the point when it came to passing moral judgements about her.

The prison chaplain, with whom she discussed the matter agreed. He did not try to get Mrs. O'Farrell pardoned, but instead informed the police of Dr. Svengali's complicity, if one could call it that, in the matter. The latter, however, had by this time vanished.

---

[2] It was in fact Alexander, not Faustus, who did this. [Ed.]

He reappeared a few months later, a changed man, in a country whose police force had the reputation of being weak and internationally uncooperative. But Mrs. O'Farrell's apprehension, conviction and subsequent demise made him realise that he was in fact deeply fond of her. Remorse at the way in which he had treated her overcame him, and he was consumed by a desire to be a better person. To a man of Dr. Svengali's outlook and training, the obvious way to accomplish this difficult feat was to alter the physiology of his own brain in such a manner as to secure the desired improvement. He found an assistant to insert Mrs. O'Farrell's control into his own skull, and himself set the dial on his short-wave radio transmitter, which he had prudently taken with him, in such a manner as to eradicate from himself any further desire towards similar misbehaviour.

Unfortunately, however, his hand slipped, and the dial fell back to the slightly worn place where it had been set to control the behaviour of Mrs. O'Farrell. From that time forward Dr. Svengali stole for himself, and his exploits became progressively more and more dangerous.

Though he, unlike Mrs. O'Farrell, had the knowledge to alter the dial setting so as to eliminate his desire to steal or, at any rate, so as to produce a counter-desire to avoid prison or a stronger dislike of his addiction to such dishonourable conduct, the machine itself, by causing him to be quite satisfied with his behaviour, brought it about that he had no motive for doing so. His very desire to steal prevented him from ordering its own extinction. Inevitably he was eventually apprehended, and the laws of his new country, which tried to make up by their extreme severity for the inefficiency of its police force, condemned him to death.

The imminence of his decease did what the death of his now beloved Geraldine had been unable to do, and he became at last overwhelmed with a readily effective remorse. Even the knowledge that he would not have been in his present plight but for a quite inadvertent slip of his fingers on the control could not prevent him from deciding to hang himself. A stool and a piece of rope had been left in his cell by thoughtful and economically minded prison authorities, but Dr. Svengali had always been a little clumsy, and in climbing on to the stool his foot slipped, and his consequent fall jolted the control in such a way as to make it function in a highly erratic manner, and Dr. Svengali to behave as one demented. The cell, of course, was not padded, and he so damaged himself against its stone sides that the prison authorities, perhaps a little inconsistently, took him to hospital to prevent him doing himself any further injury.

In the course of his treatment doctors discovered the controlling device inside his skull and removed it. His behaviour instantly became as normal as it had ever been. His solicitor appealed against the conviction on the ground that the person who was to be hanged was a different person from the person who had committed the crimes and, alternatively, on the ground that Dr. Svengali was not responsible for his actions, which were caused by the control, not by Dr. Svengali himself. The appeal court found in his favour, though one judge disagreed, on the ground that Dr. Svengali had put the control inside his own skull.

Dr. Svengali thanked God, whom he imagined in his own augmented image as a supremely powerful brain physiologist without much moral character, for his good fortune, for since his belief in the deity manifested itself only in moments of stress, he did not notice the impropriety of ascribing anything at all to luck. On his release from prison, he returned to his own country, where Mrs. O'Farrell had cached most of their booty.

His first act upon retaking up his abode in his former lodgings was to advertise for another housekeeper.

PART IV

GOODNESS NOT DEMANDED BY GOD

10

PIERRE BAYLE

The Moral Inefficacy of Theism

Introduction

Pierre Bayle (1647–1706) was (among other things) the author of a dictionary (*Dictionnaire Historique et Critique*), a precursor of the French *La Grande Encyclopedie* and *The Encyclopedia Britannica*. He was able to achieve this enormous feat partly because he had the wisdom to adhere to a decision made in early youth never to marry or accept a chair. He was one of the most famous skeptics of his age, a fact which is difficult to reconcile with his professed Calvinism.

Reading

ATHEISM DOES NOT NECESSARILY LEAD TO CORRUPTION OF MORALS.

PEOPLE ARE PERSUADED only by a false preconception concerning the light of conscience that atheism is the most abominable state into which anyone may fall, for not having discerned our true motives, they imagine that our beliefs determine our acts. This is the way they reason. Man is naturally reasonable, he never desires without a conscious motive, he necessarily seeks happiness and flees unhappiness, and he gives his preference to the objects most agreeable to him. Therefore, if he is convinced that there is a Providence which governs the world, from whose workings nothing escapes, which rewards the virtuous with an infinite bliss and punishes the wicked with an eternal torment, he will infallibly follow after virtue and flee vice. He will renounce all carnal

From Pierre Bayle, *Miscellaneous Thoughts on the Comet of 1680*, edited and translated by Karl C. Sandberg. Reprinted by permission of Karl C. Sandberg.

pleasures, knowing on the one hand that these fleeting moments of gratification will procure him an eternity of pain, and feeling on the other hand that in depriving himself of them he will find an eternity of bliss. But if he does not believe in Providence, he will regard his desires as his ultimate end and the rule of all his acts. He will scoff at what others call virtue and integrity and will follow only the movements of his own lusts. If possible, he will do away with all those who displease him. He will perjure himself for the slightest gain, and if his position puts him above human laws, as he has already placed himself above the remorse of conscience, there is no crime which we should not expect of him. He is a monster infinitely more dangerous than those fierce beasts, those lions and mad bulls from which Hercules delivered Greece. Someone else, who had nothing to fear from men, could at least be restrained by the fear of the gods, which has always been a means of bridling the passions of men. And it is sure that many crimes were prevented among the pagans by the care taken to preserve the memory of all the striking punishments visited upon scoundrels for their supposed impiety, or even to invent a few examples, such as the story spread abroad in the time of Augustus when a temple in Asia had been pillaged by the soldiers of Mark Anthony. It was said that the one who first laid his hand upon the altar of the goddess who was worshipped in that temple had immediately been struck blind and had become paralyzed in all the members of his body. (Wanting to verify the report, Augustus learned from the old officer who had done the deed that he had not only been sound and healthy ever since, but also that this act had put him in comfortable circumstances for the rest of his life.) . . . People reason that all of these accounts, true or false, which had such a good effect upon the mind of an idolater, have no power over an atheist. He is so impervious to all of these considerations that he must necessarily be the most accomplished and incorrigible scoundrel in the world.

EXPERIENCE OPPOSES THE IDEA THAT THE KNOWLEDGE OF GOD CHECKS THE EVIL INCLINATIONS OF MEN.

All of that is well and good when we regard that theoretical side of the question and make metaphysical abstractions of it, but unfortunately, the theory does not square with the findings of experience. Suppose that we asked inhabitants of another world to predict the morals of Christians after telling them that Christians are creatures endowed with reason and good sense, avid of happiness, and persuaded that there is a Paradise for those who obey the law of God and a Hell for those who do not. I admit they would undoubtedly assure us that the Christians strive to excel in observing the precepts of the Gospel and vie to distinguish themselves in works of mercy, in prayer, and in forgiving offenses, if there be any among them capable of offending his neighbor. But why would they make this complimentary judgment? It is because they would have considered only an abstract idea of the Christians, for if they considered them individually and saw everything that makes them act, they would soon lower the good opinion that they would have formed, and they would not have lived two weeks among us without declaring that in this world people do not conduct themselves according to the light of conscience.

THE REASON FOR THE DISPARITY BETWEEN BELIEF AND PRACTICE.

Here we come to the real solution of this question. When we compare the real morals of a man who has a religion with the abstract idea of what his morals should be, we are surprised not to find any conformity between reality and our expectations. According to our abstract idea, we should expect that a man who believes in a God, a Paradise, and a Hell would do everything that he knew to be pleasing to God and would do nothing he knew to be displeasing to Him, but the life of this man shows us that he does just the opposite. Do you wish to know the cause of this incongruity? Here it is — man does not decide between two possible actions by his abstract knowledge of duty, but by the particular judgment he makes of each one as he is on the point of acting. Now this decision may well be in conformity with his abstract idea of duty, but most often it is not. It is almost always determined by the dominant passion of the heart, the inclination of the temperament, the force of habit, and the taste and sensitivity which one has for certain things. The poet who has Medea say, "I see and approve the good, but I do evil"[1] has depicted perfectly the difference between the light of conscience and the particular judgment which moves us to act. Conscience recognizes the beauty of virtue in the abstract and forces us to agree that nothing is more praiseworthy than to live virtuously. But when the heart is once possessed by an unlawful love, when one sees that he will experience pleasure in satisfying it and will be plunged into chagrin and unbearable anxiety if he does not satisfy it, no light of conscience is of any avail. Nothing is consulted except passion, and judgment is rendered in favor of acting here and now against the abstract idea of duty. All of these observations only go to show that nothing is more illusory than to judge the moral character of a man by the general opinions with which he is imbued.

MAN DOES NOT ACT ACCORDING TO HIS PRINCIPLES.

Say what you will about man being a reasonable creature. It is nonetheless true that his conduct is almost never consistent with his princi-

---

[1] Ovid, *Metamorphosis*, book 7.

ples. In speculative questions he is quite capable of avoiding fallacious conclusions, because in these matters he sins much more by accepting false premises than by drawing false conclusions from them, but it is quite another thing in questions of morals. Here he very seldom adopts false principles and almost never abandons the ideas of natural equity in his conscience, and yet he almost always concludes in favor of his dissolute desires. Why is it, pray tell me, that in spite of the prodigious diversity of opinions concerning the way of serving God and living honorably, we see certain passions reigning constantly in all countries and in all ages? Why is it that ambition, avarice, envy, the desire for vengeance, fornication, and all the crimes that can satisfy these passions are seen everywhere? Why is it that the Jew and the Mohammedan, the Turk and the Moor, the Christian and the pagan, the Indian and the Tartar, the islander and the mainlander, the noble and the commoner, all of these kinds of people who in all other things are alike only in their abstract humanity, why is it that they are so alike with respect to these passions that they seem only to copy one another? Where can we find the reason for all of this except in the idea that the true principle of man's actions (I except those in whom the Holy Spirit operates with all of its efficacity) is nothing else than the temperament, the natural inclination for pleasure, the taste contracted for certain objects, the desire to please, a habit contracted through association with one's friends, or some other disposition which results from the essence of our nature, no matter where we were born or what we have been taught?

My explanation must be sound since the ancient pagans, who had an unbelievable baggage of superstitions, who were constantly appeasing the wrath of their gods, who were frightened by an endless number of wonders because they believed the gods to be the dispensers of prosperity and adversity according to one's conduct, still did not fail to commit every crime imaginable. And if my explanation were not true, how would it be possible for the Christians, who know so clearly by a revelation supported by so many miracles that they must renounce vice to be eternally happy and to avoid eternal misery; who have so many excellent preachers who are paid to compose and deliver the most cogent and compelling exhortations to virtue; who everywhere have so many learned and zealous spiritual advisers; how then would it be possible, I say, for the Christians to live as they do in the most terrible licentiousness and vice?

THE PAGANS, WHO BELIEVED FIRMLY IN MANY GODS, WERE NOT MORE VIRTUOUS THAN ATHEISTS WOULD BE.

No matter how often you object that the fear of a God is an eminently suitable means of correcting the natural corruption of man, I will still invoke the testimony of experience and ask why the pagans, who carried the fear of their gods to excessive superstitions, were so lax in correcting this corruption that every abominable vice reigned among them. In spite of the ever present memory of spectacular retribution visited by the heavens upon blasphemers and perjurers and those guilty of sacrilege; in spite of the tales forged to make the wicked tremble; in spite of the pompous descriptions of the Furies, Hell, and the Elysian Fields, temples were still pillaged when the occasion was propitious and false witnesses were found in great profusion. Juvenal is inimitable in his picture of false witnesses who have no religion and false witnesses who believe in a God. He says that the former perjure themselves without hesitation, whereas the latter reason for some time and then perjure themselves with extreme confidence. They subsequently feel remorse and imagine that the vengeance of God pursues them everywhere. Nonetheless they do not mend their ways, but sin as readily at the next opportunity as they did before.

The picture is an exact copy of Nature. We still see this same spirit reigning everywhere and drawing men to sin in spite of the fear of Hell and the remorse of conscience. So true is this observation that to argue against my thesis is nothing else than pitting metaphysical reasonings against a fact, in the manner of that philosopher [Zeno] who attempted to prove that there was no movement. No one, I am sure, will object to my use of the method of Diogenes who without answering the subtleties of Zeno point by point merely walked in his presence. Indeed, nothing is more efficacious in showing an honest man that he is reasoning upon false hypotheses than to show him that he is arguing against experience. . . .

As I have already said, we have no annals informing us of the morals and customs of a nation completely immersed in atheism. We cannot therefore refute by established fact that atheists are incapable of any moral virtue and that they are ferocious beasts more to be feared than lions and tigers. But it is not difficult to show that this conjecture is highly uncertain. For since experience shows us that those who believe in a Paradise and a Hell are capable of committing all sorts of crimes, it is evident that the inclination to do evil does not come from the ignorance of God's existence and that it is not corrected by acquiring the knowledge of a God who punishes and rewards. One may conclude therefrom that the inclination to do evil is not any greater in a soul destitute of the knowledge of God than in a soul which knows God.

Conjectures upon the morals of a society of atheists.

Now after all these remarks, if you wish to know my conjectures concerning a society of atheists, I will not hesitate to say that with regard to morals and civic affairs, it would be just like a society of pagans. It is true that very strict and well-executed laws would be needed for the punishing of criminals, but are they not needed everywhere? Would we dare to leave our houses if theft, murder, and other violences were permitted by the laws of the sovereign? In the streets of Paris, both day and night, are we protected from thieves and pickpockets by anything more than the strict enforcement of the king's laws? Without his laws, would we not be exposed to the same violences as in former reigns, even though our teachers and confessors discharged their duties even better than they formerly did? In spite of the rack, the zeal of the magistrate, and the diligence of the provost, how many murders and thefts are committed even in the places of public execution and at the moment when criminals are being executed? We can say without indulging in false oratory that human justice is the cause of the virtue of most people, for as soon as it fails to punish the sinner, few people keep themselves from the sin.

In a society of atheists there would be laws of propriety and honor.

We can now see how apparent it is that a society of atheists would practice both civic and moral actions just as other societies practice them, provided that crimes were severely punished and that honor and shame were associated with certain acts. Ignorance of a Supreme Being, the Creator and Preserver of the world, would not make the members of this society impervious to glory and scorn, to reward and punishment, and to all the passions which are seen in other men, nor would it extinguish in them the light of reason. In a society of atheists we should therefore expect to see people who would be honest in their business dealings, who would help the poor, who would oppose injustice, who would be faithful to their friends, who would scorn insults addressed to them, who would restrain their carnal appetites and who would do harm to no one. Their motives, it is true, would vary, for some would desire to be praised for all these splendid actions which the public would surely approve, while others would do them with the intention of acquiring the support of friends and protectors in case of need. Women would pride themselves on their chastity, because this quality infallibly procures them the love and esteem of men. I do not doubt that there would be crimes committed of every kind, but no more than are committed in societies of idolaters, because everything which motivates pagans, whether to good or evil, would be found in a society of atheists, that is, rewards and punishments, glory and shame, temperament and education. For as concerning this sanctifying grace which fills us with the love of God and which gives us victory over our evil habits, the pagans are just as bereft of it as atheists.

Do you wish to be fully convinced that a people deprived of the knowledge of God would make rules of honor for themselves and observe them scrupulously? You have only to look among the Christians to see a certain worldly honor which is directly contrary to the spirit of the Gospel. I would be curious to know the origin of this system of honor of which the Christians are so idolatrous and to which they sacrifice everything. When they believe that it is dishonorable to leave an offense unpunished, or to yield the first place to another, or to have less ambition or pride than their equals, is it because they believe in a God, a Gospel, a resurrection, a Paradise, and a Hell? You will surely grant me the point. Examine all of the ideas of propriety which are found among the Christians, and you will scarcely find two which have been borrowed from religion. Moreover, when improper actions become proper, it is not at all because people have consulted the morality of the Gospel. Some time ago women took it into their heads that it was more fashionable to dress in public and in presence of other people than in private, to ride horseback, to give frenetic chase to some wild animal during the hunt, etc., and because these actions have become common, we no longer look upon them as immodest. Was it religion which changed our ideas in this respect? Compare the manners of several nations which profess Christianity. Compare them, I say, one with another, and you will see that what is accounted improper in one country is not at all improper elsewhere. It must then be that the ideas of propriety which are among the Christians do not come from the religion that they profess. I admit that some of their ideas are universal, for we have no example of a Christian nation where it is shameful for women to be chaste. But to act in good faith we must confess that this idea is older than both the Gospel and Moses. It is a certain impression which is as old as the world. . . . Let us admit, then, that there are ideas of honor in the human race implanted there by nature, that is, by a general Providence. Let us especially admit that such is the case of that honor of which the brave among us are so jealous and which is so in opposition to the law of God. And how can we doubt after that, that nature could do among the atheists, where the knowledge of the Gospel would not oppose it, that which it does among the Christians?

BELIEF IN THE MORTALITY OF THE SOUL DOES NOT PREVENT PEOPLE FROM
DESIRING TO IMMORTALIZE THEIR NAME.

Perhaps people imagine that the desire to immortalize one's name, which has so much power over the minds of other men, has no effect on an atheist, who is persuaded that his soul dies with his body. But this thought is quite false, because it is certain that those who have done great deeds in order to be praised by posterity were not flattered by the hope of knowing in the next world what people would say about them after their death. We find examples even today in our brave men of war who expose themselves to so many perils and hardships in order to have their name mentioned in history. Do they imagine that the monuments which will be erected in their honor and which will inform their most distant posterity of everything great and magnificent which they have done, do they imagine, I say, that these monuments will cause them to feel any pleasure? Do they believe that they will be informed in the next world of what is happening in this one? And whether they enjoy the bliss of Paradise or whether they burn in Hell, do they not know that it would be quite useless to learn that men admire them? Therefore, it is not the belief in the immortality of the soul which causes people to love glory, and consequently atheists are quite capable of desiring an eternal reputation. The most substantial part of the love of glory is a pleasant image which one caresses in his mind during this life of many successive centuries filled with admiration for one's deeds. And after one is dead? This thought is of no further use, for there are many other things to do besides thinking of the reputation which one has left in this world.

You have no doubt heard that when M. de Castelnau was awarded the baton of a marshal of France just before his death, he said all that was very fine in this world, but he was going to depart for a country where it would be of no use to him.

Examples which show that atheists have not been especially conspicuous by the impurity of their morals.

I will perhaps be told that it would nonetheless be a strange thing for an atheist to live virtuously, a veritable prodigy beyond the forces of nature. I answer that it is not any stranger for an atheist to live virtuously than it is for a Christian to commit all sorts of crimes. If we see the latter prodigy every day, why should we believe that the other is impossible? But I will give you some even stronger reasons to show you that what I have set forth concerning the morals of a society of atheists is more than mere conjecture. I will point out that those few persons among the ancients who made an open profession of atheism, such as Diagoras, Theodorus, Evmerus and several others, caused no general outcry by their libertinism. Although they have been accused of dreadful aberrations in their reason, I am not aware that they have the reputation of extraordinary licentiousness in their conduct. On the contrary, I find that their conduct appeared so admirable to Clement of Alexandria that he felt obliged to protest against the accusation of atheism that was leveled at them. He maintained that their reputation for impiety was due only to their great zeal and perspicacity in pointing out the errors of pagan theology, and that they were called atheists only because they refused to recognize the false pagan gods.

Epicurus, who denied Providence and the immortality of the soul, was one of the philosophers of antiquity who lived in the most exemplary way, and although his sect was subsequently brought into disrepute, it is nonetheless certain that it was composed of many honorable and upright persons, and those who dishonored it by their vices were not corrupted by this school. They were people who gave themselves over to debauchery by habit and temperament and who were glad to cover their filthy passions with such a good pretext as that of following the maxims of one of the greatest philosophers in the world. They were the kind of people who imagined that as long as they hid themselves under the mantle of philosophy they could scoff at the scandal they caused. They did not become inclined to vice because they had embraced the doctrine of Epicurus, but they embraced the doctrine of Epicurus, which they did not understand, because they were inclined to vice. At least this is what Seneca says, and although he belonged to a sect which detested the memory of Epicurus, he does not hesitate to voice his belief that the pleasures of this philosopher were very sober and restrained. St. Jerome speaks very advantageously of the frugality of the same Epicurus and holds him up in sharp contrast to the licentiousness of the Christians, in order to shame the latter.

Among the Jews there was a sect which frankly denied the immortality of the soul. I speak of the Sadducees. I am not aware that with such a detestable opinion they led a life any more corrupt than the other Jews, and on the contrary it is very likely that they were more upright than the Pharisees, who prided themselves so much on their observation of the law of God.

Mr. de Balzac informs us in *The Christian Socrates* of the last words of a prince who had lived and died an atheist and he testifies that he lacked no moral virtues, swore only by "certainly," drank only herb tea, and was extremely circumspect in every outward appearance.

The detestable Vanini, who was burned in Toulouse for his atheism in 1619, had always lived moderately, and whoever would have accused him of any criminal deviation, except in his dogmas, would have run a great risk of being convicted of slander.

Under the reign of Charles IX in 1573, a man who had secretly affirmed his atheism was burned in Paris. He maintained that there was no other god in the world except the purity of his body. He was therefore reported to be yet a virgin. He had as many shirts as there are days of the year, and he sent them to Flanders to be washed in a fountain famed for the purity of its water and its property of making clothes admirably white. He had an aversion for all kinds of impurities, whether in acts or in words, and although he upheld his blasphemies with a stubbornness which he retained until his death, he always stated them in an extremely mild way.

You cannot be unaware of the account given by Mr. Ricaut, Secretary of the Count of Winchelsey, the English ambassador at Constantinople. I need not comment upon the diligence and exactitude of this author. I will say only that after giving the account of a numerous sect of atheists formed in Turkey, composed mostly of cadis and of people versed in Arabic literature, he adds that the partisans of this sect have an extraordinary affection for one another, that they render each other all kinds of good services, that they are civil and hospitable, and that if a guest of their persuasion arrives they provide him with the best food they have. I do not deny that their civilities go too far, since they provide their guest with a most improper recreation during the night, but in that they do nothing of which the other Turks are not guilty. Therefore, if we compare the life of the other Turks with that of these atheists, we will find either that there is no difference between the two or that the former are less virtuous than the latter.

I will certainly not put the Chancellor de l'Hospital among the number of atheists, for I have no doubt but that he was a good Christian. I will simply state that he was very strongly suspected of having no religion, although he lived in a most exemplary way and no one appeared to be more austere, more sober, or more dignified than he was. Mr. de Beaucaire de Peguillon, Bishop of Metz, frankly accuses him of atheism. His testimony is a little suspect because of his attachment to the Cardinal of Lorraine, whose tutor he had been. But this example nonetheless shows us that men are very careless when they state so boldly that atheism is inseparable from vice, since a Chancellor of France was suspected of atheism, although his good life was known by everybody.

11

SIGMUND FREUD

The Psychopathology of Theism

Introduction

Sigmund Freud (1856–1939) was the founder of psychoanalysis, which is both a body of theories about the causation of human behavior and a method of treating mental disorders. Freud's most basic idea—that the repression of emotion, especially of sexual desires, leads to neurosis—is now very widely accepted. However, many psychiatrists question whether his therapeutic technique produces significant improvements. Freud's publications include *The Interpretation of Dreams* (1900), *The Psychopathology of Everyday Life* (1901), *Three Contributions to Sexual Theory* (1905), and *Beyond the Pleasure Principle* (1920). Freud's impact on the thinking of educated people has been profound. Most of them now share Freud's view that many acts cannot be adequately explained without an appeal to unconscious motives and that human beings reveal their desires and feelings even in apparently meaningless behavior. Freud was a zealous naturalist and a lifelong opponent of metaphysics and religion. His most sustained criticisms of religious belief are found in *The Future of an Illusion* (1927) and in the last chapter of *New Introductory Lectures to Psychoanalysis* (1932).

Freud assumes that belief in God is rationally indefensible and that (what he thinks he has shown elsewhere) religion is a form of neurosis. The question he discusses here is whether moral prohibitions (such as that against killing) should be allowed to rest on secular foundations only or whether it is necessary for them to be believed to have a divine sanction. He thinks that the divine sanction is *certainly* unnecessary and *possibly* harmful.

Freud thinks that one disadvantage of resting religion on divine authority is that if there is in fact no God, people might discover it, the possibility of which would make morality vulnerable. He also thinks, inconsistently, that people who have faith will be too irrational to be in any danger of being converted to a secular morality.

It can be argued that basing religion on divine prohibitions that have nothing to do with the furtherance of happiness or welfare in the world has caused, and still does cause, enormous amounts of unnecessary suffering. Examples are religious prohibitions of homosexuality, suicide, euthanasia, the persecution of witches, the insistence on the wickedness of other religions, and even of different sects of the same religion.

Reading

IT IS MANIFESTLY in the interest of man's communal existence, which would not otherwise be practicable, that civilization has laid down the commandment that one shall not kill the neighbour whom one hates, who is in one's way, or whose property one covets. For the murderer would draw on to himself the vengeance of the murdered man's kinsmen and the secret envy of the others who feel as much inward inclination as he did to such an act of violence. Thus he would not enjoy his revenge or his spoil for long, but would have every prospect of being killed soon himself. Even if he could defend himself against single foes by his extraordinary strength and caution, he would be bound to succumb to a combination of these weaker foes. If a combination of this sort did not take place, then murder would continue ceaselessly, and the end of it would be that men would exterminate one another. It would be the same state of affairs among individuals that still prevails in Corsica among families, but otherwise survives only among nations. Insecurity of life, an equal danger for all, now unites men into one society, which forbids the individual to kill and reserves to itself the right to kill in the name of society the man who violates this prohibition. This, then, is justice and punishment.

We do not, however, tell others of this rational basis for the murder prohibition; we declare, on the contrary, that God is its author. Thus, making bold to divine his intentions, we find that he has no wish, either, for men to exterminate each other. By acting thus we invest the cultural prohibition with a quite peculiar solemnity, but at the same time we risk making its observance dependent on belief in God. If we retract this step, no longer saddling God with our own wishes, and content ourselves with the social justification for the cultural prohibition, then we renounce, it is true, its hallowed nature, but we also avoid endangering its existence. And we gain something else as well. Through some

From *The Future of an Illusion* by Sigmund Freud. Reprinted from *The Standard Edition of the Complete Works of Sigmund Freud*, translated and edited by James Strachey by permission of Sigmund Freud Copyrights Ltd., The Institute of Pyschoanalysis, and The Hogarth Press.

kind of diffusion or infection the character of sanctity and inviolability, of other-worldliness, one might say, has been extended from some few important prohibitions to all other cultural institutions and laws and ordinances. And often the halo becomes these none too well; not only do they invalidate each other by making conflicting decisions according to the time and place of their origin; even apart from this they betray every sign of human inadequacy. One can easily recognize among them things which can only be the product of short-sightedness and apprehensiveness, the expression of narrow interests, or the result of inadequate hypotheses. The criticism to which one must subject them also diminishes to an unwelcome extent people's respect for other and more justified cultural demands. As it is a delicate task to decide what God has himself ordained and what derives rather from the authority of an all-powerful parliament or a supreme judicial decision, it would be an indubitable advantage to leave God out of the question altogether, and to admit honestly the purely human origin of all cultural laws and institutions. Along with their pretensions to sanctity the rigid and immutable nature of these laws and regulations would also cease. Men would realize that these have been made, not so much to rule them, as, on the contrary, to serve their interests; they would acquire a more friendly attitude to them, and instead of aiming at their abolition they would aim only at improving them. This would be an important advance on the road which leads to reconciliation with the burden of culture.

But here our plea for a purely rational basis for cultural laws, that is to say, for deriving them from social necessity, is interrupted by a sudden doubt. We have chosen as our example the origin of the murder prohibition. But does our account of it correspond to historical truth? We fear not; it appears to be merely a rationalistic construction. With the help of psycho-analysis we have studied this very point in the history of human culture, and supported by this study we are bound to say that in reality it did not happen like this. Even in men to-day purely reasonable motives are of little avail against passionate impulses. How much weaker, then, must they have been in the primordial animal man! Perhaps even now his descendants would still kill one another without inhibition, if there had not been among those acts of murder one — the slaughter of the primal father — which evoked an irresistible emotional reaction, momentous in its consequences. From it arose the commandment: thou shalt not kill, which in totemism was confined to the father-substitute, and was later extended to others, but which even to-day is not universally observed.

But according to arguments which I need not repeat here, that primal father has been the prototype of God, the model after which later generations have formed their figure of God. Hence the religious explanation is right. God was actually concerned in the origin of that prohibition; his influence, not insight into what was necessary for society, brought it into being. And the process of attributing man's will to God is fully justified; for men, knowing that they had brutally set aside the father, determined, in the reaction to their outrage, to respect his will in future. And so the religious doctrine does give us the historical truth, though of course in a somewhat remodelled and disguised form; our rational explanation belies it.

We now observe that the stock of religious ideas contains not only wish-fulfilments, but also important historical memories. What matchless, what abundant power this combination of past and present must give to religion! But with the help of an analogy we may perhaps feel our way towards another view of the problem. It is not a good thing to transplant ideas far away from the soil in which they grew, but we cannot resist pointing out the resemblance which forms this analogy. We know that the human child cannot well complete its development towards culture without passing through a more or less distinct phase of neurosis. This is because the child is unable to suppress by rational mental effort so many of those instinctual impulsions which cannot later be turned to account, but has to check them by acts of repression, behind which there strands as a rule an anxiety motive. Most of these child neuroses are overcome spontaneously as one grows up, and especially is this the fate of the obsessional neuroses of childhood. The remainder can be cleared up still later by psycho-analytic treatment. In just the same way one might assume that in its development through the ages mankind as a whole experiences conditions that are analogous to the neuroses, and this for the same reasons, because in the ages of its ignorance and intellectual weakness it achieved by purely affective means the instinctual renunciations, indispensable for man's communal existence. And the residue of these repression-like processes, which took place in antiquity, has long clung on to civilization. Thus religion would be the universal obsessional neurosis of humanity. It, like the child's, originated in the Oedipus complex, the relation to the father. According to this conception one might prophesy that the abandoning of religion must take place with the fateful inexorability of a process of growth, and that we are just now in the middle of this phase of development.

So we should form our behaviour after the model of a sensible teacher, who does not oppose the new development confronting him, but seeks to further it and to temper the force of its onset. To be sure this analogy does not exhaust the essence of religion. If on the one hand religion brings with it obsessional limitations, which can only be compared to an individual obsessional neurosis, it comprises on the other hand a system of wish-illusions, incompatible with reality, such as we find in an isolated form only in Meynert's amentia, a state of blissful hallucinatory confusion. But these are only just comparisons, with whose help we can endeavour to understand social phenomena; individual psychology supplies us with no exact counterpart.

It has been shown repeatedly (by myself, and particularly by Theodor Reik) into what details the analogy of religion and the obsessional neurosis may be pursued, how much of the vicissitudes and peculiarities of the formation of religion may be understood in this way. And it accords well with this that the true believer is in a high degree protected against the danger of certain neurotic afflictions; by accepting the universal neurosis he is spared the task of forming a personal neurosis.

Our knowledge of the historical value of certain religious doctrines increases our respect for them, but it does not invalidate our proposal to exclude them from the motivation of cultural laws. On the contrary! This historical residue has given us the conception of religious dogmas as, so to speak, neurotic survivals, and now we may say that the time has probably come to replace the consequences of repression by the results of rational mental effort, as in the analytic treatment of neurotics. One may prophesy, but hardly regret, that this process of remodelling will not stop at dispelling the solemn air of sanctity surrounding the cultural laws, but that a general revision of these must involve the abolition of many of them. And this will go far to solve our appointed problem of reconciling men to civilization. We need not regret the loss of historical truth involved in accepting the rational motivation of cultural laws. The truths contained in religious doctrines are after all so distorted and systematically disguised that the mass of mankind cannot recognize them as truth. It is an instance of the same thing when we tell the child that new-born babies are brought by the stork. Here, too, we tell the truth in symbolic guise, for we know what that large bird signifies. But the child does not know it; he hears only the distortion, and feels that he has been deceived; and we know how often his refractoriness and his distrust of the grown-ups gets bound up with this impression. We have come to the conclusion that it is better to avoid such symbolic disguisings of the truth, and to allow the child knowledge of the real state of affairs in a way suitable for his stage of intellectual development.

12

JEAN-PAUL SARTRE

The Abandonment of Man by God

Introduction

Jean-Paul Sartre (1905–1980) was an eminent French literary and political figure. He was a great novelist and playwright whose philosophy also
has merit.

At the time he wrote this selection (from *Existentialism Is a Humanism*), Sartre was a leading French existentialist. According to the reading,
an existentialist is a philosopher who thinks that *existence* precedes *essence*. By this Sartre means that since there is no God, there cannot be
any antecedently existing idea of human beings, in the mind of God, an
idea to which people ought to conform. Hence it cannot be the case that
humans should live in such a manner as to fulfill God's purpose for them,
because there is no such purpose. Because the essence of humanity (in
the mind of God) thus does not precede human existence, people must
create themselves according to their own ideas; that is to say, human
existence precedes its essence.

Sartre supposed that a number of corollaries followed from this
assertion:

1. Man is (poetically speaking) abandoned by God. And since there is
   no God, everything is permitted.

Although it would indeed follow that nothing was *prohibited* by God, if
God did not exist, then it would also follow that nothing is permitted by
him either. A very large number of philosophers have held that it does
not follow from the nonexistence of God that everything is morally permissible. (See the Introduction to this section.)

2. Human beings are free.

Sartre is confused on this point. It *would* follow that humans were free from the restraints of God's commands, because there would not be any. It would *not* follow that people were free from morality, unless one thought the moral law depended on God, which it probably does not. It would *not* follow that people were free if saying that they were free meant that their actions were not determined by antecedent causes. It *would* follow that people were free in the sense that their actions were not predestined; at least, they could not be predestined by *God*. (See Part III.)

In his remarks on freedom, Sartre puts great emphasis on the extent to which human beings are free to escape enslavement by their past. A man who had been a waiter all his life could decide to give up being a waiter, in spite of habit, inertia, timidity, and all the other forces which tended to make him carry on as he always had. It would be self-deception or bad faith on his part to suppose otherwise.

However, the extent to which people are free (able) to create themselves (in spite of their past) seems to be very limited. There are in fact an enormous number of things that one cannot do. Doubtless Sartre's waiter does not have to go on being a waiter, but giving up waiting is likely to make him worse off rather than better. Human beings tend to wear blinders to the many things that are beyond their power, which saves them much time and effort. Besides, the external pressures to remain the same are simply enormous.

The question of to what extent people are capable of shaking off the past has no bearing on the truth of determinism, when determinism is interpreted to mean that everything has a cause and consequently an explanation. For example, the actions of a waiter who goes on being a waiter, and one who gives up waiting and shoots himself or runs for president, will both be in principle capable of explanation. The latter, however, may be more difficult to explain than the former.

There is a sense in which people cannot *avoid* creating themselves as they go along. Even deciding to be a waiter is the result of a decision to go on being a waiter. Hence the recommendation to create oneself is vacuous.

When Sartre says that one is able to choose to be free, the word "free" must be used in an unusual sense. For if we were not already free in one sense, we would not be *able* to choose to be free in another. Presumably one is already free in the sense in which one is able to choose. One *becomes* free in the sense that one is no longer impeded by one's husband or wife, parents, employers, or habits.

3. Because there is no God to lay down a moral law, humans must make their own morality. (This has some appearance of being inconsistent with item 1.)

Creating one's own morality does not seem to be possible. For example, how can someone who wishes it to be not immoral that stealing is wrong do anything to make it right? There is something, although not much, he or she can do to make him- or herself *think* that it is right, but this is an entirely different matter. He or she might also be able to decide what is (antecedent to and independent of his or her opinions) right.

4. Human beings are subject to anguish that results from having to make decisions about what they ought to do.

Sartre thinks that this anguish is accentuated by the fact that a person making a choice is choosing for the whole of humanity. That person is choosing for the whole of humanity, however, only in a figurative sense. What *is* true is that, if a person makes the right decision, then the same decision would be the right one to be taken by any similar person in similar circumstances. If one person making a choice were *literally* choosing for everyone, doubtless this *would* cause anguish. But because the choice is only figuratively for others, the anguish is misplaced.

Sartre, in quite correctly pointing out that even if there were a God to direct us, one still would have to make up one's own mind on whether any directive that purports to be from Him is really so, is inconsistently drawing his reader's attention to the fact that there must be a certain amount of anguish even from his opponents' point of view. (It never seemed to have occurred to Abraham that the command to kill his son did not come from God.)

Sartre (and other existentialists) may be an example of a point made by Freud in the previous reading, namely, that if one (wrongly) rests morality on divine sanctions, one is thrown into a confused state if one ceases to believe in God.

Reading

THERE IS AT least one being whose existence comes before its essence, a being which exists before it can be defined by any conception of it. That being is man or, as Heidegger has it, the human reality. What do we mean by saying that existence precedes essence? We mean that man first of all exists, encounters himself, surges up in the world—and defines himself afterwards. If man as the existentialist sees him is not definable, it is because to begin with he is nothing. He will not be anything until later, and then he will be what he makes of himself. Thus, there is no human nature, because there is no God to have a conception of it. Man simply is. Not that he is simply what he conceives himself to be, but he is what he wills, and as he conceives himself after already existing—as he wills to be after that leap towards existence. Man is nothing else but that which he makes of himself. That is the first principle of existentialism. And this is what people call its "subjectivity," using the word as a reproach against us. But what do we mean to say by this, but that man is of a greater dignity than a stone or a table? For we mean to say that man primarily exists—that man is, before all else, something which propels itself towards a future and is aware that it is doing so. Man is, indeed, a project which possesses a subjective life, instead of being a kind of moss, or a fungus or a cauliflower. Before that projection of the self nothing exists; not even in the heaven of

This selection is reprinted from "Existentialism and Humanism" by Jean-Paul Sartre. Reprinted by permission of Les Édition Nagel-Genève.

intelligence: man will only attain existence when he is what he purposes to be. Not, however, what he may wish to be. For what we usually understand by wishing or willing is a conscious decision taken —much more often than not—after we have made ourselves what we are. I may wish to join a party, to write a book or to marry—but in such a case what is usually called my will is probably a manifestation of a prior and more spontaneous decision. If, however, it is true that existence is prior to essence, man is responsible for what he is. Thus, the first effect of existentialism is that it puts every man in possession of himself as he is, and places the entire responsibility for his existence squarely upon his own shoulders. And, when we say that man is responsible for himself, we do not mean that he is responsible only for his own individuality, but that he is responsible for all men. The word "subjectivism" is to be understood in two senses, and our adversaries play upon only one of them. Subjectivism means, on the one hand, the freedom of the individual subject and, on the other, that man cannot pass beyond human subjectivity. It is the latter which is the deeper meaning of existentialism. When we say that man chooses himself, we do mean that every one of us must choose himself; but by that we also mean that in choosing for himself he chooses for all men. For in effect, of all the actions a man may take in order to create himself as he wills to be, there is not one which is not creative, at the same time, of an image of man such as he believes he ought to be. To choose between this or that is at the same time to affirm the value of that which is chosen; for we are unable ever to choose the worse. What we choose is always the better; and nothing can be better for us unless it is better for all. If, moreover, existence precedes essence and we will to exist at the same time as we fashion our image, that image is valid for all and for the entire epoch in which we find ourselves. Our responsibility is thus much greater than we had supposed, for it concerns mankind as a whole. If I am a worker, for instance, I may choose to join a Christian rather than a Communist trade union. And if, by that membership, I choose to signify that resignation is, after all, the attitude that best becomes a man, that man's kingdom is not upon this earth, I do not commit myself alone to that view. Resignation is my will for everyone and my action is, in consequence, a commitment on behalf of all mankind. Or if, to take a more personal case, I decide to marry and to have children, even though this decision proceeds simply from my situation, from my passion or my desire, I am thereby committing not only myself, but humanity as a whole, to the practice of monogamy. I am thus responsible for myself and for all men, and I am creating a certain image of man as I would have him to be. In fashioning myself I fashion man.

This may enable us to understand what is meant by such terms—perhaps a little grandiloquent—as anguish, abandonment and despair.

As you will soon see, it is very simple. First, what do we mean by anguish? The existentialist frankly states that man is in anguish. His meaning is as follows—When a man commits himself to anything, fully realising that he is not only choosing what he will be, but is thereby at the same time a legislator deciding for the whole of mankind—in such a moment a man cannot escape from the sense of complete and profound responsibility. There are many, indeed, who show no such anxiety. But we affirm that they are merely disguising their anguish or are in flight from it. Certainly, many people think that in what they are doing they commit no one but themselves to anything: and if you ask them, "What would happen if everyone did so?" they shrug their shoulders and reply, "Everyone does not do so." But in truth, one ought always to ask oneself what would happen if everyone did as one is doing; nor can one escape from that disturbing thought except by a kind of self-deception. The man who lies in self-excuse, by saying "Everyone will not do it" must be ill at ease in his conscience, for the act of lying implies the universal value which it denies. By its very disguise his anguish reveals itself. This is the anguish that Kierkegaard called "the anguish of Abraham." You know the story: An angel commanded Abraham to sacrifice his son: and obedience was obligatory, if it really was an angel who had appeared and said, "Thou, Abraham, shalt sacrifice thy son." But anyone in such a case would wonder, first, whether it was indeed an angel and secondly, whether I am really Abraham. Where are the proofs? A certain mad woman who suffered from hallucinations said that people were telephoning to her, and giving her orders. The doctor asked, "But who is it that speaks to you?" She replied: "He says it is God." And what, indeed, could prove to her that it was God? If an angel appears to me, what is the proof that it is an angel; or, if I hear voices, who can prove that they proceed from heaven and not from hell, or from my own subconsciousness or some pathological condition? Who can prove that they are really addressed to me?

Who, then, can prove that I am the proper person to impose, by my own choice, my conception of man upon mankind? I shall never find any proof whatever; there will be no sign to convince me of it. If a voice speaks to me, it is still I myself who must decide whether the voice is or is not that of an angel. If I regard a certain course of action as good, it is only I who choose to say that it is good and not bad. There is nothing to show that I am Abraham: nevertheless I also am obliged at every instant to perform actions which are examples. Everything happens to every man as though the whole human race had its eyes fixed upon what he is doing and regulated its conduct accordingly. So every man ought to say, "Am I really a man who has the right to act in such a manner that humanity regulates itself by what I do." If a man does not say that, he is dissembling his anguish. Clearly, the anguish with which we are concerned here is not one that could lead to quietism or inaction. It is anguish pure and simple, of the kind well known to all those who have borne responsibilities. When, for instance, a military leader takes upon himself the responsibility for an attack and sends a number of men to their death, he chooses to do it and at bottom he alone chooses. No doubt he acts under a higher command, but its orders, which are more general, require interpretation by him and upon that interpretation depends the life of ten, fourteen or twenty men. In making the decision, he cannot but feel a certain anguish. All leaders know that anguish. It does not prevent their acting, on the contrary it is the very condition of their action, for the action presupposes that there is a plurality of possibilities, and in choosing one of these, they realise that it has value only because it is chosen. Now it is anguish of that kind which existentialism describes, and moreover, as we shall see, makes explicit through direct responsibility towards other men who are concerned. Far from being a screen which could separate us from action, it is a condition of action itself.

And when we speak of "abandonment" — a favourite word of Heidegger — we only mean to say that God does not exist, and that it is necessary to draw the consequences of his absence right to the end. The existentialist is strongly opposed to a certain type of secular moralism which seeks to suppress God at the least possible expense. Towards 1880, when the French professors endeavoured to formulate a secular morality, they said something like this: — God is a useless and costly hypothesis, so we will do without it. However, if we are to have morality, a society and a law-abiding world, it is essential that certain values should be taken seriously; they must have an *à priori* existence ascribed to them. It must be considered obligatory *à priori* to be honest, not to lie, not to beat one's wife, to bring up children and so forth; so we are going to do a little work on this subject, which will enable us to show that these values exist all the same, inscribed in an intelligible heaven although, of course, there is no God. In other words — and this is, I believe, the purport of all that we in France call radicalism — nothing will be changed if God does not exist; we shall re-discover the same norms of honesty, progress and humanity, and we shall have disposed of God as an out-of-date hypothesis which will die away quietly of itself. The existentialist, on the contrary, finds it extremely embarrassing that God does not exist, for there disappears with Him all possibility of finding values in an intelligible heaven. There can no longer be any good *à priori*, since there is no infinite and perfect consciousness to think it. It is nowhere written that "the good" exists, that one must be honest or must not lie, since we are now upon the plane where there are only men. Dostoievsky once wrote "If God did not exist, everything would be permitted"; and that, for existentialism, is the starting point. Everything is indeed permitted if God does not exist, and man is in consequence forlorn, for he cannot find anything to depend upon either within or outside himself. He discovers forthwith, that he is without excuse. For if indeed existence precedes essence, one will never be able to explain one's action by reference to a given and specific human nature; in other words, there is no determinism — man is free, man *is* freedom. Nor, on the other hand, if God does not exist, are we provided with any values or commands that could legitimise our behaviour. Thus we have neither behind us, nor before us in a luminous realm of values, any means of justification or excuse. We are left alone, without excuse. That is what I mean when I say that man is condemned to be free. Condemned, because he did not create himself, yet is nevertheless at liberty, and from the moment that he is thrown into this world he is responsible for everything he does. The existentialist does not believe in the power of passion. He will never regard a grand passion as a destructive torrent upon which a man is swept into certain actions as by fate, and which, therefore, is an excuse for them. He thinks that man is responsible for his passion. Neither will an existentialist think that a man can find help through some sign being vouchsafed upon earth for his orientation: for he thinks that the man himself interprets the sign as he chooses. He thinks that every man, without any support or help whatever, is condemned at every instant to invent man. As Ponge has written in a very fine article, "Man is the future of man." That is exactly true. Only, if one took this to mean that the future is laid up in Heaven, that God knows what it is, it would be false, for then it would no longer even be a future. If, however, it means that, whatever man may now appear to be, there is a future to be fashioned, a virgin future that awaits him — then it is a true saying. But in the present one is forsaken.

As an example by which you may the better understand this state of abandonment, I will refer to the case of a pupil of mine, who sought me out in the following circumstances. His father was quarrelling with his mother and was also inclined to be a "collaborator"; his elder brother had been killed in the German offensive of 1940 and this young man, with a sentiment somewhat primitive but generous, burned to avenge him. His mother was living alone with him, deeply afflicted by the semi-treason of his father and by the death of her eldest son, and her one consolation was in this young man. But he, at this moment, had the choice between going to England to join the Free French Forces or of staying near his mother and helping her to live. He fully realised that this woman lived only for him and that his disappearance — or perhaps his death — would plunge her into despair. He also realised that, concretely and in fact, every action he performed on his mother's behalf would be sure of effect in the sense of aiding her to live, whereas anything he did in order to go and fight would be an ambiguous action which might vanish like water into sand and serve no purpose. For instance, to set out for England he would have to wait indefinitely in a Spanish camp on the way through Spain; or, on arriving in England or in Algiers he might be put into an office to fill up forms. Consequently, he found himself confronted by two very different modes of action; the one concrete, immediate, but directed towards only one individual; and the other an action addressed to an end infinitely greater, a national collectivity, but for that very reason ambiguous — and it might be frustrated on the way. At the same time, he was hesitating between two kinds of morality; on the one side the morality of sympathy, of personal devotion and, on the other side, a morality of wider scope but of more debatable validity. He had to choose between those two. What could help him to choose? Could the Christian doctrine? No. Christian doctrine says: Act with charity, love your neighbour, deny yourself for others, choose the way which is hardest, and so forth. But which is the harder road? To whom does one owe the more brotherly love, the patriot or the mother? Which is the more useful aim, the general one of fighting in and for the whole community, or the precise aim of helping one particular person to live? Who can give an answer to that *à priori*? No one. Nor is it given in any ethical scripture. The Kantian ethic says, Never regard another as a means, but always as an end. Very well; if I remain with my mother, I shall be regarding her as the end and not as a means: but by the same token I am in danger of treating as means those who are fighting on my behalf; and the converse is also true, that if I go to the aid of the combatants I shall be treating them as the end at the risk of treating my mother as a means.

13

P. T. GEACH

God and Evil

Introduction

P. T. Geach is Emeritus Professor of Philosophy at the University of Leeds (U.K.), a Fellow of the British Academy, and the author of numerous books, including *Mental Acts*, *Logic Matters*, *God and the Soul* (from which this excerpt is taken), *Providence and Evil*, a work on McTaggart, and numerous articles.

This reading is mainly a criticism of Plato's argument in his dialogue *Euthyphro*. Plato raises the question, discussed in the Introduction, whether certain acts are unjust because God has forbidden them or whether God has forbidden them because they are unjust. Geach thinks that, although we can obtain some moral knowledge independently of knowledge of God's commands, knowledge of God is necessary to know, as we do, that it is wrong to do evil in order that good may result. If there were no God, it *would* be the case that we might do evil, if good were to come of it.

Geach's argument for this view is as follows. It is usually wrong to lie, or even to contemplate lying. Hence God (assuming that there is one) must prohibit *all* lying. Otherwise, when we had to decide whether it was right to lie or not, we would be judges in our own cause and have to rely on very dubious knowledge of the consequences of lying in this or that case. If there are any divine edicts on this matter, they must be capable of being put into practice by simple people. A law prohibiting lying, which had exceptions, would be too complicated. Hence God's law prohibiting lying will not have exceptions. Because it is always wrong to do what God prohibits, it is *always* wrong to lie.

1. No one has sufficient insight into God's intentions to be sure what He would or would not command. (The ninth commandment prohibits

161

bearing false witness against one's neighbor, but not lying as such.) But there is a point to make concerning one of Geach's premises, that is, the premise that lying is usually but not always wrong. In those cases when lying is *not* wrong, is it positively wrong *not* to lie, or is it just a matter of indifference whether one lies or not? (It could be that *sometimes* it was wrong not to lie and *sometimes* just a matter of indifference whether one lied or not.) If Geach thinks that sometimes, when it is not wrong to lie, it is positively wrong *not* to lie, he has to suppose that God positively prohibits our performing actions which are *right*, which means that we can do what God does permit only by performing actions which are wrong.

2. If I were the deity and had wanted people to know that I absolutely prohibited lying, I would have given them the knowledge that lying was always wrong, not the knowledge that it was sometimes wrong.

3. Geach produces a formally valid argument for the existence of God: (a) it is always wrong to do evil that good may come; (b) it would not always be wrong to do evil that good may come if there were no God; therefore (c) there is a God. This argument, although formally valid, suffers from two defects: its first premise is not true, and it would be impossible to prove its first premise to be true without proving its conclusion. This means that it is circular.

4. I myself think that lying is sometimes positively commendable. I was once visited by a student who told me that he was the leader of a large organization whose object was the reformation of the human race. I naturally concluded that he was insane and tried to get him to accept treatment. When he explained that he could not do this, as there would be no one to lead this organization in his absence, I assured him that I had both the will and the ability to act as a temporary substitute and promised to be his deputy. He was sufficiently unbalanced to put complete faith in my integrity, went to the hospital, and was cured. I have never regretted my duplicity.

5. The statement that it is wrong to do evil that good may result is ambiguous. It may mean that it is wrong to do what is wrong, in order that good may come. This statement is true and follows logically from the tautology that it is wrong to do what is wrong. There is the statement that an action which *would* be wrong, in circumstances in which good did not come of it, would still be wrong, however much good came of it. This statement is obviously false. The first sense is true whether there is a God or not. The second sense is false whether there is a God or not.

6. Geach correctly points out that, if the fact that breaking promises was *usually* wrong meant that it was *always* prohibited, and the fact that not helping those in distress was also usually wrong also meant that it too was always prohibited, we might be in a situation where we could not avoid disobeying God's commands. His reply is that we can conclude that there *can* be no such conflicts of duties, because God would not put us in a situation in which we were faced with a conflict between two of his commandments.

Because we can be more sure that we *are* in situations where there is a conflict of duties than we can be of the nature of God's commands, Geach's argument ought to be reversed. Since we are sometimes in a situation where there would be a conflict between God's commands, if they universally prohibited both lying and not helping others in distress, it cannot be that God commands universal obedience to both rules.

7. Geach urges us to forget about the sense of duty. Beliefs about it are irrational.

Whether or not our beliefs about duty are irrational, the tendency to act on these irrational beliefs is one which human beings could not do without. It has been pointed out elsewhere in this collection that there must be some way of getting people to perform actions which are against their individual interest but necessary to society, and appealing even to an irrational tendency to act from duty is as good a way as any. In any case, beliefs such as that it is the duty of army doctors to relieve the suffering of maimed soldiers are not irrational, for it is the task, arising from their station in life, allocated by human superiors to army doctors. Furthermore, one quite properly condemns army doctors who do not do this duty.

Geach (and Professor Foot) think that it is rational, instead of acting from duty, to acquire the virtues (although it is not obvious that one cannot do both). For reasons mentioned in the discussion of Plato, this remark is ill considered. Some virtues are predominantly in the interest of the agent, others in the interest of others. Hence it is rational to acquire the former but not the latter. Since virtuous action is usually, although not always, admirable, it follows that it is not always rational to be admirable.

8. Plato takes for granted something of which Geach seems not to be clearly aware: the question of whether someone has done something wrong is one thing; the question of whether we ought to make this kind of action illegal if it is not illegal already, punish people for doing it, tell the police about it, or bring a private prosecution against its perpetrators is quite another thing. From the fact that an action is wrong it does not follow that it is right to prevent it, and people who, like Euthyphro, go about trying to punish even crimes committed by near relations are likely to find themselves doing more harm than good and having few friends. Sometimes, for a variety of reasons, of which the expense of enforcement is only one, it is right to *tolerate* actions that are wrong.

9. In condemning Euthyphro's father, too, Geach does not make adequate allowance for the fact that this man acted in a society where killing slaves, or, at any rate, not striving desperately hard to keep them alive, would not necessarily be thought wrong. It would be difficult to accept the view that if an action is thought by the agent to be right (in one sense), it must actually always be right (in another). (See the Introduction to Part VII.) But surely it would be just plain wrong to treat a slave-owning Greek living centuries before the birth of Christ in the same way as a slave-owning American living centuries later.

Reading

IN MODERN ETHICAL treatises we find hardly any mention of God; and the idea that if there really is a God, his commandments might be morally relevant is wont to be dismissed by a short and simple argument that is generally regarded as irrefutable. "If what God commands *is not* right, then the fact of his commanding it is no moral reason for obedience, though it may in that case be dangerous to disobey. And if what God commands *is* right, even so it is not God's commanding it that makes it right; on the contrary, God as a moral being would command only what was right apart from his commanding it. So God has no essential place in the foundations of morals."

The use of this argument is not confined to a recent or narrowly local school of philosophers; it was used by the British Idealists when they dominated British philosophy, and, as we shall see, it was used much earlier than that. Nor is its use confined to people who do not believe in God; on one occasion when I attacked the argument, my chief opponents were not atheists but professing Christians. This is not surprising; for the argument was used by Christians of an earlier generation, the Cambridge Platonists, as a stick to beat that dreadful man Hobbes with. (I shall have more to say about Hobbes later on.) And they in turn got the argument from Plato's *Euthyphro*.

Let me summarize that dialogue. Euthyphro and Socrates are discussing the trial in which Euthyphro is to appear as prosecutor of his own father. Euthyphro's father had tied up a peasant who killed another peasant in a drunken brawl, notified the authorities, thrown the prisoner into a ditch, and put the matter out of his mind; meanwhile the prisoner died of hunger and cold. Euthyphro (Mr. Right-mind, as Bunyan might have called him) feared lest the gods might punish him if he sat at meat with a man who had done such a deed, unless he set matters right by prosecuting the offender. He must have known that this would be an ineffectual gesture; the old-fashioned Homeric idea that Zeus will punish men for callous insolence to the poor was not going to impress the Athenian court.

Socrates (that is, I presume, Plato) finds it outrageous that a man prosecutes his own father over the death of a no-good peasant (he reiterates this term *"thēs,"* to rub it in how little the man's death mattered) and he tries to dissuade Euthyphro by tricky arguments, in a style much admired and imitated by modern moral philosophers. Euthyphro is easily tied in knots by asking him whether pious deeds are pious because they please the gods, or please the gods because they are pious deeds; whether men ever disagree except about moral matters, for which there is no decision procedure like arithmetical calculation or

From *God and the Soul* by P. T. Geach. Reprinted by permission of Routledge, a division of Routledge, Chapman, and Hall Ltd.

physical measurements; and so on. But Mr. Right-mind is not convinced; again and again he cuts himself loose from these dialectical knots with the assertion that it doesn't matter who was the murderer and what relation he was to the prosecutor and whether the victim was a peasant, but only whether a man was foully done to death in a way that all the gods must hate. The dialogue ends with Euthyphro telling Socrates he has no more time for discussion and going off on his legal business.

Was this, as the received view represents, a victory for Socrates? Or was it a victory for simple piety over sophistical tricks? Euthyphro admittedly had one weak point: he believed in many gods who were sometimes at variance with one another and so might command different things. But this is irrelevant for our purposes; for Euthyphro's unswerving fidelity to the divine law would be no less objectionable to modern moral philosophers if he had believed in one God. The main issue is whether a man's moral code ought to be influenced in this way by beliefs about Divine commands.

In the first place, I want to reject a view—which some Christians have at least approached—that all our appraisals of good and bad logically depend on knowledge of God. To get a clear and indisputable example I shall take a bad sort of act. For there is a logical asymmetry between good and bad acts: an act is good only if everything about it is good, but may be bad if *anything* about it is bad; so it might be risky to say we knew an act to be good *sans phrase*, rather than to have some good features. But there is no such risk in saying that we know certain kinds of act to be bad. Lying, for example, is bad, and we all know this; giving a man the lie is a deadly insult the world over.

If a philosopher says he doubts whether there is anything objectionable in the practice of lying, he is not to be heard. Perhaps he is not sincere in what he says; perhaps his understanding is debauched by wickedness; perhaps, as often happens to philosophers, he has been deluded by a fallacious argument into denying what he really knows to be the case. Anyhow, it does not lie in his mouth to say that here I am abandoning argument for abuse; there is something logically incongruous, to use Newman's phrase, if we take the word of a Professor of Lying that he does not lie. Let me emphasize that I am not saying a sane and honest man must think one should *never* lie; but I say that, even if he thinks lying is sometimes a necessary evil, a sane and honest man must think it an evil.

Now it is logically impossible that our knowledge that lying is bad should depend on revelation. For obviously a revelation from a deity whose "goodness" did not include any objection to lying would be worthless; and indeed, so far from getting our knowledge that lying is bad from revelation, we may use this knowledge to test alleged revelations. Xenophanes rejected traditional Greek religious beliefs because the gods were represented as liars and cheats; and (if Browning could be trusted) it would be a fatal objection to the claims of the Druses' Messiah Hakim that he commanded his followers to lie about their religion under persecution. It is not that it would be too dreadful to believe in mendacious deities; a revelation destroys its own credibility if it is admitted to come from deities or from a prophet who may lie. We know lying to be bad before needing to examine any alleged revelation. Sir Arnold Lunn has jeered at unbelievers for esteeming truthfulness apart from any supernatural hopes or fears, and has quoted with approval a remark of Belloc that one can't be loyal to an abstraction like truth; a pagan Greek would have retorted that Lunn and Belloc were *akolastoi*, incorrigibly wicked, if they could not see directly the badness of lying.

The knowledge of God is thus *not* prerequisite to one having *any* moral knowledge. I shall argue however that we do need it in order to see that we must not do evil that good may come, and that this principle actually follows from a certain conception of God. If I can make this out, the sophistry from which I started will have been completely refuted; for accepting or rejecting this principle makes an enormous difference to one's moral code.

I must first clear up an ambiguity in the phrase "doing evil that good may come." We cannot ask whether e.g. Caesar's death was a good or bad *thing to happen*; there are *various* titles under which it may be called good or bad. One might very well say e.g. that a violent death was a bad *thing to happen to a living organism* but a good *thing to happen to a man who claimed divine worship*, and this would again leave it open whether doing Caesar to death was a good or bad *thing to do* for Brutus and the rest. Now when I speak of "not doing evil that good may come," what I mean is that certain sorts of act are such *bad things to do* that they must never be done to secure any good or avoid any evil. For A to kill a man or cut off his arm is not necessarily at *bad thing to do*, though it is necessarily bad that such a thing should happen to a living organism. Only by a fallacy of equivocation can people argue that if you accept the principle of not doing evil that good may come, then you must be against capital punishment and surgical operations.

Suppose that A and B are agreed that adultery is a bad sort of behaviour, but that A accepts the principle of not doing evil that good may come, whereas B rejects it. Then in A's moral deliberations adultery is simply out: as Aristotle said, there can be no deliberating when and how and with whom to commit it. For B, on the other hand, the *prima facie* objection to adultery is defeasible, and in some circumstances he may decide: Here and now adultery is the best thing. Similarly, Sir David Ross holds that the objection to punishing the innocent, viz. that then we are not "respecting the rights of those who have respected the rights of others," is only a *prima facie* objection; in the general interest it may have to be overruled, "that the whole nation perish not" — a Scripture quotation that we may hope Sir David made without remembering who was speciously justifying whose judicial murder.

It is psychologically possible to hold the principle of not doing evil that good may come independently of any belief in Divine commandments: I have already cited the example of Aristotle on adultery. We have to see whether this is also logically consistent.

We must first settle what sort of answer is relevant if a man asks "Why shouldn't I commit adultery?"; only then can we see what reason against, if any, is decisive. One obviously relevant sort of reply to a question "Why shouldn't I?" is an appeal to something the questioner wants, and cannot get if he does so-and-so. I maintain that only such a reply is relevant and rational. In post-Kantian moral theory another sort of reply has been offered as relevant — an appeal not to an agent's Inclinations but to his Sense of Duty. Now indeed you can so train a man that "You *must* not," said in a peculiar manner, strikes him as a sufficient answer to "Why shouldn't I?"; he may feel a peculiar awe at hearing this from others, or even on saying it himself; it may even be part of the training to make him think he *must* not ask why he *must* not. (Cf. Lewis Carroll's juvenile poem "My Fairy.") The result of such training is what people like Sir David Ross call "apprehending obligation." When I speak of the Sense of Duty (in capitals) I shall always be referring to this notion.

Now, as we know, a totalitarian regime can make a man "apprehend" all sorts of things as his "obligations," if Providence does not specially protect him. But on the Sense of Duty theory a man so trained is admirable if he does what he thinks he *must* do, regardless of the nature and quality of his acts; for is he not acting from the highest of motives, the Sense of Duty? If a young Nazi machine-guns a column of refugees till he bleeds to death, instead of retiring for medical treatment, is not his Sense of Duty something to fill us with awe?

To myself, it seems clear that although *"You mustn't"* said in this peculiar way may psychologically work as a final answer to "Why shouldn't I?," it is no rational answer at all. This Sense of Duty, as Bradley said (*Appearance and Reality*, c. 25) "is empty self-will and self-assurance, which swollen with private sentiment or chance desire, wears the mask of goodness. And hence that which professes itself moral would be the same as mere badness, if it did not differ, even for the worse, by the addition of hypocrisy. We may note here that our country, the chosen home of Moral Philosophy, has the reputation abroad of being the chief home of hypocrisy and cant."

Let us forget about the Sense of Duty, for I think it can be shown that an action's being a good or bad thing for a human being to do is of itself a fact calculated to touch an agent's inclinations. I shall here appropriate the powerful arguments, in the spirit of Aristotle, recently developed by Mrs. Philippa Foot. Moral virtues, she argues, are habits of action and avoidance; and they are such as a man cannot rationally choose to go without, any more than he can rationally choose to be blind, paralytic, or stupid; to choose to lack a virtue would be to choose a maimed life, ill-adapted to this difficult and dangerous world. But if you opt for virtue, you opt for being the sort of man who *needs* to act virtuously (just as if you choose to take up smoking you opt to be the kind of man who *needs* to smoke); moreover, you cannot decide at the outset to act virtuously only when it is not too awkward or dangerous or unpleasant — that is deciding not to have the habit of virtue at all. If, for example, you opt for courage, you may perish through facing danger a coward would have shirked; but our world is such that it is not even safe not to be brave — as Horace said, death pursues after cowards too. And if you opt for chastity, then you opt to become the sort of person who *needs* to be chaste; and then for you, as Aristotle said, there can be no deliberating when and with whom to commit adultery; adultery is out.

But somebody might very well admit that not only is there something bad about certain acts, but also it is desirable to become the sort of person who needs to act in the contrary way; and yet *not* admit that such acts are to be avoided in all circumstances and at any price. To be sure, a virtuous person cannot be ready in advance to do such acts; and if he does do them they will damage his virtuous habits and perhaps irreparably wreck his hard-won integrity of soul. But at this point someone may protest "Are you the only person to be considered? Suppose the price of your precious integrity is a most fearful disaster! Haven't you got a hand to burn for your country (or mankind) and your friends?" This sort of appeal has not, I think, been adequately answered on Aristotelian lines, either by Aristotle or by Mrs. Foot.

It is just at this point, I think, that the law of God becomes relevant. I shall not argue as to the truth of the theological propositions I shall use in the following discussion; my aim in this essay is to show that *if* a man accepts them he may rationally have quite a different code from someone who does not. And the propositions I shall use all belong to natural theology; in Hobbes's language, I am considering only "the Kingdom of God by Nature."

If God and Man are voluntary agents, it is reasonable to believe that God will not only direct men to his own ends willy-nilly like the irrational creatures, but will govern them by command and counsel. The question is then whether God has given laws to man which forbid whole classes of actions, as human laws do. There appear strong reasons for doubting whether God's commands could be like this.

Laws have to be framed in broad general terms because the foresight of legislation is limited, and because the laws would be unmanageably complicated if the legislators even tried to bring in all the contingencies they could themselves foresee; nor can there be somebody always at every man's elbow to give him commands suiting the particular contingency. But God is subject to none of these human limitations; so is it not a grossly anthropomorphic view of God to imagine him legislating in general terms because hard cases make bad law?

It is not a question, I reply, of God's knowledge and power, but of man's. Man's reason can readily discern that certain practices, like lying, infanticide, and adultery, are generally undesirable, even to the point that it is generally desirable that men should not *think* of resorting to them. But what man is competent judge in his own cause, to make exception in a particular case? Even apart from bias, our knowledge of the present relevant circumstances is grossly fallible; still more, our foresight of the future. Some men, like Dr. Buchman's disciples, have claimed to have Divine guidance in all conjunctures of life; but such claims are open to doubt, and certainly most men are not thus favoured. So unless the rational knowledge that these practices are *generally undesirable* is itself a promulgation of the Divine law *absolutely forbidding* such practices, God has left most men without any promulgation of commands to them on these matters at all; which, on the theological premises I am assuming, is absurd.

The rational recognition that a practice is generally undesirable and that it is best for people on the whole not even to think of resorting to it is thus *in fact* a promulgation to a man of the Divine law forbidding the practice, even if he does not realise that this is a promulgation of the Divine law, even if he does not believe there is a God.

This is not a paradox. You have had a city's parking regulation promulgated to you by a No Parking notice, even if you are under the illusion that you may ignore the notice and think it has been put up by a neighbour who dislikes cars. And similarly anyone who can see the general objectionableness of lying and adultery has had God's law against such actions promulgated to him, even if he does not recognize it as God's law.

This means that the Divine law is in some instances promulgated to all men of sound understanding. No man can sincerely plead ignorance that lying, for example, is generally objectionable. I am *not* saying that a sane and honest man must see that lying is *absolutely excluded*; but he must have some knowledge of the *general objectionableness* of lying, and this is in fact a promulgation to him of the Divine law against lying. And he can advance from this knowledge to recognition of the Divine law as such, by a purely rational process.

To make this point clearer, let us consider a modern ethical philosopher who says "I do on the whole object to lying, but this is just a practical attitude I take up — it is quite wrong to call it 'knowledge.'" I do *not* say of him what I should of a man who professed to have no special objection to lying: that he is just a vicious fellow, or a fool talking at random, who deserves no answer. What I do say is that his very protest shows that he does possess that sort of knowledge which is in fact God's promulgation of a law to him. His erroneous philosophy will not allow him to call it knowledge; but that does not prevent it from *being* knowledge — philosophers in fact know many things that their own theories would preclude them from knowing. And since he has this knowledge, he has had God's law against lying promulgated to him, even if he does not believe in God.

Thus, whatever a man may think, his rational knowledge that it is a bad way of life for a man to be a liar or an adulterer is in fact a promulgation to him of the Divine law; and he is able to infer that it is such a promulgation if he rightly considers the matter. As Hobbes said:

> These dictates of reason men use to call by the name of laws, but improperly: for they are but conclusions or theorems concerning what conduceth to the conservation and defence of themselves: whereas law, properly, is the word of him that by right hath command over others. But yet if we consider the same theorems as delivered in the word of God that by right commandeth over all things, then are they properly called laws.

There is a current malicious interpretation of Hobbes on which "the word of God" would mean whatever the sovereign chooses to decree to be canonical Scripture. High-minded people are prepared to talk about Hobbes with reckless disregard of the truth: the late Lord Lindsay, in his Preface to the Everyman *Leviathan*, perpetrated a serious garbling of Hobbes' text, giving the false text an air of authenticity by the use of antique spelling.° But what Hobbes himself says elsewhere is: "God declareth his word by the dictates of natural reason." As an historical footnote I add that a very similar line of reasoning is to be found in Berkeley's youthful sermon on Passive Obedience. The debt Berkeley owes to Hobbes is quite obvious: but no doubt a clergyman could hardly cite such an authority explicitly without destroying the edifying effect of his discourse.

But what if somebody asks "Why should I obey God's Law?" This is really an insane question. For Prometheus to defy Zeus made sense because Zeus had not made Prometheus and had only limited power over him. A defiance of an Almighty God is insane: it is like trying to cheat a man to whom your whole business is mortgaged and who you know is well aware of your attempts to cheat him, or again, as the prophet said, it is as if a stick tried to beat, or an axe to cut, the very hand that was wielding it. Nebuchadnezzar had it forced on his atten-

---

° Page xvi of Everyman edition. Lindsay's garbling confounds Law and Right of Nature; which Hobbes emphatically distinguishes in the very passage that Lindsay claims to be quoting!

tion that only by God's favour did his wits hold together from one end of a blasphemous sentence to another—and so he saw that there was nothing for him but to bless and glorify the King of Heaven, who is able to abase those who walk in pride. To quote Hobbes again "God is King, though the nations be angry: and he that sitteth upon the cherubim, though the earth be moved. Whether men will or no they must be subject always to the divine power. By denying the existence or providence of God, men may shake off their ease, but not their yoke."

This reasoning will not convince everybody; people may still *say* that it makes sense, given that there is a God, to defy him; but this is so only because, as Prichard said, you can no more make a man think than you can make a horse drink. A moral philosopher once said to me: "I don't think I am morally obliged to obey God unless God is good: and surely it is a synthetic proposition that God is good." I naturally asked him how he understood the proposition that God is good; he replied "Well, I have no considered view how it should be analysed; but provisionally I'd say it meant something like this: God is the sort of God whom I'd choose to be God if it were up to me to make the choice." I fear he has never understood why I found the answer funny.

I shall be told by such philosophers that since I am saying not: It is your supreme moral duty to obey God, but simply: It is insane to set about defying an Almighty God, my attitude is plain power worship. But since this is worship of the Supreme Power, it is as such wholly different from, and does not carry with it, a cringing attitude towards earthly powers. An earthly potentate does not compete with God, even unsuccessfully: he may threaten all manner of afflictions, but only from God's hands can any affliction actually come upon us. If we fully realize this, we shall have such fear of God as destroys all earthly fear: "I will show you whom you shall fear," said Jesus Christ to his disciples.

"But now you are letting your view of the facts distort your values." I am not sure whether this piece of claptrap is meant as moral reprobation or as a logical objection; either way, there is nothing in it. Civilized men know that sexual intercourse is liable to result in child-bearing; they naturally have quite different sexual morals, one way or another, from savages who do not know this. And they are logically justified in evaluating sexual intercourse differently; for they have a different view of what sort of act it is. Now for those who believe in Almighty God, a man's every act is an act either of obeying or of ignoring or of defying that God; so naturally and logically they have quite different standards from unbelievers—they take a different view as to what people are in fact doing.

"But suppose circumstances are such that observance of one Divine law, say the law against lying, involves breach of some other absolute Divine prohibition?"—If God is rational, he does not command the impossible; if God governs all events by his providence, he can see to it that circumstances in which a man is inculpably faced by a choice between forbidden acts do not occur. Of course such circumstances (with the clause "and there is no way out" written into their description) are consistently describable; but God's providence could ensure that they do not in fact arise. Contrary to what unbelievers often say, belief in the existence of God does make a difference to what one expects to happen.

Let us then return to our friend Euthyphro. Euthyphro regarded his father's act of leaving a poor man to die forgotten in a ditch as not just *prima facie* objectionable, but as something *forbidden* by the gods who live for ever; and he was horribly afraid for himself if he went on living with the offender as if nothing had happened. He did well to be afraid, the fear of God is the beginning of wisdom. To be sure, it is not all of wisdom.

The fear of God of which I have spoken is such fear as restrains even the wish to disobey him; not merely servile fear, which restrains the outward act, but leaves behind the wish "If only I could do it and get away with it!" And, as is proper in a paper of this kind, I have confined myself to what Hobbes called the Kingdom of God by Nature. It is no part of our merely natural knowledge of God that we can boldly call God our Father and serve him in filial love: we are his children, if we are, purely by his free gift of the Spirit of adoption, and not by birthright: and the fear of God for his power irresistible is at least the *beginning* of wisdom — without it there is only pitiable folly. I agree, indeed, with Hobbes that gratitude for God's benefits would not be a sufficient ground for *unreserved* obedience if it were severed from fear of God's irresistible power.

That fear is an ultimate suasion. We cannot balance against our obedience to God some good to be gained, or evil to be avoided, by disobedience. For such good or evil could in fact come to us only in the order of God's Providence; we cannot secure good or avoid evil, either for ourselves or for others, in God's despite and by disobedience. And neither reason nor revelation warrants the idea that God is at all likely to be lenient with those who presumptuously disobey his law because of the way they have worked out the respective consequence of obedience and disobedience. Eleazar the scribe (2 Maccabees 6), with only Sheol to look forward to when he died, chose rather to go thereby martyrdom — *praemitti se velle in infernum* — than to break God's law. "Yet should I not escape the hand of the Almighty, neither alive nor dead."

The wicked can for the moment use God's creation in defiance of God's commandments. But this is a sort of miracle or mystery; as St. Paul said, God has made the creature subject to vanity against its will. It is reasonable to expect, if the world's whole *raison d'être* is to effect God's good pleasure, that the very natural agents and operations of the world should be such as to frustrate and enrage and torment those who set their wills against God's. If things are not at present like this, that is only a gratuitous mercy, on whose continuance the sinner has no reason to count. "The world shall fight with him against the unwise. . . . Yea, a mighty wind shall stand up against them, and like a storm shall blow them away."

14

A. J. AYER

Morality Without Religion

Introduction

Ayer was an early and influential logical positivist, and the author of numerous books on philosophy. The first and perhaps best of these was the deservedly celebrated *Language, Truth and Logic*, one of the most important books on philosophy ever written. Among his other works, which are too numerous to be listed here, are *The Foundations of Empirical Knowledge, Philosophical Essays, The Concept of Person, The Central Questions of Philosophy* (from which this selection is taken), and *Probability and Evidence*. He was one of the most outstanding and influential philosophers of this century.

In this selection, Ayer claims that there is little to choose between his view, on the relationship between morals and theology, and objectivism. He is right in saying that, in the last resort, objectivists will be unable to prove that their moral views are correct. (In the last resort, Copernicus was unable to prove that the earth went around the sun.) But at least objectivists will be able to believe that their views *are* correct, and correct whether they believe them to be so or not. The trouble with Ayer's own view is that it precludes one from thinking that the principles one has chosen to live by are right and that principles incompatible with them are wrong. I think that my own moral beliefs are correct—I would not hold them if I did not—and rather suspect that Ayer also thought the same of his.

Reading

IS THERE ANY support for religious belief in the fact that men have moral sentiments to which their actions sometimes answer? The view that there is has been quite widely held. The main arguments which have been advanced in its favour are, first, that only the agency of God can account for the existence of morality, and, secondly, that God's authority is needed to give our moral standards some objective validity.

The first of these arguments seems very weak. The assumption which underlies it is that it is natural for men to behave only in a purely selfish manner. Consequently, if they sometimes forgo their interests, or what they believe to be their interests, in order to serve others, or because they think that the action which promotes their interests is wrong, or that some other course of action is morally binding on them, the ability to behave in this unnatural way must have been given to them by a higher power. Even if the starting-point of this argument were true, the reasoning would not be cogent, since it ignores the possibility that moral behaviour can be adequately explained in terms of social conditioning, but in fact it is not true. Antecedently to any actual observations that are made of human behaviour, there is no reason to expect it either to be selfish or to be unselfish; there is no reason to expect it either to conform or not to conform to any particular moral code. If it seems to us more natural for men to pursue their individual interests, this is only because they most commonly do so, at any rate in our own form of society. I believe that there are, or have been, societies in which it is more common for men to pursue the interest of some group of which they are members, their family or clan or tribe. But even if the prevalent tendency in all societies were for men to behave selfishly, it would not follow that unselfish behaviour was unnatural, in the sense of being contrary to nature. Nothing that actually happens is contrary to nature, though there are some actions that we misleadingly call unnatural as a way of expressing our disapproval of them. In fact, I think that a good case can be made for saying that altruistic impulses are innate, though they may be initially weaker in small children than the self-regarding or aggressive impulses. If they are not innate, at least the evidence shows that we have the capacity to acquire them. But how did we obtain this capacity? This question is on a level with any other question about the causes of human behaviour. It is no more and no less difficult than the question how we obtain our capacity to injure one another. If there were any good reason to believe that men were the outcome of a God's creation, their creator would be equally responsible for all their characteristics, however much or little we esteem them. Conversely, if there is otherwise no good reason to believe that men

From A. J. Ayer, *The Central Questions in Philosophy*, Chapter X, George Weidenfeld & Nicholson Ltd., 1973. Reprinted by permission.

were so created, the fact that they behave unselfishly as well as selfishly to each other does not provide one.

In dealing with the argument that a God is required to ensure the objectivity of moral standards, we need to distinguish carefully between the motives for morality and its possible grounds. There is no doubt that belief in a God has frequently been the source of moral incentives. Sometimes the motive has been the altruistic one of love for a deity or a saint whose wishes one believes oneself to be carrying out, or love for other human beings on the ground that they are equally the children of God. Perhaps more frequently it has been the prudential motive of fear of future punishment or hope of future reward. It was the belief that men were not generally capable of behaving decently without this prudential motive that led Voltaire to say that if God did not exist it would be necessary to invent him.[1] This is a good epigram, but like many good epigrams, it probably distorts the truth. I do not know that a scientific study has ever been made of this question, but if one were to be made I doubt if it would reveal any strong correlation either of morally admirable behaviour with religious belief or of morally reprehensible behaviour with its absence. Much good has been done in the name of religion but also very much evil. When the long history of religious intolerance and persecution is taken into account, together with the tendency of religious hierarchies to side with the oppressors rather than the oppressed, it is arguable that the evil has outweighed the good. Many bad men have indeed been irreligious, but many agnostics and atheists have led very decent lives. Neither do those who are sincerely religious always live up to their good principles. My own conjecture is that the factors which make for the observance or disregard of morality are mainly psychological and social, and that religious belief has had a smaller influence either way than is commonly supposed. However this may be, it is clear that to show that belief in God had had a predominantly good effect would not be to show that the belief was true, any more than showing that it had had a predominantly bad effect would be to show that it was false.

I suspect that the widespread assumption that religious belief is necessary for the maintenance of moral standards arises not so much from any assessment of the empirical evidence as from a tacit or explicit acceptance of the proposition that if there is no God there is no reason to be moral. What is meant is that there is then no justification for morality, but because of the ambiguity of the word "reason," the fallacious inference is drawn that there is neither any ground nor any motive. The conclusion sought is that since there is reason to be moral, there is a God. This is the obverse of the Nietzschean idea that since God is dead, everything is permitted.

[1] Voltaire. *Epistles* XCVI.

Whichever way it is taken, this proposition contains two serious errors, apart from the fallacy of thinking that the absence of grounds for morality entails the absence of motives. The first error is to suppose that morality needs an ulterior justification. The second error is to suppose that a God could supply it. The fallacy which is involved in thinking that morals could be founded on divine authority has been exposed by many philosophers, but perhaps most clearly and succinctly by Russell. "Theologians have always taught that God's decrees are good, and that this is not a mere tautology: it follows that goodness is logically independent of God's decrees."[2] The point is that moral standards can never be justified merely by an appeal to authority, whether the authority is taken to be human or divine. There has to be the additional premiss that the person whose dictates we are to follow is good, or that what he commands is right, and this cannot be the mere tautology that he is what he is, or that he commands what he commands. This does not mean that we cannot look for guidance in conduct to those whom we judge to be better or wiser or more experienced than ourselves. To a greater or lesser extent, we can and do take our morals on trust but in so doing we are making a moral decision. We are at least implicitly judging that the rules which we have been brought up to respect, or the verdicts of our mentor, are morally right: and again this is not the mere tautology that these rules and verdicts just are what they are.

But if a moral code cannot be founded on authority, neither can it be founded on metaphysics or on science or on empirical matters of fact. Scientific and factual considerations are indeed relevant to morals, because of the bearing which they have upon the application of our moral principles. We have to know what the situation is in which we are placed and what the consequences of different actions are likely to be. If, for example, we think it right to try to maximize human happiness, a scientific approach to the practical problems may instruct us how best to set about it. The adoption of such a principle is, however, something which is not dictated to us by the facts. It is a decision for which it may be that we are not able to give any further reason, just as we may not be able to give any further reason for the value that we attach to justice or to liberty. In the end, it is a matter of finding principles which one is prepared to stand by and when they conflict, as for most of us they sometimes will, of giving more weight to one or another according to the circumstances of the particular case.

This does not mean that we have to regard every moral standpoint as equally correct. In holding a moral principle, one regards it as valid for others besides oneself, whether they think so or not. In cases where they do not think so, it will depend on their circumstances whether one

[2]Bertrand Russell. *Human Society in Ethics and Politics*, p. 48.

judges that they are unenlightened or morally at fault. What has to be admitted is that there is no way of proving that they are mistaken. The most that one can do is argue *ad hominem*. One may be able to show that their principles are inconsistent, or that they are based on factual assumptions which are false, or that they are the product of bad reasoning, or that they lead to consequences which their advocates are not prepared to stand by. Even if we are successful in this, we may not persuade them to change their principles, but at least we shall have advanced some reason why they should. It may be, however, that we cannot find any such flaws in their position and still want to regard it as morally untenable. In that case discussion can go no further. This stage is seldom reached because it is nearly always possible to find a sufficient basis of moral agreement for the argument to proceed, but it has to be accepted as a possibility. Neither is this just the outcome of a subjective attitude to morals. The position is no different from one who believes that value-predicates stand for objective, unanalyzable ethical properties. In the case where his intuitions of what is good or right conflict with those of some other moralist he has no means of proving that they are correct. The difference between him and the subjectivist is that whereas the subjectivist is content to say that these are his principles and leave it at that, the believer in absolute values wants to say that his moral judgements are objectively true. Since, however, his only criterion of their truth is his own intuition, the difference is negligible. The merit of this sort of objectivism is that it avoids any suggestion of moral nihilism. Its demerit is its implication that value-judgements are descriptive of something other-worldly, whereas fundamentally they are not descriptive judgements at all. I say "fundamentally" because they sometime are descriptive of natural states of affairs; they convey the implication that the objects or actions in question come up to standard, or fail to do so. But then the acceptance of these standards is presupposed.

PART V

BEING GOOD INVOLVES BEING THE DUPE OF SOMEONE ELSE

15

PLATO

Virtue the Interest of the Stronger?

Introduction

Although Plato depicts Thrasymachus as vulgar, self-seeking, conceited, and exhibitionistic—a mildly reprehensible rhetorical device used to discredit his views—variants on Thrasymachus' view, that morality is an expedient by which those clever enough to see through it use to impose their wishes on those who are not, have had enormous importance in the history of morals and politics. Although both Socrates and Plato think that Thrasymachus is *defining* justice as that which is in the interest of the stronger, it is better to regard him as maintaining the following propositions: (a) being just (or perhaps being *good*) consists (by definition) in obeying the law; (b) the laws are in fact made by the strong in their own interest; (c) hence justice deserves no respect; (d) real excellence involves ignoring justice and pursuing one's own interest in spite of conventional morality; if possible, one should join the rulers, or depose them and rule in their stead. In addition, it may be that Thrasymachus does not clearly separate the following views: (a) *Justice* consists in obedience to law, which is made in the interest of the stronger; (b) it is only *supposed* justice that consists in obedience to law; *true* justice consists in seeking one's own interest.

There is a further ambiguity in the contention that justice is in the interest of the stronger. It may mean (a) that it is just for the strong to seek their own interest; (b) that it is just for other people to seek the interest of the strong. Thrasymachus seems to wish to maintain both of these propositions. Even though they are not inconsistent, the argument would be clearer had they been clearly distinguished. It could be that Thrasymachus thought that it was in the interest only of the strong, not of everybody, to seek his own interest. The weak were too feeble to do so, and were much better off obeying the laws made by the strong.

Criticisms of Thrasymachus' view (which would for the most part have been accepted by Socrates) are

1. The strong will sometimes make laws that are not in their interest. In that case, if the weak obey the law, they will *not* be doing what is in the interest of the strong.

2. The law is not always or exclusively in the interests of the strong (see "Summing Up" in the Introduction), although it will tend to favor the ruling classes and may well be preponderantly in their interest. It should, however, be obeyed, even when it *is* preponderantly in favor of the strong, because rebellion would only make things worse.

3. It *is* wrong, whatever Thrasymachus may think, to seek one's own interest exclusively (see Part I). In any case Thrasymachus is somewhat conventionally minded in his views about what one might do if freed from the restraints of morality.

Reading

TO WHICH I replied, "It's quite true, Thrasymachus, to say I learn from others, but it's not true to say I'm not grateful. I am generous with my praise — the only return I can give, as I have no money. You'll see in a moment how ready I am to praise any view I think well founded, for I'm sure the answer you're going to give me will be that."

"Listen then," he replied. "I define justice or right as what is in the interest of the stronger party. Now where is your praise? I can see you're going to refuse it."

"You shall have it when I understand what you mean, which at present I don't. You say that what is in the interest of the stronger party is right; but what do you mean by interest? For instance, Polydamas the athlete is *stronger* than us, and it's in his *interest* to eat beef to keep fit; we are *weaker* than he, but you can't mean that the same diet is in our *interest* and so *right* for us."

"You're being tiresome, Socrates," he returned, "and taking my definition in the sense most likely to damage it."

"I assure you I'm not," I said; "you must explain your meaning more clearly."

"Well then, you know that some states are tyrannies, some democracies, some aristocracies? And that in each city power is in the hands of the ruling class?"

From Plato's *Republic*, Book I, translated by B. Jowett, Oxford University Press, 1931. Reprinted with permission of Oxford University Press.

"Yes."

"Each ruling class makes laws that are in its own interest, a democracy democratic laws, a tyranny tyrannical ones and so on; and in making these laws they define as 'right' for their subjects what is in the interest of themselves, the rulers, and if anyone breaks their laws he is punished as a 'wrongdoer.' That is what I mean when I say that 'right' is the same thing in all states, namely the interest of the established ruling class; and this ruling class is the 'strongest' element in each state, and so if we argue correctly we see that 'right' is always the same, the interest of the stronger party."

"Now," I said, "I understand your meaning, and we must try to find out whether you are right or not. Your answer defines 'right' as 'interest' (though incidentally this is just what you forbade me to do), but adds the qualification 'of the stronger party.'"

"An insignificant qualification, I suppose you will say."

"Its significance is not yet clear; what is clear is that we must consider whether your definition is true. For I quite agree that what is right is an 'interest'; but you add that it is the interest 'of the stronger party,' and that's what I don't know about and want to consider."

"Let us hear you."

"You shall," said I. "You say that obedience to the ruling power is right and just?"

"I do."

"And are those in power in the various states infallible or not?"

"They are, of course, liable to make mistakes," he replied.

"When they proceed to make laws, then, they may do the job well or badly."

"I suppose so."

"And if they do it well the laws will be in their interest, and if they do it badly they won't, I take it."

"I agree."

"But their subjects must obey the laws they make, for to do so is right."

"Of course,"

"Then according to your argument it is *right* not only to do what is in the interest of the stronger party but also the opposite."

"What do you mean?" he asked.

"My meaning is the same as yours, I think. Let us look at it more closely. Did we not agree that when the ruling powers order their subjects to do something they are sometimes mistaken about their own best interest, and yet that it is *right* for the subject to do what his ruler enjoins?"

"I suppose we did."

"Then you must admit that it is *right* to do things that are *not* in the interest of the rulers, who are the *stronger* party; that is, when the rulers mistakenly give orders that will harm them and yet (so you say) it is right for their subjects to obey those orders. For surely, my dear Thrasymachus, in those circumstances it follows that it is 'right' to do the opposite of what you say is right, in that the weaker are *ordered* to do what is against the interest of the stronger."

"A clear enough conclusion," exclaimed Polemarchus.

"No doubt," interrupted Cleitophon, "if we are to take *your* word for it."

"It's not a question of *my* word," replied Polemarchus; "Thrasymachus himself agrees that rulers sometimes give orders harmful to themselves, and that it is right for their subjects to obey them"

"Yes, Polemarchus, that was because he said that it was right to obey the orders of those in power."

"*And* that the interest of the stronger was right. And having put forward both views he had to admit that the stronger sometimes give orders which are not in their interest which their weaker subjects obey. From which admission it follows that what is in the interest of the stronger is no more right than the reverse."

"But," objected Cleitophon, "what Thrasymachus meant by the interest of the stronger was what the stronger *thinks* to be in his interest; this is what the subject must do and what was intended by the definition."

"Well, it was not what he said," replied Polemarchus.

"It does not matter, Polemarchus," I said. "If this is Thrasymachus' meaning let us accept it. Tell me, Thrasymachus, was this how you meant to define what is right, that it is that which seems to the stronger to be his interest, whether it really is or not?"

"Certainly not," he replied; "do you think that I call someone who is making a mistake 'stronger' just when he is making his mistake?"

"I thought," I said, "that that was what you meant when you agreed that rulers are not infallible but sometimes make mistakes."

"That's because you're so malicious in argument, Socrates. Do you, for instance, call a man who has made a mistaken diagnosis a doctor by virtue of his mistake? Or when a mathematician makes a mistake in his calculations do you call him a mathematician by virtue of his mistake and when he makes it? We use this form of words, of course, and talk of a doctor or a mathematician or a scholar 'making a mistake'; but in fact, I think, each of them, in so far as he is what we call him, is infallible. And so to be precise (and precision is what you aim at) no skilled craftsman ever makes a mistake. For he makes his mistake because his skill fails him, and he is then no longer a skilled craftsman. So no craftsman or scientist ever makes a mistake, nor does a ruler so long as he is a ruler; though it's true that in common parlance one may *talk* about the doctor or ruler making a mistake as I did in what I was saying just now. To be really precise one must say that the ruler, in so far as he is a ruler, makes no mistake, and so infallibly enacts what is best for himself, which his subjects must perform. And so, as I said to begin with, 'right' means the interest of the stronger party."

"Well," said I, "so you think I'm malicious, do you, Thrasymachus?"

"I certainly do."

"You think my questions were deliberately framed to distort your argument?"

"I know perfectly well they were. But they won't get you anywhere; you can't fool me, and if you don't you won't be able to crush me in argument."

"My dear chap, I wouldn't dream of trying," I said. "But, to stop this sort of thing happening again, will you make this point clear; when you speak of the ruler and stronger party whose interest it is right that the weaker should serve, do you use the words in their more general sense or in the precise sense which you have just defined?"

"I mean ruler in the precisest sense," he replied. "Try your low tricks on that if you can — I ask no mercy. But you are not likely to succeed."

"Surely," I said, "you don't think I'm foolish enough to try to beard the lion and trick Thrasymachus?"

"You tried just now," he answered, "but nothing came of it."

"Well, let us leave it at that," I said; "but tell me, this doctor in the precise sense you have just been talking about, is he a business-man or a medical practitioner? I mean the man who really is a doctor."

"A medical practitioner."

"And a ship's captain? Is he a member of the crew or in command of it?"

"In command."

"For it would, I take it, be wrong to take account of his mere presence on board to call him a member of the crew. For he is not captain by virtue of being on board, but because of his professional skill and command of the crew."

"True."

"And each group has its own particular interest."

"Yes."

"And in each case the object of the profession concerned is to further that interest?"

"That is its object."

"Then has any form of professional skill any interest at which it aims over and above its own perfection?"

"What do you mean by that?"

"Suppose, for example," I replied, "that you were to ask me whether the body were self-sufficient, with no needs beyond itself, I should answer 'It certainly has needs. That is the reason why medicine has been discovered, because the body has its defects and these need curing; medical skill was, in fact, acquired to look after the interests of the body.' Would that be a correct answer, do you think?''

"It would."

"Then is the science or art of medicine itself defective? Does it or any other skilled activity need anything to complete it? I mean as the eyes need sight and the ears hearing, so they also need an art to look to their interests and provide them with what they need in this respect. But is it a characteristic of skilled activity as such to be defective, so that each activity needs another to look after its interests, and this one another, and so *ad infinitum*? Or does each look after its own interest? Is it not rather true that each has no need either of its own or another's supervision to check its faults and watch its interests? For there is no fault or flaw in any science or art, nor is it its business to seek the interest of anything but its subject matter; each is faultless and flawless and right, so long as it is entirely and precisely what it is. And it is in your precise sense that I want you to tell me if I am right."

"You are right," he said.

"Medicine therefore looks to the interest not of medicine but of the body."

"Yes."

"And training to the interest of the horse and not its own. Nor does any art or science seek its own interest (it needs nothing) but that of its subject matter."

"It looks like it."

"Yet surely," I said, "the arts and sciences rule and control their subject-matter."

Thrasymachus only agreed to this very reluctantly.

"Then no science studies or enforces the interest of the controlling or stronger party, but rather that of the weaker party subjected to it."

He agreed to this, too, in the end, though he tried to make a fight of it. Having secured his agreement I proceeded, "Then it follows that the doctor *qua* doctor prescribes with a view not to his own interest but that of his patient. For we agreed that a doctor in the precise sense controlled the body and was not in business for profit, did we not?"

He assented.

"And did we not also agree that a ship's captain in the precise sense controlled the crew but was not one of them? So that a captain in this sense will not give his orders with his own interest in view, but that of the crew which he controls."

He agreed reluctantly.

"And therefore, my dear Thrasymachus," I concluded, "no ruler of any kind, *qua* ruler, exercises his authority, whatever its sphere, with his own interest in view, but that of the subject of his skill. It is his subject and his subject's proper interest to which he looks in all he says and does."

At this stage of the argument it was obvious to everyone that the definition of justice had been reversed, and Thrasymachus, instead of replying, remarked, "Tell me, Socrates, have you a nurse?"

"What do you mean?" I returned. "Why not answer my question, instead of asking that sort of thing?"

"Well, she lets you go round snivelling and drivelling, and you can't even tell her the difference between sheep and shepherd."

"And why exactly should you say that?" I asked.

"Because you suppose that shepherds and herdsmen study the good of their flocks and herds and fatten and take care of them with some other object in view than the good of their masters and themselves; and don't realize that the rulers of states, if they are truly such, feel towards their subjects as one might towards sheep, and think about nothing all the time but how they can make a profit out of them. Your view of right and wrong is indeed wide of the mark. You are not aware that justice or right is really what is good for someone else, namely the interest of the stronger party or ruler, exacted at the expense of the subject who obeys him. Injustice or wrong is just the opposite of this, and dictates to the simple and the just, while they serve its interests because it is stronger than they, and as subjects promote not their own but their rulers' happiness. I'm afraid you're very simple-minded, Socrates; but you ought to consider how the just man always comes off worse than the unjust. For instance, in any business relations between them, you won't find the just man better off at the end of the deal than the unjust. Again, in their relations with the state, when there are taxes to be paid the just man will pay less on the same income, and when there's anything to be got he'll get it all. Thus if it's a question of office, if the just man loses nothing else he will suffer from neglecting his private affairs; his honesty will prevent him appropriating public funds, and his relations and friends will detest him because his principles will not allow him to push their interests. But quite the reverse is true of the unjust man. I'm thinking of the man I referred to just now who can make profits in a big way: he's the man to study if you want to find how much more private profit there is in wrong than in right. You can see it most easily if you take the extreme of injustice and wrongdoing, which brings the highest happiness to its practitioners and plunges its victims and their honesty in misery—I mean, of course, tyranny. Tyranny is not a matter of minor theft and violence, but of wholesale plunder, sacred or profane, private or public. If you are caught committing such crimes in detail you are punished and disgraced: sacrilege, kidnapping, burglary, fraud, theft are the names we give to such petty forms of wrongdoing. But when a man succeeds in robbing the whole body of citizens and reducing them to slavery, they forget these ugly names and call him happy and fortunate, as do all others who hear of his unmitigated wrongdoing. For, of course, those who abuse wrongdoing and injustice do so because they are afraid of suffering from it, not of doing it. So we see that injustice, given scope, has greater strength and freedom and power than justice; which proves what I started by saying, that justice is the interest of the stronger party, injustice the interest and profit of oneself."

After deluging us with this oratorical shower-bath, Thrasymachus intended to leave; the others, however, would not let him, but compelled him to stay and be cross-examined. I supported their pleas, saying, "My dear Thrasymachus, you can't mean to throw a theory like that at us and then leave us without explaining it or examining its truth. Surely it's no small matter to define the course we must follow if we're to live our lives to the best advantage?"

16

BERNARD MANDEVILLE

Virtue the Offspring of Flattery Begat upon Pride

Introduction

Bernard Mandeville (1670–1733) was of Dutch extraction, a doctor and a writer on moral and social problems. His best-known work, *The Fable of the Bees, or Private Vices, Public Benefits*, was written to show that certain vices (e.g., luxury and vanity) were necessary to modern society, because they increase the demand for commodities. (The reader who doubts this need only consider what would happen to American and British society if everyone's debts were paid off.) Considering the excellence and the number of Mandeville's philosophical works, it is difficult to resist the conclusion that his quite considerable reputation would have been greater than it was had he been more pretentious and a bigger hypocrite.

Mandeville was among those who thought that morality is a device, employed by law givers and other Wisemen, which enables people to be more easily ruled. He differs from Thrasymachus in that he does not suggest that conventional morality is produced in the interest of rulers only. Almost everybody has an interest in others being conventionally good.

According to Mandeville, morality is the offspring of flattery based on pride. Although conventionally good people were necessary to society, it was not in the real interest of good people to be good. Hence a substitute interest had to be found. This substitute and imaginary interest was love of honor (a manifestation of pride). Love of honor is a very strong motive in humankind. British civil servants, for example, are partly rewarded for their services by honors such as knighthoods, which induce them to accept relatively low rates of pay.

If one does not probe too deeply into people's motivation, it might seem that the cavalrymen celebrated in Tennyson's "The Charge of the Light Brigade" were induced to lose their lives from a love of honor. Because they were acting in obedience to an absurd order given by an incompetent officer, it would seem that as a means of securing cohesive action, love of honor has disadvantages. From Mandeville's viewpoint, Tennyson was simply (unwittingly) perpetuating a usually useful delusion. It would have been in the collective interest of the cavalrymen to disobey their officers and go home, provided they acted in concert. But it was in the interest of each individual cavalryman to obey. Left to themselves, no individual could have disobeyed the order because he would have been shot by the others. But in this particular case, love of honor does *not* promote the (collective) interest of those who have it. Indeed, it works in the opposite direction since it causes them to lose their lives. It is presumably considered by those who train soldiers that it is better to have soldiers who unthinkingly obey all orders, however stupid, than it is to have soldiers who obey some orders but not others. The gain from having them disobey bad orders is outweighed by the loss that would otherwise be occasioned by the facts that (a) they will not always know or agree which orders *are* bad orders, (b) they will not act quickly enough to meet an emergency unless they are taught instant obedience, and (c) without obedience they will not all go in the same direction.

A difficulty for Mandeville is that the *satisfaction* humans get from the praise of others is not an *imaginary* one; it is something from which they get very real pleasure. However, Mandeville thought not so much that the satisfaction of honor was imaginary, as that the belief that some ways of behaving are honorable is something like a *delusion*. By means of this device people are made to sacrifice their real interest to obtain honor.

Besides making people more likely to perform the actions for which they are flattered, flattering people will cause them to regard not performing these actions as dishonorable. But being honorable is not an objective characteristic of the action that is honorable. All there is in nature are the feelings in us which honorable actions arouse. Before this conditioning, an action arouses no such feelings. If, *before* being conditioned to regard it as dishonorable not to accept a challenge to a duel, a man were to say that not to do so was dishonorable, he would be abusing the word "dishonorable," even if he understood what it meant. But, if *after* he has, by means of flattery, been made to feel that it is dishonorable not to accept challenges, he says this is dishonorable, he will be using the word "dishonorable" *correctly*. Hence people have by flattery the power to *make* it correct to say that something is dishonorable when before their saying this it was not. They have the power to produce (possibly but not necessarily because they think that it is in their interest to produce it) some sort of *illusion*.

Thus a woman can be trained to regard it dishonorable to sleep with a man who is not her husband, or alternatively, to regard it as dishonorable (because it is inhospitable) not to sleep with one of her husband's guests if requested by him to do so. If she receives the first training, the remark that she will subsequently make — that it is dishonorable to sleep with a man who is not her husband—no more reflects objective fact than the remark that she will make if she is subjected to the second process of indoctrination and is taught that it is dishonorable *not* to sleep with her husband's guests. (There could however be a great deal of difference between the *usefulness* of these two practices.)

It is not necessary that Mandeville hold that the pleasure from satisfying one's love of honor should be greater than the loss which inculcating it is designed to compensate. He could have held that, although a strong-minded person could ignore honor and maximize interest, most of us, through weakness of will, find desire for honorable conformity too much for us and sacrifice our long-term interest to the short-term pleasure of feeling we deserve honor, and (if we are lucky) actually *being* honored by our society.

Although Mandeville says little about guilt, it is obvious that a sense of guilt can be produced in much the same way as a sense of honor.

Reading

ALL UNTAUGHT ANIMALS are only Sollicitous of pleasing themselves, and naturally follow the bent of their own Inclinations, without considering the good or harm that from their being pleased will accrue to others. This is the Reason, that in the wild State of Nature those Creatures are fittest to live peaceably together in great Numbers, that discover the least of Understanding, and have the fewest Appetites to gratify, and consequently no Species of Animals is without the Curb of Government, less capable of agreeing long together in Multitudes than that of Man; yet such are his Qualities, whether good or bad, I shall not determine, that no Creature besides himself can ever be made sociable: But being an extraordinary selfish and headstrong as well as cunning Animal, however he may be subdued by superior Strength, it is impossible by force alone to make him tractable, and receive the Improvements he is capable of.

The chief Thing therefore, which Law-givers and other Wise Men, that have laboured for the Establishment of Society, have endeavour'd, has been to make the People they were to govern, believe, that it was more beneficial for every body to conquer than indulge his Appetites, and much better to mind the Publick than what seem'd his private Interest. As this has always been a very difficult Task, so no Wit or Eloquence has been left untried to compass it; and the Moralists and Philosophers of all Ages employ'd their utmost Skill to prove the truth

From "An Enquiry into Virtue" by Bernard Mandeville in *Mandeville: The Fable of the Bees*, edited by Phillip Hotuh, Pelican Classics, 1970. Reprinted by permission of Penguin Books.

of so useful an Assertion. But whether Mankind would have ever be-
liev'd it or not, it is not likely that any body could have perswaded them
to disapprove of their natural Inclinations, or prefer the good of others
to their own, if at the same time he had not shew'd them an Equivalent to be enjoy'd as a Reward for the Violence, which by so doing they
of necessity must commit upon themselves. Those that have under-
taken to civilise Mankind, were not ignorant of this; but being unable to
give so many real Rewards as would satisfy all Persons for every individual Action, they were forc'd to contrive an imaginary one, that as a
general Equivalent for the trouble of Self-denial should serve on all
occasions, and without costing any thing either to themselves or others,
be yet a most acceptable Recompence to the Receivers.

They thoroughly examin'd all the Strength and Frailties of our Nature, and observing that none were either so savage as not to be
charm'd with Praise, or so despicable as patiently to bear Contempt,
justly concluded, that Flattery must be the most powerful Argument
that cou'd be used to Human Creatures. Making use of this bewitching
Engine, they extoll'd the Excellency of our Nature above other Animals, and setting forth with unbounded Praises the Wonders of our
Sagacity and vastness of Understanding, bestow'd a thousand Encomiums on the Rationality of our Souls, by the help of which we were
capable of performing the most noble Atchievements. Having by this
artful way of Flattery insinuated themselves into the Hearts of Men,
they began to instruct them in the Notions of Honour and Shame;
representing the one as the worst of all Evils, and the other as the
highest good to which Mortals could aspire: Which being done, they
laid before them how unbecoming it was the Dignity of such sublime
Creatures to be sollicitous about gratifying those Appetites, which they
had in common with Brutes, and at the same time unmindful of those
higher qualities that gave them the pre-eminence over all visible
Beings. They indeed confess'd, that those impulses of Nature were very
pressing; that it was troublesome to resist, and very difficult wholly to
subdue them: But this they only used as an Argument to demonstrate,
how glorious the Conquest of them was on the one hand, and how
scandalous on the other not to attempt it.

To introduce moreover an Emulation amongst Men, they divided the
whole Species in two Classes, vastly differing from one another: The
one consisted of abject, low minded People, that always hunting after
immediate Enjoyment, were wholly incapable of Self-denial, and without regard to the good of others, had no higher Aim than their private
Advantage; such as being enslaved by Voluptuousness, yielded without
Resistance to every gross desire, and made no use of their Rational
Faculties but to heighten their Sensual Pleasures. These vile grov'ling
Wretches, they said, were the Dross of their kind, and having only the

Shape of Men, differ'd from Brutes in nothing but their outward Figure. But the other Class was made up of lofty high-spirited Creatures, that free from sordid Selfishness, esteem'd the Improvements of the Mind to be their fairest Possessions; and setting a true value upon themselves, took no delight but in imbellishing that Part in which their Excellency consisted; such as despising whatever they had in common with irrational Creatures, opposed by the help of Reason their most violent Inclinations; and making a continual War with themselves to promote the Peace of others, aim'd at no less than the Publick Welfare and the Conquest of their own Passions.

> *Fortior   est   qui   se   quam   qui   fortissima   Vincit*
> *Mænia* ————[1]

These they call'd the true Representatives of their sublime Species, exceeding in worth the first Class by more degrees, than that it self was superior to the Beasts of the Field.

As in all Animals that are not too imperfect to discover Pride, we find, that the finest and such as are the most beautiful and valuable of their kind, have generally the greatest Share of it; so in Man, the most perfect of Animals, it is so inseparable from his very Essence (how cunningly soever some may learn to hide or disguise it) that without it the Compound he is made of would want one of the chiefest Ingredients: Which, if we consider, it is hardly to be doubted but Lessons and Remonstrances, so skillfully adapted to the good Opinion Man has of himself, as those I have mentioned, must, if scatter'd amongst a Multitude, not only gain the assent of most of them, as to the Speculative part, but likewise induce several, especially the fiercest, most resolute, and best among them, to endure a thousand Inconveniences, and undergo as many hardships, that they may have the pleasure of counting themselves Men of the second Class, and consequently appropriating to themselves all the Excellencies they have heard of it.

From what has been said we ought to expect in the first place, that the Heroes who took such extraordinary Pains to master some of their natural Appetites, and prefer'd the good of others to any visible Interest of their own, would not recede an Inch from the fine Notions they had receiv'd concerning the Dignity of Rational Creatures; and having ever the Authority of the Government on their side, with all imaginable Vigour assert the Esteem that was due to those of the second Class, as well as their superiority over the rest of their kind. In the second, that those who wanted a sufficient Stock of either Pride or Resolution, to buoy them up in mortifying of what was dearest to them, follow'd the

---

[1] "He who conquers himself is stronger than one who takes the greatest fortress." Mandeville may be giving an inexact paraphrase of *Proverbs*, xvi, 32. — Ed.

sensual dictates of Nature, would yet be asham'd of confessing themselves to be those despicable Wretches that belong'd to the inferior Class, and were generally reckon'd to be so little remov'd from Brutes; and that therefore in their own Defence they would say, as others did, and hiding their own Imperfections as well as they could, cry up Self-denial and Publick spiritedness as much as any: For it is highly probable, that some of them, convinced by the real Proofs of Fortitude and Self-Conquest they had seen, would admire in others what they found wanting in themselves; others be afraid of the Resolution and Prowess of those of the second Class, and that all of them were kept in awe by the Power of their Rulers, wherefore it is reasonable to think, that none of them (whatever they thought in themselves) would dare openly contradict, what by every body else was thought Criminal to doubt of.

This was (or at least might have been) the manner after which Savage Man was broke; from whence it is evident, that the first Rudiments of Morality, broach'd by skilfull Politicians, to render Men useful to each other as well as tractable, were chiefly contriv'd; that the Ambitious might reap the more Benefit from, and govern vast Numbers of them with the greater Ease and Security. This Foundation of Politicks being once laid, it is impossible that Man should long remain uncivilis'd: For even those who only strove to gratify their Appetites, being continually cross'd by others of the same Stamp, could not but observe, that whenever they check'd their Inclinations, or but follow'd them with more Circumspection, they avoided a world of Troubles, and often escap'd many of the Calamities that generally attended the too eager pursuit after Pleasure.

First, they receiv'd, as well as others, the benefit of those Actions that were done for the good of the whole Society, and consequently could not forbear wishing well to those of the superior Class that perform'd them. Secondly, the more intent they were in seeking their own Advantage, without Regard to others, the more they were hourly convinced, that none stood so much in their way as those that were most like themselves.

It being the Interest then of the very worst of them, more than any, to preach up Publick-spiritedness, that they might reap the Fruits of the Labour and Self-denial of others, and at the same time indulge their own Appetites with less disturbance, they agreed with the rest, to call every thing, which, without Regard to the Publick, Man should commit to gratify any of his Appetites, VICE; if in that Action there could be observ'd the least prospect, that it might either be injurious to any of the Society, or ever render himself less serviceable to others: And to give the Name of VIRTUE to every Performance, by which Man, contrary to the impulse of Nature, should endeavour the Benefit of others, or the Conquest of his own Passions, out of a Rational Ambition of being good.

It shall be objected, that no Society was ever any ways civilis'd before the major part had agreed upon some Worship or other of an over ruling Power, and consequently that the Notions of Good and Evil, and the Distinction between *Virtue* and *Vice*, were never the Contrivance of Politicians, but the pure effect of Religion. Before I answer this Objection, I must repeat what I have said already, that in this *Enquiry into the Origin of Moral Virtue* I speak neither of *Jews* or *Christians*, but Man in his State of Nature and Ignorance of the true Deity; and then I affirm, that the Idolatrous Superstitions of all other Nations, and the pitiful Notions they had of the Supreme Being were incapable of exciting Man to Virtue, and good for nothing but to awe and amuse a rude and unthinking Multitude. It is evident from History, that in all considerable Societies, how stupid or ridiculous soever Peoples received Notions have been, as to the Deities they worship'd, Human Nature has ever exerted itself in all its branches, and that there is no Earthly Wisdom or Moral Virtue, but at one time or other Men have excell'd in it in all Monarchies and Commonwealths, that for Riches and Power have been any ways remarkable.

The Ægyptians not satisfy'd with having Deify'd all the ugly Monsters they could think on, were so silly as to adore the Onions of their own sowing; yet at the same time their Country was the most famous Nursery of Arts and Sciences in the World, and themselves more eminently skill'd in the deepest Mysteries of Nature than any Nation has been since.

No States or Kingdoms under Heaven have yielded more or greater Paterns in all sorts of Moral Virtues than the *Greek* and *Roman* Empires, more especially the latter; and yet how loose, absurd, and ridiculous were their Sentiments as to Sacred Matters: For without reflecting on the extravagant Number of their Deities, if we only consider the infamous Stories they father'd upon them, it is not to be denied but that their Religion, far from teaching Men the Conquest of their Passions, and the way to Virtue, seem'd rather contriv'd to justify their Appetities, and encourage their Vices. But if we would know what made 'em excel in Fortitude, Courage and Magnanimity, we must cast our Eyes on the Pomp of their Triumphs, the Magnificence of their Monuments and Arches, their Trophies, Statues, and Inscriptions; the variety of their Military Crowns, their Honours decreed to the Dead, Publick Encomiums on the Living, and other imaginary Rewards they bestow'd on Men of Merit; and we shall find, that what carried so many of them to the utmost Pitch of Self-denial, was nothing but their Policy in making use of the most effectual Means that human Pride could be flatter'd with.

It is visible then that it was not any Heathen Religion or other

Idolatrous Superstition, that first put Man upon crossing his Appetites and subduing his dearest Inclinations, but the skilful Management of wary Politicians; and the nearer we search into human Nature, the more we shall be convinc'd, that the Moral Virtues are the Political Offspring which Flattery begot upon Pride.

There is no Man of what Capacity or Penetration soever, that is wholly Proof against the witchcraft of Flattery, if artfully perform'd, and suited to his Abilities. Children and Fools will swallow Personal Praise, but those that are more cunning, must be manag'd with greater Circumspection; and the more general the Flattery is, the less it is suspected by those it is levell'd at. What you say in Commendation of a whole Town is receiv'd with Pleasure by all the Inhabitants: Speak in Commendation of Letters in general, and every Man of Learning will think himself in particular obliged to you. You may safely praise the Employment a Man is of, or the Country he was born in; because you give him an opportunity of screening the Joy he feels upon his own account, under the Esteem which he pretends to have for others.

It is common among cunning Men, that understand the Power which Flattery has upon Pride, when they are afraid they shall be impos'd upon to enlarge, tho' much against their Conscience, upon the Honour, fair Dealing and Integrity of the Family, Country, or sometimes the Profession of him they suspect; because they know that Men often will change their Resolution, and act against their Inclination, that they may have the Pleasure of continuing to appear in the Opinion of some what they are conscious not to be in reality. Thus Sagacious Moralists draw Men like Angels, in hopes that the Pride at least of some will put 'em upon copying after the beautiful Originals which they are represented to be.

17

FRIEDRICH NIETZSCHE

Against Morality

Introduction

Friedrich Nietzsche (1844–1900) was born in Prussia. He was so brilliant that he was given a chair at Basel, in Switzerland, without ever having completed a doctorate. He died insane as a result of tertiary syphilis of unknown origin. He wrote brilliant prose (which frequently resembles poetry). His works were composed despite severe illness.

Nietzsche can be regarded, up to a point, as an ally of Thrasymachus, only Nietzsche regarded morality not as being a delusion that favored the strong, but as a delusion that favored the weak, as well as favoring the self-indulgent, lazy, commonplace, and comfortable. Morality was to the strong as a snare to a hawk — it enslaved them. Like Thrasymachus, but for more elevated reasons (if an immoralist like Nietzsche can consistently think that anything is elevated), Nietzsche thought the strong should ignore morality. But in ignoring morality, the strong were avoiding subjection by the weak, not by other members of the fraternity of the strong.

It is very difficult to find out from reading Nietzsche, who was more prone to aphorism than to careful reasoning, *how*, if they really did, the weak produced in the strong the delusion that the weak ought to be protected. But there is no reason he should not accept the account of the genesis of this delusion provided by Mandeville, with guilt substituted for shame.

It is also difficult to find out exactly how Nietzsche thought the strong, when released from the delusion of morality, ought to behave. If the strong man was a general, he might exhibit Napoleonic virtues from a place well behind the front line. Nietzsche must regard any compassion a Napoleon might have for his soldiers as irrational. Another thing that the strong might perhaps do would be to devote themselves to excellence (e.g., artistic excellence), for which they might have more time and energy if they were released from moral ties. On the other hand, it is doubtful whether an artist would not lose more time than he saved by behaving in such a way as to be pestered by creditors and ex-mistresses, and incapacitated by hangovers.

Although what Nietzsche thought was often obscure, it is abundantly clear that he was against Christian morality, a morality which, superficially at any rate, favored the weak. By trying to inculcate virtues like meekness, for example, it encouraged what might be described as weakness.

It is a Marxist view that Christianity favors (in a different way) the strong, by teaching the weak obedience, meekness, other-worldliness, and forgiveness. It exhorts them to love the strong and to leave the strong in possession of power and money, things which Christianity teaches the weak to despise. (When a number of Penang set up a roadblock defended with blowguns to protect their home from being destroyed with their tropical rain forest, the government of Borneo sent both soldiers armed with rifles to dislodge them and a priest to tell them about brotherly love.) Nietzsche, however, might have thought that the emphasis on qualities such as meekness favored the weak rather than the strong because, since the weak had no alternative to being meek but the strong did, the strong were giving up something by their meekness, while the weak were not.

Nietzsche's view that morality is useful to the weak, and Marx's view that it is useful to the strong, could both be correct. Indeed, they would be correct if morality is useful to everybody.

It is very difficult to regard Nietzsche, despite what he himself says, as an immoralist rather than as a moralist with eccentric, but passionately held, views. The admiration for ruthlessness, which has in part stemmed from Nietzsche, is deplorable. But on the other hand, Christianity has overemphasized the need to keep the weak (in this case, the sick, maimed, and dying) alive, when it might be better for them and for everybody else if they were helped to die in peace. The hostile attitude to elitism in education, which in the short run, at any rate, favors the weak, tends to encourage waste of talent and human resources.

Reading

THE DAWN OF THE DAY

3.

A TIME FOR EVERYTHING. — When man assigned a sex to all things, he did not believe that he was merely playing; but he thought, on the contrary, that he had acquired a profound insight: — it was only at a much later period, and then only partly, that he acknowledged the enormity of his error. In the same way, man has attributed a moral relationship to everything that exists, throwing the cloak of *ethical significance* over the world's shoulders. One day all that will be of just as much value, and no more, as the amount of belief existing to-day in the masculinity or femininity of the sun.

97.

ONE BECOMES MORAL. — but not because one is moral! Submission to morals may be due to slavishness or vanity, egoism or resignation, dismal fanaticism or thoughtlessness. It may, again, be an act of despair, such as submission to the authority of a ruler; but there is nothing moral about it *per se*.

100.

AWAKING FROM A DREAM. — Noble and wise men once upon a time believed in the music of the spheres; there are still noble and wise men who believe in "the moral significance of existence," but there will come a day when this music of the spheres also will no longer be audible to them. They will awake and perceive that their ears have been dreaming.

101.

OPEN TO DOUBT. — To accept a belief simply because it is customary implies that one is dishonest, cowardly, and lazy. — Must dishonesty, cowardice, and laziness, therefore, be the primary conditions of morality?

103.

THERE ARE TWO CLASSES OF PEOPLE WHO DENY MORALITY. — To deny morality may mean, in the first place, to deny the moral inducements which,
men pretend, have urged them on to their actions, — which is equivalent to saying that morality merely consists of words and forms, part of
that coarse and subtle deceit (especially self-deceit) which is characteristic of mankind, and perhaps more especially of those men who are
celebrated for their virtues. In the second place, it may mean our
denying that moral judgments are founded on truths. It is admitted in
such a case that these judgments are, in fact, the motives of the actions,
but that in this way it is really errors as the basis of all moral judgments
which urge men on to their moral actions. This is my point of view; but
I should be far from denying that in very many cases a subtle suspicion
in accordance with the former point of view — *i.e.* in the spirit of La
Rochefoucauld — is also justifiable, and in any case of a high general
utility. — Therefore I deny morality in the same way as I deny alchemy,
i.e. I deny its hypotheses; but I do not deny that there have been
alchemists who believed in these hypotheses and based their actions
upon them. I also deny immorality — not that innumerable people feel
immoral, but that there is any true reason why they should feel so. I
should not, of course, deny — unless I were a fool — that many actions
which are called immoral should be avoided and resisted; and in the
same way that many which are called moral should be performed and
encouraged; but I hold that in both cases these actions should be
performed from motives other than those which have prevailed up to
the present time. We must learn anew in order that at last, perhaps very
late in the day, we may be able to do something more: feel anew.

104.

OUR VALUATIONS. — All actions may be referred back to valuations, and
all valuations are either one's own or adopted, the latter being by far
the more numerous. Why do we adopt them? Through fear, *i.e.* we
think it more advisable to pretend that they are our own, and so well do
we accustom ourselves to do so that it at last becomes second nature to
us. A valuation of our own, which is the appreciation of a thing in
accordance with the pleasure or displeasure it causes us and no one
else, is something very rare indeed! — But must not our valuation of our
neighbour — which is prompted by the motive that we adopt his valuation in most cases — proceed from ourselves and by our own decision?
Of course, but then we come to these decisions during our childhood,
and seldom change them. We often remain during our whole lifetime
the dupes of our childish and accustomed judgments in our manner of

judging our fellowmen (their minds, rank, morality, character, and reprehensibility), and we find it necessary to subscribe to their valuations.

105.

PSEUDO-EGOISM. — The great majority of people, whatever they may think and say about their "egoism," do nothing for their ego all their life long, but only for a phantom of this ego which has been formed in regard to them by their friends and communicated to them. As a consequence, they all live in a haze of impersonal and half-personal opinions and of arbitrary and, as it were, poetic valuations: the one always in the head of another, and this head, again, in the head of somebody else — a queer world of phantoms which manages to give itself a rational appearance! This haze of opinions and habits grows in extent and lives almost independently of the people it surrounds; it is it which gives rise to the immense effect of general judgments on "man" — all those men, who do not know themselves, believe in a bloodless abstraction which they call "man," *i.e.* in a fiction; and every change caused in this abstraction by the judgments of powerful individualities (such as princes and philosophers) produces an extraordinary and irrational effect on the great majority, — for the simple reason that not a single individual in this haze can oppose a real ego, an ego which is accessible to and fathomed by himself, to the universal pale fiction, which he could thereby destroy.

THINKING EVIL MEANS MAKING EVIL. — The passions become evil and insidious when they are considered evil and insidious. Thus Christianity has succeeded in turning Eros and Aphrodite — great powers, capable of idealization — into hellish goblins. . . . In themselves the sexual feelings, like those of pity and adoration, are such that one human being thereby gives pleasure to another human being through his delight; one does not encounter such beneficent arrangements too frequently in nature. And to slander just such a one and to corrupt it through bad conscience! To associate the procreation of man with bad conscience!

In the end this transformation of Eros into a devil wound up as a comedy: gradually the "devil" Eros became more interesting to men than all the angels and saints, thanks to the whispering and the secret-mongering of the Church in all erotic matters: this has had the effect, right into our own time, of making the *love story* the only real interest shared by *all* circles — in an exaggeration which would have been incomprehensible in antiquity and which will yet be laughed at someday. . . .

Notes (1880–1881)

A GIRL WHO surrenders her virginity to a man who has not first sworn solemnly before witnesses that he will not leave her again for the rest of her life not only is considered imprudent but is also called immoral. She did not follow the *mores*; she was not only imprudent but also disobedient, for she knew what the mores commanded. Where the mores command differently, the conduct of the girl in such a case would not be called immoral either; in fact, there are regions where it is considered moral to lose one's virginity before marriage. Thus the reproach is really directed against disobedience: it is this that is immoral. Is this sufficient? Such a girl is considered contemptible—but what kind of disobedfience is it that one despises? (Imprudence is not despised.) One says of her: she could not control herself, that is why she was disobedient against the mores; thus it is the blindness of the desire that one despises, the animal in the girl. With this in mind, one also says: she is unchaste, by this one could not mean that she is doing what the lawfully wedded wife does, too, without being called unchaste. The mores are then seen to demand that one bear the displeasure of unsatisfied desire, that the desire be able to *wait*. To be immoral means therefore, in this case, not to be able to bear a displeasure despite the thought of the power that makes the rules. *A feeling is supposed to be subdued by a thought*—more precisely, by the thought of fear (whether it be fear of the sacred mores or of the punishment and shame threatened by the mores). In itself, it is not at all shameful, but natural and fair, that a desire be satisfied immediately. Therefore what is really contemptible in this girl is the *weakness of her fear*. Being moral means being highly accessible to fear. Fear is the power by which the community is preserved.

If one considers, on the other hand, that every original community requires a high degree of fearlessness in its members in other respects, then it becomes clear that what is to be feared in the case of morality must inspire fear in the very highest degree. Therefore mores have been introduced everywhere as functions of a divine will, hiding under the fearfulness of gods and demonic means of punishment—and being immoral would then mean: not fearing the infinitely fearful.

Of anyone who denied the gods one expected anything: he was automatically the most fearsome human being, whom no community could suffer because he tore out the roots of fear on which the community had grown. It was supposed that in such a person desire raged unlimited: one considered every human being without such fear infinitely evil. . . .

The more peaceful a community has become, the more cowardly the citizens become; the less accustomed they are to standing pain, the more will worldly punishments suffice as deterrents, the faster will religious threats become superfluous. . . . In highly civilized peoples, finally, even punishments should become highly superfluous deterrents; the mere fear of shame, the trembling of vanity, is so continually effective that immoral actions are left undone. The refinement of morality increases together with the refinement of fear. Today the fear of disagreeable feelings in other people is almost the strongest of our own disagreeable feelings. One would like ever so much to live in such a way as to do nothing except what causes others *agreeable* feelings, and even to take pleasure in nothing any more that does not also fulfill this condition.

Thus Spake Zarathustra

I WALK AMONG this people and I keep my eyes open; they do not forgive me that I do not envy their virtues. They bite at me because I say to them: small people need small virtues—and because I find it hard to accept that small people are needed. . . .

And at that time it also happened—and verily, it happened for the first time—that his word pronounced *selfishness* blessed the wholesome, healthy selfishness that wells from a powerful soul—from a powerful soul to which belongs the high body, beautiful triumphant, refreshing around which everything becomes a mirror—the supple, persuasive body, the dancer whose parable and epitome is the self-enjoying soul. The self-enjoyment of such bodies and souls calls itself "virtue."

With its words about good and bad, such self-enjoyment screens itself as with sacred groves; with the names of its happiness it banishes from its presence whatever is contemptible. From its presence it banishes whatever is cowardly; it says: bad—*that is* cowardly! Contemptible to its mind is anyone who always worries, sighs, is miserable, and also anyone who picks up even the smallest advantages. It also despises all wisdom that wallows in grief, for verily, there is also wisdom that blooms in the dark, a nightshade wisdom, which always sighs: all is vain. . . .

"Thou shalt not rob! Thou shalt not kill!" Such words were once called holy; one bent the knee and head and took off one's shoes before them. But I ask you: where have there ever been better robbers and killers in this world than such holy words?

Is there not in all life itself robbing and killing? And that such words were called holy—was not truth itself killed thereby? Or was it the preaching of death that was called holy, which contradicted and contravened all life? O my brothers, break, break the old tablets!

You higher men, learn this from me: in the market place nobody believes in higher men. And if you want to speak there, very well! But the mob blinks: "We are all equal."

"You higher men"—thus blinks the mob—"there are no higher men, we are all equal, man is man, before God we are all equal."

Before God! But now this god had died. And before the mob we do not want to be equal. You higher men, go away from the market place.

You higher men, this god was your greatest danger. It is only since he lies in his tomb that you have been resurrected. Only now the great noon comes; only now the higher man becomes—lord.

Have you understood this word, O my brothers? You are startled? Do your hearts become giddy? Does the abyss yawn before you? Does the hellhound howl at you? Well then, you higher men! Only now is the mountain of man's future in labor. God died: now *we* want the overman to live.

Do not be virtuous beyond your strength! And do not desire anything of yourselves against probability. . . .

What is good? Everything that heightens the feeling of power in man, the will to power, power itself.

What is bad? Everything that is born of weakness.

What is happiness? The feeling that power is *growing*, that resistance is overcome.

Not contentedness but more power: not peace but war; not virtue but fitness (Renaissance virtue, *virtu*, virtue that is morality-free).

The weak and the failures shall perish; first principle of *our* love of man. And they shall even be given every possible assistance.

What is more harmful than any vice? Active pity for all the failures and all the weak: Christianity.

18

STEVEN LUKES

Marxism and Morality

Introduction

Karl Marx (1818–1883) was a German who emigrated first to France and then to England, where he spent most of his life working in the British Museum. His principal works were (with Friedrich Engels) *The Communist Manifesto* and *Das Kapital*, most of which was reconstructed by Engels from a draft. He was one of the founders of modern communism and one of the most influential thinkers of modern times.

Steven Lukes is the author of a number of well-known books on politics and sociology. This reading by him is included in lieu of a suitable selection from Marx himself.

The *type* of view discussed in this section — that the good are the dupes of other people — was (roughly) sometimes held by Marx. A society's moral beliefs are an illusion (or false consciousness) produced by certain economic forces. These moral beliefs reflect the interest of the economically dominant social class, which in Marx's day was the bourgeoisie. Members of this class, consciously or unconsciously, use their control over law, education, the judicial system, and the press to inculcate and enforce a morality which is to their own advantage. For example, the common moral belief that one ought to be sober, industrious, punctual, content with one's station in life, and respectful in the presence of one's social superiors favors the bourgeoisie by securing for them a cheap, reliable, and docile work force. If it was argued that sobriety, industry, and so forth were also in the interests of the workers themselves, the reply would be that, in Europe and North America at the time at which Marx wrote, the conditions of many of them were so dreadful that they

had nothing to lose but their chains by refusing to cultivate these character traits. (In developed countries things are now better.) It was then
more to their interest to overthrow the system than to acquire those
virtues that made more fortunate people successful within it.

The prevailing morality, of course, frowned on rebellion, but that it
should do so was just another instance of the workers being kept in their
place by a moral delusion inculcated by the bourgeoisie. If religion is the
opium of the masses, morality is their policeman. The only salvation for
the proletariat is to trample over morality, overthrow the bourgeoisie,
and set up the dictatorship of the proletariat. (It would be wrong to say
that such a violent solution is a case of the end justifying the means, for it
would be only a bourgeois delusion that the means were wrong, and, if
rightness is a delusion, the means *cannot* be justified, i.e., *shown* to be
right.)

Marx gives no account of the mechanism by which the interest of the
dominant social class produced a delusive morality. He could have said
that morality was partly the result of education and that the bourgeoisie
could produce a morality that was in their own interests by hiring
teachers to inculcate such a morality in their pupils. For example, an
imperialist set of moral beliefs would be in the interest of the bourgeoisie, if it would help open new markets for their goods. It could be that any
teachers who were anti-imperialist would be sacked by the school governors, who were likely to be members of the bourgeoisie; this has happened. It would be excessively crude to hold that the bourgeoisie will
always know what they are doing. They will be as much subject to
self-deception and wishful thinking on these matters as everybody else.

Marx does not seem to be aware of the obvious difficulty that if *all*
moralities are false consciousnesses produced in the interest of the dominant social class, a Marxist morality must be as delusive as any other.
When the proletariat eventually becomes economically dominant, a new
morality will be produced, but this will be just as much the product of
economic (and social) forces, and so just as delusive, as its predecessor.
Hence Marx, in arguing for the irrationality of morality, is cutting the
ground from under his own feet.

Marx might have replied to this difficulty in two ways. First, he could
have said that although *almost* all moralities were a delusion produced by
social forces, *Marxist* morality was an exception. Reflecting on the forces
that produce moralities, which is what Marxist philosophers have done,
gives one exemption from dominance of these forces. (Freedom is the
consciousness of necessity.) Once people know the power of economic
forces, they are able to see the truth without being influenced by them,
and the truth is that Marxist moral beliefs are correct.

The second Marxist reply would be to say that all morality *is* a delusion,
but that morality will not be necessary when the communist millennium
actually arrives. Hence there would be *no* Marxist morality to *be* the
irrational product of economic forces. It was an overoptimistic Marxist
view that after the communist revolution the state would eventually
become redundant, and so wither away. Marx could have held that morality would wither away with the state. Antisocial behavior, perhaps, is

produced by a competitive society and will disappear when society ceases to be competitive, as it will when the state withers away (e.g., in an ideal society there will be no lawyers).

It has been held, not implausibly, by the philosopher David Hume, that justice would not be necessary, and so not exist, in a society in which everybody loved one another sufficiently. (He did not think, however, that they ever *would* love one another sufficiently.) There would be no rules prohibiting violence because no one would have any enemies, and there would be no rules allocating and protecting property (including, although Hume does not say so, property in men and women) because everyone would freely give to one another anything that was needed. Marx could have held (again overoptimistically) that the communist millennium would be a society in which morality was made unnecessary by everybody's loving one another.

(There is an interesting parallel to be drawn between Marxism and antinomianism, the Christian heresy which holds that when Christians have attained a state of grace, they are absolved from obedience to the moral law. Christian antinomian communities, however, were very small. It is difficult to understand how a large industrial society could manage without moral rules.)

Reading

The moment anyone started to talk to Marx about morality, he would roar with laughter.

K. Vorländer

ON THE ONE hand it is claimed that morality is a form of ideology, and thus social in origin, illusory in content, and serving class interests; that any given morality arises out of a particular stage in the development of the productive forces and relations and is relative to a particular mode of production and particular class interests; that there are no objective truths or eternal principles of morality; that the very form of morality, and general ideas such as freedom and justice that are "common to all states of society," cannot "completely vanish except with the total disappearance of class antagonisms;" that the proletarian sees morality, along with law and religion, as "so many bourgeois prejudices, behind which lurk in ambush just as many bourgeois interests"; that marxism is

From "Marxism and Morality" by Steven Lukes, pp. 3–4, 27, and 95–96, Oxford University Press, 1985. Reprinted by permission of Oxford University Press.

opposed to all moralizing and rejects as out of date all moral vocabulary, and that the marxist critique of both capitalism and political economy is not moral but scientific.

On the other hand, no one can fail to notice that Marx's and marxist writings abound in moral judgements, implicit and explicit. From his earliest writings, where Marx expresses his hatred of servility, through the critique of alienation and the fragmentary visions of communism in the Paris Manuscripts and *The German Ideology*, to the excoriating attacks on factory conditions and the effects of exploitation in *Capital*, it is plain that Marx was fired by outrage and indignation and the burning desire for a better world that it is hard not to see as moral. The same applies to Engels, author of *The Condition of the Working Class in England*, a work full of moral criticism of the social conditions created by advancing industrial capitalism, which remained basic to his thought, and which Marx explicitly endorsed for its depiction of the "moral degradation caused by the capitalistic exploitation of women and children." The same applies to their followers down to the present day. Open practically any Marxist text, however aseptically scientific or academic, and you will find condemnation, exhortation, and the vision of a better world. As for the socialist leaders, as Irving Howe has well said, few "were of proletarian origin, few acted out of direct class needs, and most were inspired by moral visions their ideology somehow inhibited them from expressing' (Howe 1981: 492).

Notice that the paradox, the seeming contradiction, lies at the level of general belief. On the one hand, morality, as such, is explained, unmasked, and condemned as an anachronism; on the other, it is believed in and appealed to, and indeed urged upon others as relevant to political campaigns and struggles. I am not referring to a contrast between, say, bourgeois morality on the one hand, and authentic proletarian morality on the other. As we shall see, Marxists have sometimes drawn this distinction, but it is no contradiction. I am concerned rather with Marxist beliefs about morality and moral judgement *per se* and in general: in the absence of further explanation, these certainly do look contradictory. Nor am I referring to the contrast between theory and practice, between what Marxists say and what they do. Often, where this contrast exists, it does constitute a contradiction, but it is one common to all political ideologies and creeds, and it is no paradox. In short, what is striking about Marxism is its apparent commitment to both the rejection and the adoption of moral criticism and exhortation. . . . The key to resolving the paradox lies, I believe, in drawing a distinction, to be found in Marx, between what I shall call, following Marx, the morality of *Recht* and the morality of *emancipation*.

Marx and Engels scorned "the faith of individuals in the conceptions of *Recht*," conceptions which "they ought to get out of their heads."

"As far as *Recht* is concerned," they wrote, "we with many others have stressed the opposition of communism to *Recht*, both political and private, as also in its most general form as the rights of man." This is an accurate statement about all their writings—and indeed about the marxist tradition in general—from "On the Jewish Question" onwards.

In that work, Marx spoke of "the so-called *rights of man*" as "nothing but the rights of a *member of civil society*, i.e. the rights of egoistic man, of man separated from other men and from the community." The "right of man to liberty is based not on the association of man with man, but on the separation of man from man. It is the *right* of this separation, the right of the *restricted* individual, withdrawn into himself," its practical application being the right to private property.

"Emancipation" is a term which derives from the Latin "amancipare," which in turn derives from "e + maxims + capere" meaning "to set free a child or wife from the patria potestas" and later of course to be set free from slavery, and hence generally from civil disabilities. For Marx emancipation denoted a setting free from the pre-history of human bondage, culminating in wage-slavery and exploitation, and thus it refers to that ideal of transparent social unity and individual self-realization in which "the contradiction between the interest of the separate individuals who have intercourse with one another has been abolished". . . .

My suggestion then is this: that the paradox in Marx's attitude to morality is resolved once we see that it is the morality of *recht* that it condemns as ideological and anachronistic, and the morality of emancipation that it adopts as its own. Indeed, as I shall argue in this chapter, human emancipation in part precisely consists in emancipation from *recht*, and the conditions that call it into being.

PART VI

MORAL BELIEFS: THE IRRATIONAL PRODUCTS OF EVOLUTION

19

THOMAS HUXLEY

Against Evolutionary Morality

Introduction

Thomas Huxley (1825–1895) was an eminent Victorian scientist. He was most famous for defending and publicizing the ideas of Charles Darwin, but he also wrote extensively and ably on metaphysics, epistemology, religion, and ethics. He was, incidentally, the grandfather of Aldous Huxley (the author of *Brave New World*) and Julian Huxley (the well-known biologist).

In an earlier part of *Evolution and Ethics*, Huxley states the fundamental idea that human beings, like other animals, came to have the features they have because possessing these features was of advantage to them in competing with other humans and animals. He thinks that this process has now virtually stopped. With the exception of criminals and the destitute, who comprise only a tiny percentage of the population, no one fails to survive, which gives people considerable latitude over the choice of a moral code.

Huxley seems to forget, however, that *sexual* selection will still operate. If women prefer tall or strong or reliable men—reliability is a characteristic that is partly congenital and partly acquired—then tall or strong or reliable men will have children while others do not. In addition, certain people still have an ethos which is either conducive or not conducive to their having large families. If blacks have more children than whites, or Catholics (on account of their antagonism to birth control) than Protestants, the poorly educated than the well-educated, then being white or Protestant or well-educated will, to that extent, be characteristics hostile to the survival of white or Protestant or well-educated people. The color problem, indeed, could be solved by everyone's eventually becoming black Catholics, and a universal religion more the result of the fecundity of its adherents than of the truth of its doctrine.

Huxley professes to be opposed to eugenics, the practice of deliberately producing better breeds of human beings, as gardeners produce better breeds of plant, by deliberately planned selective breeding. He opposes it on the grounds that it overlooks the fact that although selection of plants is conducted by gardeners and not by plants, selection of humans would have to be conducted by people themselves. He thinks that there are no people with the judgment necessary to make such decisions. There can, however, be little disagreement about the desirability of eliminating various serious incurable illnesses which are known to be inherited.

In this reading, Huxley advances the following two objections to evolutionary ethics, which, although enormously influential, seem to be ill considered.

1. He says that undesirable characteristics have evolved as well as desirable ones. The view Huxley *ought* to be attacking is that our moral standards have become what they are by a process of selection, and the fact that the character traits they condemn as well as the traits they approve have both been selected is not to the point.

2. He thinks that we must oppose the progress of evolution, on ethical grounds, for it tends to favor the strong and the ruthless. Here he is making a mistake analogous to the one he condemns in his opponents. He is being misled by the metaphor "struggle for existence." There is no struggle for existence, in the literal sense of "struggle," of plants and animals fighting with other plants and animals to survive. Plants cannot fight. It is a mistake, made both by Huxley and by his opponents, to suppose that evolution favors animals which *literally* struggle and which are strong and fierce in order to fit them for strife. The deer survives because of its camouflage, speed, and readiness to run away, and other animals survive for a variety of extraordinary reasons, some even because they are kept for food by other animals (not necessarily human ones).

It also is a mistake to suppose that ferocity is necessarily an advantage to humankind. A certain amount of ferocity, mostly directed against members of other tribes, would be selected, but a great deal of altruism, directed at mates, children, and others in need, would fairly obviously increase a tribe's ability to survive, also. Hence a moral code that approved of these traits, and so encouraged people not to struggle, would *increase* the ability to survive of those who possessed it. It would, indeed, be more successful in the metaphorical struggle for survival than a code that constantly encouraged people literally to struggle with one another to more than a limited extent.

Not only is Huxley, then, in urging us to combat the process of evolution, failing to realize that evolution can positively favor altruism. He also is unreflectingly applying a belief in the value of altruism that has itself been reached as a result of evolution.

Reading

THE PROPOUNDERS OF what are called the "ethics of evolution," when the "evolution of ethics" would usually better express the object of their speculations, adduce a number of more or less interesting facts and more or less sound arguments, in favour of the origin of the moral sentiments, in the same way as other natural phenomena, by a process of evolution. I have little doubt, for my own part, that they are on the right track; but as the immoral sentiments have no less been evolved, there is, so far, as much natural sanction for the one as the other. The thief and the murderer follow nature just as much as the philanthropist. Cosmic evolution may teach us how the good and the evil tendencies of man may have come about; but, in itself, it is incompetent to furnish any better reason why what we call good is preferable to what we call evil than we had before. Some day, I doubt not, we shall arrive at an understanding of the evolution of the æsthetic faculty; but all the understanding in the world will neither increase nor diminish the force of the intuition that this is beautiful and that is ugly.

There is another fallacy which appears to me to pervade the so-called "ethics of evolution." It is the notion that because, on the whole, animals and plants have advanced in perfection of organization by means of the struggle for existence and the consequent "survival of the fittest"; therefore men in society, men as ethical beings, must look to the same process to help them towards perfection. I suspect that this fallacy has arisen out of the unfortunate ambiguity of the phrase "survival of the fittest." "Fittest" has a connotation of "best"; and about "best" there hangs a moral flavour. In cosmic nature, however, what is "fittest" depends upon the conditions. Long since, I ventured to point out that if our hemisphere were to cool again, the survival of the fittest might bring about, in the vegetable kingdom, a population of more and more stunted and humbler and humbler organisms, until the "fittest" that survived might be nothing but lichens, diatoms, and such microscopic organisms as those which give red snow its colour; while, if it became hotter, the pleasant valleys of the Thames and Isis might be uninhabitable by any animated beings save those that flourish in a tropical jungle. They, as the fittest, the best adapted to the changed conditions, would survive.

From *Evolution and Ethics* by Thomas Huxley.

Men in society are undoubtedly subject to the cosmic process. As among other animals, multiplication goes on without cessation, and involves severe competition for the means of support. The struggle for existence tends to eliminate those less fitted to adapt themselves to the circumstances of their existence. The strongest, the most self-assertive, tend to tread down the weaker. But the influence of the cosmic process on the evolution of society is the greater the more rudimentary its civilization. Social progress means a checking of the cosmic process at every step and the substitution for it of another, which may be called the ethical process; the end of which is not the survival of those who may happen to be the fittest, in respect of the whole of the conditions which obtain, but of those who are ethically the best.

As I have already urged, the practice of that which is ethically best —what we call goodness or virtue—involves a course of conduct which, in all respects, is opposed to that which leads to success in the cosmic struggle for existence. In place of ruthless self-assertion it demands self-restraint; in place of thrusting aside, or treading down, all competitors, it requires that the individual shall not merely respect, but shall help his fellows; its influence is directed, not so much to the survival of the fittest, as to the fitting of as many as possible to survive. It repudiates the gladiatorial theory of existence. It demands that each man who enters into the enjoyment of the advantages of a polity shall be mindful of his debt to those who have laboriously constructed it; and shall take heed that no act of his weakens the fabric in which he has been permitted to live. Laws and moral precepts are directed to the end of curbing the cosmic process and reminding the individual of his duty to the community, to the protection and influence of which he owes, if not existence itself, at least the life of something better than a brutal savage.

It is from neglect of these plain considerations that the fanatical individualism of our time attempts to apply the analogy of cosmic nature to society. Once more we have a misapplication of the stoical injunction to follow nature; the duties of the individual to the state are forgotten, and his tendencies to self-assertion are dignified by the name of rights. It is seriously debated whether the members of a community are justified in using their combined strength to constrain one of their number to contribute his share to the maintenance of it; or even to prevent him from doing his best to destroy it. The struggle for existence, which has done such admirable work in cosmic nature, must, it appears, be equally beneficent in the ethical sphere. Yet if that which I have insisted upon is true; if the cosmic process has no sort of relation to moral ends; if the imitation of it by man is inconsistent with the first principles of ethics; what becomes of this surprising theory?

Let us understand, once for all, that the ethical progress of society depends, not on imitating the cosmic process, still less in running away from it, but in combating it. It may seem an audacious proposal thus to pit the microcosm against the macrocosm and to set man to subdue nature to his higher ends; but I venture to think that the great intellectual difference between the ancient times with which we have been occupied and our day, lies in the solid foundation we have acquired for the hope that such an enterprise may meet with a certain measure of success.

The history of civilization details the steps by which men have succeeded in building up an artificial world within the cosmos. Fragile reed as he may be, man, as Pascal says, is a thinking reed: there lies within him a fund of energy, operating intelligently and so far akin to that which pervades the universe, that it is competent to influence and modify the cosmic process. In virtue of his intelligence, the dwarf bends the Titan to his will. In every family, in every polity that has been established, the cosmic process in man has been restrained and otherwise modified by law and custom; in surrounding nature, it has been similarly influenced by the art of the shepherd, the agriculturist, the artisan. As civilization has advanced, so has the extent of this interference increased; until the organized and highly developed sciences and arts of the present day have endowed man with a command over the course of non-human nature greater than that once attributed to the magicians. The most impressive, I might say startling, of these changes have been brought about in the course of the last two centuries; while a right comprehension of the process of life and of the means of influencing its manifestations is only just dawning upon us. We do not yet see our way beyond generalities; and we are befogged by the obtrusion of false analogies and crude anticipations. But Astronomy, Physics, Chemistry, have all had to pass through similar phases, before they reached the stage at which their influence became an important factor in human affairs. Physiology, Psychology, Ethics, Political Science, must submit to the same ordeal. Yet it seems to me irrational to doubt that, at no distant period, they will work as great a revolution in the sphere of practice.

The theory of evolution encourages no millennial anticipations. If, for millions of years, our globe has taken the upward road, yet, some time, the summit will be reached and the downward route will be commenced. The most daring imagination will hardly venture upon the suggestion that the power and the intelligence of man can ever arrest the procession of the great year.

Moreover, the cosmic nature born with us and, to a large extent, necessary for our maintenance, is the outcome of millions of years of severe training, and it would be folly to imagine that a few centuries will suffice to subdue its masterfulness to purely ethical ends. Ethical nature may count upon having to reckon with a tenacious and powerful enemy as long as the world lasts. But, on the other hand, I see no limit to the extent to which intelligence and will, guided by sound principles of investigation, and organized in common effort, may modify the conditions of existence, for a period longer than that now covered by history. And much may be done to change the nature of man himself. The intelligence which has converted the brother of the wolf into the faithful guardian of the flock ought to be able to do something towards curbing the instincts of savagery in civilized men.

But if we may permit ourselves a larger hope of abatement of the essential evil of the world than was possible to those who, in the infancy of exact knowledge, faced the problem of existence more than a score of centuries ago, I deem it an essential condition of the realization of that hope that we should cast aside the notion that the escape from pain and sorrow is the proper object of life.

We have long since emerged from the heroic childhood of our race, when good and evil could be met with the same "frolic welcome"; the attempts to escape from evil, whether Indian or Greek, have ended in flight from the battle-field; it remains to us to throw aside the youthful overconfidence and the no less youthful discouragement of nonage. We are grown men, and must play the man

> strong in will
> To strive, to seek, to find, and not to yield,

cherishing the good that falls in our way, and bearing the evil, in and around us, with stout hearts set on diminishing it. So far, we all may strive in one faith towards one hope:

> It may be that the gulfs will wash us down,
> It may be we shall touch the Happy Isles,
>
> . . . . but something ere the end,
> Some work of noble note may yet be done.

20

E. O. WILSON

Ethics and Sociobiology

Introduction

E. O. Wilson, an eminent biologist, is Frank B. Baird, Jr., Professor of Science and Curator in Entomology at the Museum of Comparative Zoology, Harvard University. His most recent book, *On Human Nature*, has been awarded the Pulitzer Prize for general nonfiction.

It is unfortunate that Wilson's wise and fundamentally sound remarks on evolution and ethics are vitiated by ignorance of moral epistemology. For example, one would not expect a moral view to predict how people would behave, and so it could not be a valid criticism of one that it did not do this. It is not a criticism of the moral view that people *ought* to give to charity that they seldom *do*.

However, it may be that Wilson does not mean quite what he says, and what he does mean is that an ethical view (he uses Rawls's *A Theory of Justice* as an example) cannot be morally evaluated unless we can predict the consequences of its adoption and that the consequences of the adoption of certain views (for example, Rawls's) are not likely to be beneficial. This would be a valid criticism of these views if (a) the effects of the adoption of the view in question *would not* be beneficial and (b) one assumed the truth of utilitarianism, according to which (roughly) the rectitude of various human practices is determined by their effects, good or ill, on the welfare and happiness of humankind. Wilson, throughout his more recent book, constantly evaluates the morality of humankind according to whether its consequences are good or bad.

But this is to adopt a moral view. According to Wilson, however, no

216

moral view can be the product of rational insight. Instead, "ethical philosophers [seem to] intuit the deontological canons of morality by consulting the emotive centres of their own hypothalamic-limbic system."
But if all moral views are irrational, it would follow that utilitarianism,
which is itself a moral view, is just as irrational as any other moral view.
Therefore Wilson is cutting off the branch on which he is sitting.

Although the word is not in Wilson's useful glossary, the hypothalamic-
limbic system determines our emotions. Hence Wilson is suggesting that
one makes moral pronouncements because they appeal to one emotion-
ally, which Wilson thinks shows that our moral views are irrational.

It may be that Wilson thinks that Rawls (in A *Theory of Justice*) can be
used as an example of the way in which philosophers come to moral
conclusions apparently as the result of reasoning, but in fact because they
have evolved to be the kind of animal to whose moral emotions certain
forms of behavior appeal. Rawls held that a society was just if it was the
kind of society which people would choose to live in if they did not know
what their own place in it would be. However, no one knows what society
frail and fallible human beings would choose to live in if they were in
such a situation. That Rawls thinks that they would choose a society
which bears a resemblance to American society (in which he has been
brought up) must be because he himself has been conditioned to approve
of it as a result of countless years of selective adaptation. In other words,
nature has hoodwinked him into cooking his results.

It can be held that it is rational to regard certain things as wrong if it is
useful to humankind that they be regarded as wrong. Hence people like
Wilson could say with a clear conscience that it was wrong to break
promises because, although they thought they had shown that all such
judgments were irrational, they were irrational judgments that it would
be rational for people *to make*. It would be rational to make them if, as it
is, making them was conducive to the welfare of humankind. This view
may not be totally true. But people who, like Wilson and Russell, think
that moral judgments are false or irrational but who at the same time
want to throw out some (but not all) such judgments as being inconducive
to human welfare, need such a view in order to make their theory consistent. According to this view, morality is a delusion to which it is rational
to subscribe in order to obtain ends which are good.

Wilson also seems to think that some kind of relativism has been established (in a survey conducted quite recently by Lawrence Kohlberg) by
empirical investigation. What *has* been established by empirical investigation is that different age groups have different moral attitudes, which,
by itself, does not establish relativism. It would establish relativism only if
these different moral attitudes could not be deduced from one overall
principle (and perhaps not even then); Wilson has adduced no evidence
to show that this is so. Indeed, he produces some evidence that would
tend to show that it is *not* so, for he says that the adolescents' morality is
useful to adolescents whereas their elders' morality is useful to the
elders. This assertion suggests that people have moral principles and
attitudes that are useful to the group to which they belong. The fact that

different beliefs are useful to different groups would no more establish relativism than the fact that water flows in different directions in different places would establish that there was no law of gravity. (The example is Hume's.)

It may sometimes be beneficial to a society for it to contain communities with different moral principles, living side by side. Relativism, however, needs to maintain that these different principles are all *true*, and it is not at all necessary for them to be true in order for their existence to be beneficial. They can also all be true, but constitute no evidence for relativism, because they are not incompatible with one another. A society which contains a race of Xs who think that Xs ought to behave in such-and-such a way, and a race of Ys who think that Ys ought to behave in a different way, does not support relativism because there is no earthly reason it should not be true both that Xs should behave in one way and that Ys behave in another. These two opinions are not remotely incompatible. The trouble starts only when the Xs think that all people, including Ys, should behave in such-and-such a way and the Ys think that all people, including Xs, should behave differently.

Reading

SCIENTISTS AND HUMANISTS should consider together the possibility that the time has come for ethics to be removed temporarily from the hands of the philosophers and biologized. The subject at present consists of several oddly disjunct conceptualizations. The first is *ethical intuitionism*, the belief that the mind has a direct awareness of true right and wrong that it can formalize by logic and translate into rules of social action. The purest guiding precept of secular Western thought has been the theory of the social contract as formulated by Locke, Rousseau, and Kant. In our time the precept has been rewoven into a solid philosophical system by John Rawls.[1] His imperative is that justice should be not merely integral to a system of government but rather the object of the original contract. The principles called by Rawls "justice and fairness" are those which free and rational persons would choose if they were beginning an association from a position of equal advantage and wished to define the fundamental rules of the association. In judging the appropriateness of subsequent laws and behavior, it would be

[1] *A Theory of Justice* (Cambridge, MA: Belknap Press of Harvard University Press, 1971).

necessary to test their conformity to the unchallengeable starting position.

The Achilles heel of the intuitionist position is that it relies on the emotive judgment of the brain as though that organ must be treated as a black box. While few will disagree that justice as fairness is an ideal state for disembodied spirits, the conception is in no way explanatory or predictive with reference to human beings. Consequently, it does not consider the ultimate ecological or genetic consequences of the rigorous prosecution of its conclusions. Perhaps explanation and prediction will not be needed for the millenium. But this is unlikely — the human genotype and the ecosystem in which it evolved were fashioned out of extreme unfairness. In either case the full exploration of the neural machinery of ethical judgment is desirable and already in progress. One such effort, constituting the second mode of conceptualization, can be called *ethical behaviorism*. Its basic proposition, which has been expanded most fully by J. F. Scott,[2] holds that moral commitment is entirely learned, with operant conditioning being the dominant mechanism. In other words, children simply internalize the behavioral norms of the society. Opposing this theory is the *developmental-genetic conception* of ethical behavior. The best-documented version has been provided by Lawrence Kohlberg.[3] Kohlberg's viewpoint is structuralist and specifically Piagetian, and therefore not yet related to the remainder of biology. Piaget has used the expression "genetic epistemology" and Kohlberg "cognitive-developmental" to label the general concept. However, the results will eventually become incorporated into a broadened developmental biology and genetics. Kohlberg's method is to record and classify the verbal responses of children to moral problems. He has delineated six sequential stages of ethical reasoning through which an individual may progress as part of his mental maturation. The child moves from a primary dependence on external controls and sanctions to an increasingly sophisticated set of internalized standards (see table). The analysis has not yet been directed to the question of plasticity in the basic rules. Intracultural variance has not been measured, and heritability therefore not assessed. The difference between ethical behaviorism and the current version of developmental-genetic analysis is that the former postulates a mechanism (operant conditioning) without evidence and the latter presents evidence without postulating a mechanism. No great conceptual difficulty underlies this disparity. The study of moral development

---

[2]*Internalization of Norms: A Sociological Theory of Moral Commitment* (Englewood Cliffs, NJ, 1971).

[3]"Stage and Sequence: the cognitive development approach to socialization theory and research," D. A. Goslin, ed., *Handbook of Socialization Theory and Research* (Chicago: Rand McNally Co., 1969), pp. 347–480.

The classification of moral judgment into levels and stages of development.
(Based on Kohlberg[4])

Level	Basis of moral judgment	Stage of development
I	Moral value is defined by punishment and reward	1. Obedience to rules and authority to void punishment 2. Conformity to obtain rewards and to exchange rewards and to exchange favors
II	Moral value resides in filling the correct roles, in maintaining order and meeting the expectations of others	3. Good-boy orientation: conformity to avoid dislike and rejection by others 4. Duty orientation: conformity to avoid censure by authority, disruption of order, and resulting guilt
III	Moral value resides in conformity to shared standards, rights, and duties	5. Legalistic orientation: recognition of the value of contracts, some arbitrariness in rule formation to maintain the common good 6. Conscience or principle orientation: primary allegiance to principles of choice, which can overrule law in cases where the law is judged to do more harm than good

is only a more complicated and less tractable version of the genetic variance problem. With the accretion of data the two approaches can be expected to merge to form a recognizable exercise in behavioral genetics.

Even if the problem were solved tomorrow, however, an important piece would still be missing. This is the *genetic evolution of ethics.* In the first chapter of this book I argued that ethical philosophers intuit the deontological canons of morality by consulting the emotive centers of their own hypothalamic-limbic system. This is also true of the developmentalists, even when they are being their most severely objective. Only by interpreting the activity of the emotive centers as a biological

---

[4]"Stage and Sequence: The cognitive development approach to socialization theory and research," pp. 347–480.

adaptation can the meaning of the canons be deciphered. Some of the activity is likely to be outdated, a relic of adjustment to the most primitive form of tribal organization. Some of it may prove to be *in statu nascendi*, constituting new and quickly changing adaptations to agrarian and urban life. The resulting confusion will be reinforced by other factors. To the extent that unilaterally altruistic genes have been established in the population by group selection, they will be opposed by allelomorphs favored by individual selection. The conflict of impulses under their various controls is likely to be widespread in the population, since current theory predicts that the genes will be at best maintained in a state of balanced polymorphism. Moral ambivalency will be further intensified by the circumstance that a schedule of sex- and age-dependent ethics can impart higher genetic fitness than a single moral code which is applied uniformly to all sex-age groups. Some of the differences in the Kohlberg stages could be explained in this manner. For example, it should be of selective advantage for young children to be self-centered and relatively disinclined to perform altruistic acts based on personal principle. Similarly, adolescents should be more tightly bound by age-peer bonds within their own sex and hence unusually sensitive to peer approval. The reason is that at this time greater advantage accrues to the formation of alliances and rise in status than later, when sexual and parental morality become the paramount determinants of fitness. Genetically programmed sexual and parent-offspring conflict of the kind predicted by the Trivers models are also likely to promote age differences in the kinds and degrees of moral commitment. Finally, the moral standards of individuals during early phases of colony growth should differ in many details from those of individuals at demographic equilibrium or during episodes of overpopulation. Metapopulations subject to high levels of r extinction[5] will tend to diverge genetically from other kinds of populations in ethical behavior.

If there is any truth to this theory of innate moral pluralism, the requirement for an evolutionary approach to ethics is self-evident. It should also be clear that no single set of moral standards can be applied to all human populations, let alone all sex-age classes within each population. To impose a uniform code is therefore to create complex, intractable moral dilemmas — these, of course, are the current condition of mankind.

---

[5]R extinction is the tendency toward extinction of populations who are struggling to maintain their hold on a new environment. It is presented by such traits as clustering, mutual defense, and cooperative foraging and nest building.

21

MICHAEL RUSE

Evolution and Moral Skepticism

Introduction

Michael Ruse holds the chair in history and philosophy at the University of Guelph (Ontario). He is the author of a number of well-known books on sociobiology and editor of the excellent *Philosophy of Biology* in the *Philosophical Topics Series*.

In this reading he tries to defend intuitionism against an attack by E. O. Wilson. (Intuitionism is the view that we have a rational insight into the truth of certain moral judgments, although it is not contradictory to deny them and although they cannot be established empirically by observation and experiment.) Ruse has, incidentally, changed his views since he wrote this selection. As we have already seen, sociobiology throws doubt on intuitionism, because its study might suggest that current moral beliefs are prevalent not because people intuit them to be rational, but simply because those without these moral beliefs have not survived to tell the tale.

Consider the following comments on Ruse's attempt to defend the rationality of ethics.

1. There is no need for someone believing that our moral beliefs have a sociobiological explanation to be a relativist. It is certainly the case that sociobiological factors will produce different apparent or pseudo-intuitions in different places. But it is also the case, as any sane philosopher would agree, that a mode of action that can be right at one time and place can be wrong at another time and place. Utilitarians, for example, are

nonrelativists to the extent that they believe that at absolutely all times and places people ought to act in such a way as to produce the maximum amount of good. But at the same time, they would be stupid if they did not realize that a kind of action that produced good at one time and place would not necessarily produce it at another.

2. Ruse argues that our biology might just as well deceive us over matters of fact or logic as over morals. But this is not so. Having true beliefs helps the organism that has the belief in question to survive because acting on it leads it to do things that are the correct means to its ends. All false beliefs about matters of fact, mathematics, or logic can cause one to take incorrect means to one's ends, and an organism which produced false beliefs about the means to its ends *would* be impossibly handicapping itself in the struggle for survival. It is not at all obvious, however, that incorrect *moral* beliefs would cause one to take the incorrect means to one's ends. Moral beliefs are not beliefs about the means to ends.

It may be a problem for the view that false beliefs are biologically disadvantageous that *religious* beliefs — or so it seems to some — are an ideal example of *false* beliefs that *do* help their possessors to survive. A partial solution to this problem may be that having false beliefs does not matter if they are about only what will happen to us in another world. (But false beliefs to the effect that what we do in this world will have certain consequences in the next could have very serious consequences in *this* world.)

Furthermore, if religious beliefs are *not* acted on — as some people say — the religious person can gain sustenance and encouragement from having beliefs that are false, without the disadvantages of acting in ways that are *not* conducive to his or her ends.

3. Ruse argues against Wilson that he fails to distinguish reasons from causes. The reader is referred to remarks on this subject in the section on evolution in the Introduction.

Reading

WILSON'S ATTACK ON INTUITIONISM

THERE ARE TWO parts to E. O. Wilson's assault on the problems of ethics, the combined effect of which is an argument concluding that we must accept evolution, its results and its processes, as the good, because in some sense almost by definition that is what the good has to be. At least, I think this is what Wilson's conclusion is, although as I shall show, he is contradictory. The two parts to Wilson's analysis are first an attack on what he takes to be the accepted justification of ethical

From Michael Ruse, "Sociobiology: Sense or Nonsense?" *Episteme* 8, pp. 204–209.
Copyright (©) 1979 by D. Reidel Publishing Company, Dordrecht, Holland.

positions and secondly an affirmation of moral relativism based on the findings of sociobiological theory. Let us take them in turn and see where they lead us.

First Wilson attacks what he sees as the primary philosophical justification offered today for ethical views, namely *intuitionism*, that is "the belief that the mind has a direct awareness of true right and wrong that it can formalize by logic and translate into rules of social action."[1] He is not entirely clear as to what he finds wrong with this position, but the primary fault seems to be that it does not take into account the fact that the organ of intuition is a product of evolution.

> The Achilles heel of the intuitionist position is that it relies on the emotive judgment of the brain as though that organ must be treated as a black box. While few will disagree that justice as fairness is an ideal state for disembodied spirits, the conception is in no way explanatory or predictive with reference to human beings. Consequently, it does not consider the ultimate ecological or genetic consequences of the rigorous prosecution of its conclusions. Perhaps explanation and prediction will not be needed for the millennium. But this is unlikely — the human genotype and the ecosystem in which it evolved were fashioned out of extreme unfairness. In either case the full exploration of the neural machinery of ethical judgment is desirable and already in progress.

One feels still one would like to have spelt out a little more clearly the reason why this should all count against intuitionism, but, reading a little between the lines, presumably the main cause for complaint is that because the brain is a product of evolution, we cannot rely on its perceptions or judgements or what have you in a way that is centrally presupposed by intuitionism. We know that different people have different evolutionary interests. We know, from sociobiology, that people will "see" that which it is in their (evolutionary) interests to see. This seeing or perceiving is not necessarily of the truth. Hence, an ethical intuitionism, that is an ethical belief that we have a direct insight into the moral truth, whether it be that we ought to maximize happiness or that we ought to treat humans as ends, just cannot be accepted. It is all too possible (nay probable) that our genes are deceiving us and filling us full of a glow of having achieved absolute truth. Totally deceived moralists are far more evolutionarily efficient than conscious hypocrites.

I think this is Wilson's position. Certainly it sits well with the moral relativism that we shall see him adopting shortly. And certainly it seems the kind of position that [R. L.] Trivers would support, for he is quite explicit in his belief that because of evolution we cannot trust — ought indeed mistrust — the perceived or intuited "truths" we hold dear:

---

[1] E. O. Wilson, *Sociobiology: The New Synthesis* (Cambridge, MA: Harvard University Press, 1975). p. 562.

" . . . the conventional view that natural selection favours nervous systems which produce ever more accurate images of the world must be a very naive view of mental evolution."[2]

Before turning to examine this argument critically, in fairness to philosophers as a tribe it should perhaps be noted that it is a little strange that they should be saddled with the claim that intuition is the main support of ethical judgements. It is true that in the first part of this century intuitionism was popular, but for nearly fifty years now — indeed from the rise of logical positivism — other meta-ethical theories have found favour with many philosophers. One thinks of emotivism, its descendent prescriptivism, and, more recently, naturalism. Indeed, without necessarily endorsing any one of these positions or, in fact, rejecting intuitionism, on the surface it would seem that intuitionism was a rather unfair choice to show that evolution destroys philosophical justifications of ethics. Actually, another choice might have led entirely to the opposite conclusion, for something like emotivism seems almost tailor-made for the evolutionist. The emotivist, in fact, entirely side-steps the difficulties that the sociobiologists think that evolutionary theory raises for the ethicist. When the emotivist says that one ought to do x, what he or she thinks one is saying is that he or she approves of doing x and "Do thou likewise." The truth-claim refers to one's own personal feelings, and (without wanting to get unduly psychoanalytic) seems to be an introspection the truth of which not even sociobiology can take away from one. And, for the emotivist, the rest of a moral claim is exhortation, which is neither true nor false. In other words, ethical statements for the emotivist cannot involve the possible divorce from reality, which the sociobiologists seem to think can make so suspect philosophical claims about ethics.

But this is all a bit by way of preliminary: By making his case against ethics in terms of intuitionism, Wilson rather strikes me as being like a philosopher who rejects genetics because he or she finds fault with the classical gene concept of T. H. Morgan. However, even against intuitionism the case is not as devastating as all that. At least, I think one can invoke a strong and effective *tu quoque* argument. Every argument which can be made against ethics, can be made against other truth-claiming statements, particularly those of science — and even more particularly those of sociobiology! In other words, using sociobiology to undercut ethics is hopelessly circular. Consider: The supposed problem with ethics is that we get at it only through evolved organs, and unfortunately these might lead us astray because it may well be in our evolutionary interests to be deceived. But, with respect, how do we get to know the facts of science, or of mathematics, or of logic, other than through organs that have evolved through natural selection? Of course

---

[2]Richard Dawkins, *The Selfish Gene* (Oxford University Press, 1976), p. vi.

one might argue that these organs would not deceive one, but that surely is to assume the whole point! If they are deceiving us, then because we use these very organs to understand them, they will fill us with confidence about their veracity.

Nor can it be argued that biology shows that deception would come only over matters of morals and not over matters of science and logic. It is clear that our science and our logic are just as much of adaptive value as is our ethics, and so deception is possible. Moreover, if one argues that a mark of possible divorce from reality is a chopping and changing of minds (not possible if one is tuned right into the truth), and since morality seems so changeable this shows ethics not absolutely true, I would suggest that science seems no less changeable — for all that the science of the day seems so overwhelmingly certain. Compared to the two-thousand-year Christian code, astronomy seems positively fickle. One can still follow Socrates in ethics; one would look a bit silly following Ptolemy in astronomy. Finally, if it be argued that ethics cannot be intuited because different people arrive at different conclusions — children and idiots, for instance, have trouble with understanding morality — exactly the same argument can be brought against science. My small children, for example, certainly have at least as much of a grasp of the differences between right and wrong as they do of the principles of modern physics.

In short, the case against intuitionism does not succeed. One might, of course, conclude that what the above argument shows is not that intuition is infallible but that all of our knowledge is fallible, in which case, presumably, one has to adopt some sort of pragmatic attitude, arguing that one assumes what works for the time being. But even here, ethics is no worse off than anything else, and one certainly cannot use science against it. Simply speaking, what has gone wrong with the sociobiological argument at this point is that a confusion has been made between *causes* and *reasons*. It is more than likely that we have ethics and a moral sense because of evolution, that is through evolutionary causes. This does not mean that the reasons, the justification of ethics, are evolutionary, any more than the fact that we have science and mathematics because of evolved organs means that the reasons for the principles of science and mathematics are evolutionary.

Wilson's Moral Relativism

We come now to the second part of Wilson's argument. Having supposedly disposed of philosophers' justifications of ethics, he argues that different people have different evolutionary interests and thus we are stuck with a total moral relativism. Sociobiology shows that different people, young and old, female and male, have different evolutionary interests. But:

> If there is any truth to this theory of innate moral pluralism, the requirement for an evolutionary approach to ethics is self-evident. It should also be clear that no single set of moral standards can be applied to all human populations, let alone all sex-age classes with each population. To impose a uniform code is therefore to create complex, intractable moral dilemmas — these, of course, are the current condition of mankind.[3]

Fortunately, this appalling conclusion is no more well-taken than Wilson's previous conclusion about intuitionism. For a start, given his previous argument, Wilson has absolutely no right to talk of "moral pluralism," or moral anything else for that matter. If, as I understand him to think he has done, he has negated philosophical (or other rational) justifications of ethics, then all we are left with are organisms with different, clashing, evolutionary strategies. The only difference between the human case and any animal case is that humans lay over their strategies this layer of beliefs that there are genuine moral standards. But, essentially, that is, from the viewpoint of the logic of morals, humans are no different from the animals: there is no "real" morality.

However, if this is so, then Wilson ought not talk about moral pluralism. A pluralism of desires maybe; but when did a desire automatically have moral force? I want the chocolate cake. My sister wants the chocolate cake. There is no question of morality here. We certainly do not need to invoke a theory of moral pluralism. The only way in which we could achieve such a conclusion in Wilson's case is if we were to argue that, traditional arguments for morality having collapsed, we are therefore entitled to define morality as that which is in the interests of an evolutionary strategy. But this is at best a stipulative definition, and should not be presented as the outcome of an analysis of how we do and ought properly to use the world "moral."

The second point about Wilson's argument is that there is a conflation between different levels, of a kind noted more than once already in this book. We, or more precisely although metaphorically, our genes, have different evolutionary strategies. But as we know full well, at the phenotypic level, which gets us to the level of actual desires, of culture generally and of moral beliefs particularly, we do not necessarily have a plurality of wants (which Wilson's argument presupposes). Indeed, what we find is that although people have different evolutionary strategies, even manifesting different desires, they tend to share the same moral code. In other words, in another sense they want the same thing.

Consider: I expect most heterosexual men have felt as I do occasionally that there is some particular woman that they find sexually attractive and that they would really like to go to bed with. Now, from a biological viewpoint, this is all to my interest. If I can carry out my desires then I may well impregnate yet another female and thus pass on

[3]*Sociobiology: The New Synthesis*, p. 564.

yet more genes (assuming that the foetus is not aborted, and so forth). And yet, without wanting to appear unduly burdened with a moral sense, I think I can genuinely say that because of my moral beliefs there are times when I have even stronger wants not to have intercourse with a woman toward whom I feel a strong sexual urge: suppose, for example, that she is a married woman and that if her infidelity were discovered it would cause great hurt to her whole family, including herself. The conclusion from such a case seems to be that although we may all have different evolutionary strategies, we may all want the same moral code — even those of us who break it! Hence, even our desires do not necessarily commit us to a moral pluralism.

Finally, in case it is objected that people do not all share the same moral code and that the differences may well represent different genetic backgrounds as the results of different evolutionary forces, I would suggest that this problem may well be overcome by drawing a distinction between different levels of a moral code. Suppose it is pointed out that, in the West, we practice monogamy and that this is backed by moral sanctions (at least, it used to be!); but that some societies practice polyandry, several husbands with one wife, where this is considered ethically acceptable if not obligatory. Suppose also that this is offered as evidence for moral relativism, and that this were backed by pointing to Alexander's[4] explanation of polyandry in terms of parental manipulation. One can still argue — indeed, I would argue — that all of these different marital practices can be fitted under a higher common rubric, namely that all people ought to have a chance to get married. And this rubric, in turn, fits under a totally universal Kantian or utilitarian ethic: that people not just be means (e.g. sex objects for other's gratification) and have the opportunity for maximum happiness, they ought to have the opportunity of long-term relationships with a partner (this is not to imply that this ought to be obligatory or that it is what everyone would want). Hence, because different situations have different needs, all does not collapse into a morass of relativism.

Wilson's arguments therefore do not work. This is perhaps just as well, for he himself blithely ignores his conclusions as soon as he has drawn them, arguing quite inconsistently that our present existential predicament demands that we start planning for the good of the whole, putting aside selfishness. Of course, what one might argue, and what I myself have indeed argued, is that although human culture as it presently stands is both a product of evolution and, in some general sense, biologically adaptive, it gives us the power to transcend our biology in certain respects. This means that we are no longer helpless pawns of

---

[4]"The Evolution of Social Behavior," *Annual Review of Ecology and Systematics*. Vol. 5 (1974).

our biology, but can act morally even though our basic desires drive us in other ways. Thus, suppose we accept (what I do not accept) that biologically, in some absolute way, men are dominant over women, this is not to deny that we have reached the point where our culture enables us to alter this state: that by freeing women from childbearing and so forth, we can now direct women into equal power with men. However, even if one argues this way, or rather because one can argue this way, Wilson's pluralistic selfish moral relativism fails. And the same holds if one tries related tactics, arguing for example as Alexander[5] does sometimes, that we humans have now got to the point where our selfish interests and group interests coincide. There is nothing to stop us from consistently accepting human sociobiology and rejecting moral relativism.

[5]"The Search for an Evolutionary Philosophy," Proceedings of the Royal Society of Victoria, Vol. 84, 1971.

22

RICHARD DAWKINS

You Scratch My Back, and I'll Ride on Yours

Introduction

Richard Dawkins is a fellow of New College, Oxford, and the author of the deservedly well-known *The Selfish Gene* and *The Blind Watchmaker*.

In this reading, Dawkins envisages a group of birds that can survive satisfactorily only if they (altruistically) pick debilitating ticks off one another's heads. Birds that (not knowing their Kant) did not pick the ticks off other birds' heads, but nevertheless allowed other birds to do this to them would save time and energy. Hence they would survive at other birds' expense and pass on the lack of altruism to their offspring. But if *all* birds were to become highly rational and decided to benefit from having other birds pick ticks off their heads, without wasting time and energy on reciprocation, all birds would have ticks. They would become diseased and miserable and eventually perish.

Although a society of birds in which *none* picked ticks off other birds would be temporarily *unhappy*, and permanently extinct, a society of birds whose entire population picked ticks off one another's heads would be unstable. This is because they would be vulnerable to any bird and its offspring that might by some chance mutation come to be born without this tendency. Dawkins believes that a stable and advantageous state would eventually be reached whenever all or almost all birds picked ticks off other birds' heads only so long as their tick picking was reciprocated.

Reflecting on this example reinforces the earlier suggestion that one function of moral sentiment in human society is to encourage the belief that altruism is necessary for cooperation. Perhaps birds pick the ticks off other birds from an altruistic love of bird-kind or because they like the taste. But if they felt guilty if they did *not* pick the ticks off other birds, the beneficial effect would be the same.

Although Dawkins's book is called *The Selfish Gene* — selfish in only a metaphorical sense — it does not at all follow from anything he says that all human motivation is selfish. It may be that we are altruistic because altruism is conducive to the survival of our own genes rather than to other genes of the species *homo sapiens*. But from this it no more follows that altruism is not a disinterested desire for the welfare of others than it follows, from the fact that hunger is *conducive* to the survival of our genes, that hunger is a *desire for* the survival of our genes.

Reading

SEVERAL SPECIES OF ants in the New World, and, quite independently, termites in Africa, cultivate "fungus gardens." The best known are the so-called parasol ants of South America. These are immensely successful. Single colonies with more than two million individuals have been found. Their nests consist of huge spreading underground complexes of passages and galleries going down to a depth of ten feet or more, made by the excavation of as much as 40 tons of soil. The underground chambers contain the fungus gardens. The ants deliberately sow fungus of a particular species in special compost beds which they prepare by chewing leaves into fragments. Instead of foraging directly for their own food, the workers forage for leaves to make compost. The "appetite" of a colony of parasol ants for leaves is gargantuan. This makes them a major economic pest, but the leaves are not food for themselves but food for their fungi. The ants eventually harvest and eat the fungi and feed them to their brood. The fungi are more efficient at breaking down leaf material than the ants' own stomachs would be, which is how the ants benefit by the arrangement. It is possible that the fungi benefit too, even though they are cropped: the ants propagate them more efficiently than their own spore dispersal mechanism might achieve. Furthermore, the ants "weed" the fungus gardens, keeping them clear of alien species of fungi. By removing competition, this may benefit the ants' own domestic fungi. A kind of relationship of mutual altruism could be said to exist between ants and fungi. It is remarkable that a very similar system of fungus-farming has evolved independently, among the quite unrelated termites.

From *The Selfish Gene* by Richard Dawkins, pp. 194–202, Oxford University Press, 1976. Reprinted by permission of Oxford University Press.

Ants have their own domestic animals as well as their crop plants. Aphids — greenfly and similar bugs — are highly specialized for sucking the juice out of plants. They pump the sap up out of the plants' veins more efficiently than they subsequently digest it. The result is that they excrete a liquid which has had only some of its nutritious value extracted. Droplets of sugar-rich "honeydew" pass out of the back end at a great rate, in some cases more than the insect's own body-weight every hour. The honeydew normally rains down on to the ground — it may well have been the providential food known as "manna" in the Old Testament. But ants of several species intercept it as soon as it leaves the bug. The ants "milk" the aphids by stroking their hindquarters with their feelers and legs. Aphids respond to this, in some cases apparently holding back their droplets until an ant strokes them, and even withdrawing a droplet if an ant is not ready to accept it. It has been suggested that some aphids have evolved a backside which looks and feels like an ant's face, the better to attract ants. What the aphids have to gain from the relationship is apparently protection from their natural enemies. Like our own dairy cattle they lead a sheltered life, and aphid species which are much cultivated by ants have lost their normal defensive mechanisms. In some cases ants care for the aphid eggs inside their own underground nests, feed the young aphids, and finally, when they are grown, gently carry them up to the protected grazing grounds.

A relationship of mutual benefit between members of different species is called mutualism or symbiosis. Members of different species often have much to offer each other because they can bring different "skills" to the partnership. This kind of fundamental asymmetry can lead to evolutionarily stable strategies of mutual cooperation. Aphids have the right sort of mouthparts for pumping up plant sap, but such sucking mouthparts are no good for self-defence. Ants are no good at sucking sap from plants, but they are good at fighting. Ant genes for cultivating and protecting aphids have been favoured in ant gene-pools. Aphid genes for cooperating with the ants have been favoured in aphid gene-pools.

Symbiotic relationships of mutual benefit are common among animals and plants. A lichen appears superficially to be an individual plant like any other. But it is really an intimate symbiotic union between a fungus and a green alga. Neither partner could live without the other. If their union had become just a bit more intimate we would no longer have been able to tell that a lichen was a double organism at all. Perhaps then there are other double or multiple organisms which we have not recognized as such. Perhaps even we ourselves?

Within each one of our cells there are numerous tiny bodies called mitochondria. The mitochondria are chemical factories, responsible for providing most of the energy we need. If we lost our mitochondria we would be dead within seconds. Recently it has been plausibly argued that mitochondria are, in origin, symbiotic bacteria who joined forces with our type of cell very early in evolution. Similar suggestions have been made for other small bodies within our cells. This is one of those revolutionary ideas which it takes time to get used to, but it is an idea whose time has come. I speculate that we shall come to accept the more radical idea that each one of our genes is a symbiotic unit. We are gigantic colonies of symbiotic genes. One cannot really speak of "evidence" for this idea, but, as I tried to suggest in earlier chapters, it is really inherent in the very way we think about how genes work in sexual species. The other side of this coin is that viruses may be genes who have broken loose from "colonies" such as ourselves. Viruses consist of pure DNA (or a related self-replicating molecule) surrounded by a protein jacket. They are all parasitic. The suggestion is that they have evolved from "rebel" genes who escaped, and now travel from body to body directly through the air, rather than via the more conventional vehicles — sperms and eggs. If this is true, we might just as well regard ourselves as colonies of viruses! Some of them cooperate symbiotically, and travel from body to body in sperms and eggs. These are the conventional "genes." Others live parasitically, and travel by whatever means they can. If the parasitic DNA travels in sperms and eggs, it perhaps forms the "paradoxical" surplus of DNA which I mentioned in Chapter 3. If it travels through the air, or by other direct means, it is called "virus" in the usual sense.

But these are speculations for the future. At present we are concerned with symbiosis at the higher level of relationships between many-celled organisms, rather than within them. The word symbiosis is conventionally used for associations between members of different species. But, now that we have eschewed the "good of the species" view of evolution, there seems no logical reason to distinguish associations between members of different species as things apart from associations between members of the same species. In general, associations of mutual benefit will evolve if each partner can get more out than he puts in. This is true whether we are speaking of members of the same hyena pack, or of widely distinct creatures such as ants and aphids, or bees and flowers. In practice it may be difficult to distinguish cases of genuine two-way mutual benefit from cases of one-sided exploitation.

The evolution of associations of mutual benefit is theoretically easy to imagine if the favours are given and received simultaneously, as in the case of the partners who make up a lichen. But problems arise if there is a delay between the giving of a favour and its repayment. This is because the first recipient of a favour may be tempted to cheat and refuse to pay it back when his turn comes. The resolution of this problem is interesting and is worth discussing in detail. I can do this best in terms of a hypothetical example.

Suppose a species of bird is parasitized by a particularly nasty kind of tick which carries a dangerous disease. It is very important that these ticks should be removed as soon as possible. Normally an individual bird can pull off its own ticks when preening itself. There is one place, however — the top of the head — which it cannot reach with its own bill. The solution to the problem quickly occurs to any human. An individual may not be able to reach his own head, but nothing is easier than for a friend to do it for him. Later, when the friend is parasitized himself, the good deed can be paid back. Mutual grooming is in fact very common in both birds and mammals.

This makes immediate intuitive sense. Anybody with conscious foresight can see that it is sensible to enter into mutual back-scratching arrangements. But we have learnt to beware of what seems intuitively sensible. The gene has no foresight. Can the theory of selfish genes account for mutual back-scratching, or "reciprocal altruism," where there is a delay between good deed and repayment? Williams briefly discussed the problem in his 1966 book, to which I have already referred. He concluded, as had Darwin, that delayed reciprocal altruism can evolve in species which are capable of recognizing and remembering each other as individuals. Trivers, in 1971, took the matter further. When he wrote, he did not have available to him Maynard Smith's concept of the evolutionarily stable strategy. If he had, my guess is that he would have made use of it, for it provides a natural way to express his ideas. His reference to the "prisoner's dilemma" — a favourite puzzle in Game Theory — shows that he was already thinking along the same lines.

Suppose B has a parasite on the top of his head. A pulls it off him. Later, the time comes when A has a parasite on his head. He naturally seeks out B in order that B may pay back his good deed. B simply turns up his nose and walks off. B is a cheat, an individual who accepts the benefit of other individuals' altruism, but who does not pay it back, or who pays it back insufficiently. Cheats do better than indiscriminate altruists because they gain the benefits without paying the costs. To be sure, the cost of grooming another individual's head seems small compared with the benefit of having a dangerous parasite removed, but it is not negligible. Some valuable energy and time has to be spent.

Let the population consist of individuals who adopt one of two strategies. As in Maynard Smith's analyses, we are not talking about conscious strategies, but about unconscious behaviour programs laid down by genes. Call the two strategies Sucker and Cheat. Suckers groom anybody who needs it, indiscriminately cheats accept altruism from suckers, but they never groom anybody else, not even somebody who has previously groomed them. As in the case of the hawks and doves, we arbitrarily assign pay-off points. It does not matter what the exact values are, so long as the benefit of being groomed exceeds the cost of grooming. If the incidence of parasites is high, any individual sucker in a population of suckers can reckon on being groomed about as often as he grooms. The average pay-off for a sucker among suckers is therefore positive. They all do quite nicely in fact, and the word sucker seems inappropriate. But now suppose a cheat arises in the population. Being the only cheat, he can count on being groomed by everybody else, but he pays nothing in return. His average pay-off is better than the average for a sucker. Cheat genes will therefore start to spread through the population. Sucker genes will soon be driven to extinction. This is because, no matter what the ratio in the population, cheats will always do better than suckers. For instance, consider the case when the population consists of 50 per cent suckers and 50 per cent cheats. The average pay-off for both suckers and cheats will be less than that for any individual in a population of 100 per cent suckers. But still, cheats will be doing better than suckers because they are getting all the benefits —such as they are— and paying nothing back. When the proportion of cheats reaches 90 per cent, the average pay-off for all individuals will be very low: many of both types may by now be dying of the infection carried by the ticks. But still the cheats will be doing better than the suckers. Even if the whole population declines toward extinction, there will never be any time when suckers do better than cheats. Therefore, as long as we consider only these two strategies, nothing can stop the extinction of the suckers and, very probably, the extinction of the whole population too.

But now, suppose there is a third strategy called Grudger. Grudgers groom strangers and individuals who have previously groomed them. However, if any individual cheats them, they remember the incident and bear a grudge: they refuse to groom that individual in the future. In a population of grudgers and suckers it is impossible to tell which is which. Both types behave altruistically towards everybody else, and both earn an equal and high average pay-off. In a population consisting largely of cheats, a single grudger would not be very successful. He would expend a great deal of energy grooming most of the individuals he met—for it would take time for him to build up grudges against all of them. On the other hand, nobody would groom him in return. If grudgers are rare in comparison with cheats, the grudger gene will go extinct. Once the grudgers manage to build up in numbers so that they reach a critical proportion, however, their chance of meeting each other becomes sufficiently great to off-set their wasted effort in grooming cheats. When this critical proportion is reached they will start to average a higher pay-off than cheats, and the cheats will be driven at an accelerating rate towards extinction. When the cheats are nearly extinct their rate of decline will become slower, and they may survive as a minority for quite a long time. This is because for any one rare cheat there is only a small chance of his encountering the same grudger twice: therefore the proportion of individuals in the population who bear a grudge against any given cheat will be small.

I have told the story of these strategies as though it were intuitively obvious what would happen. In fact it is not all that obvious, and I did take the precaution of simulating it on a computer to check that intuition was right. Grudger does indeed turn out to be an evolutionarily stable strategy against sucker and cheat, in the sense that, in a population consisting largely of grudgers, neither cheat nor sucker will invade. Cheat is also an ESS, however, because a population consisting largely of cheats will not be invaded by either grudger or sucker. A population could sit at either of these two ESSs. In the long term it might flip from one to the other. Depending on the exact values of the pay-offs — the assumptions in the simulation were of course completely arbitrary — one or other of the two stable states will have a larger "zone of attraction" and will be more likely to be attained. Note incidentally that, although a population of cheats may be more likely to go extinct than a population of grudgers, this in no way affects its status as an ESS. If a population arrives at an ESS which drives it extinct, then it goes extinct, and that is just too bad.

It is quite entertaining to watch a computer simulation which starts with a strong majority of suckers, a minority of grudgers which is just about the critical frequency, and about the same-sized minority of cheats. The first thing that happens is a dramatic crash in the population of suckers as the cheats ruthlessly exploit them. The cheats enjoy a soaring population explosion, reaching their peak just as the last sucker perishes. But the cheats still have the grudgers to reckon with. During the precipitous decline of the suckers, the grudgers have been slowly decreasing in numbers, taking a battering from the prospering cheats, but just managing to hold their own. After the last sucker has gone and the cheats can no longer get away with selfish exploitation so easily, the grudgers slowly begin to increase at the cheats' expense. Steadily their population rise gathers momentum. It accelerates steeply, the cheat population crashes to near extinction, then levels out as they enjoy the privileges of rarity and the comparative freedom from grudges which this brings. However, slowly and inexorably the cheats are driven out of existence, and the grudgers are left in sole possession. Paradoxically, the presence of the suckers actually endangered the grudgers early on in the story because they were responsible for the temporary prosperity of the cheats.

By the way, my hypothetical example about the dangers of not being groomed is quite plausible. Mice kept in isolation tend to develop unpleasant sores on those parts of their heads which they cannot reach. In one study, mice kept in groups did not suffer in this way, because they licked each others' heads. It would be interesting to test the theory of reciprocal altruism experimentally and it seems that mice might be suitable subjects for the work.

Trivers discusses the remarkable symbiosis of the cleaner-fish. Some fifty species, including small fish and shrimps, are known to make their living by picking parasites off the surface of larger fish of other species. The large fish obviously benefit from being cleaned, and the cleaners get a good supply of food. The relationship is symbiotic. In many cases the large fish open their mouths and allow cleaners right inside to pick their teeth, and then to swim out through the gills which they also clean. One might expect that a large fish would craftily wait until he had been thoroughly cleaned, and then gobble up the cleaner. Yet instead he usually lets the cleaner swim off unmolested. This is a considerable feat of apparent altruism because in many cases the cleaner is of the same size as the large fish's normal prey.

Cleaner-fish have special stripy patterns and special dancing displays which label them as cleaners. Large fish tend to refrain from eating small fish who have the right kind of stripes, and who approach them with the right kind of dance. Instead they go into a trance-like state and allow the cleaner free access to their exterior and interior. Selfish genes being what they are, it is not surprising that ruthless, exploiting cheats have cashed in. There are species of small fish that look just like cleaners and dance in the same kind of way in order to secure safe conduct into the vicinity of large fish. When the large fish has gone into its expectant trance the cheat, instead of pulling off a parasite, bites a chunk out of the large fish's fin and beats a hasty retreat. But in spite of the cheats, the relationship between fish cleaners and their clients is mainly amicable and stable. The profession of cleaner plays an important part in the daily life of the coral reef community. Each cleaner has his own territory, and large fish have been seen queuing up for attention like customers at a barber's shop. It is probably this site-tenacity which makes possible the evolution of delayed reciprocal-altruism in this case. The benefit to a large fish of being able to return repeatedly to the same "barber's shop," rather than continually searching for a new one, must outweigh the cost of refraining from eating the cleaner. Since cleaners are small, this is not hard to believe. The presence of cheating cleaner-mimics probably indirectly endangers the bona-fide cleaners by setting up a minor pressure on large fish to eat stripy dancers. Site-tenacity on the part of genuine cleaners enables customers to find them and to avoid cheats.

A long memory and a capacity for individual recognition are well developed in man. We might therefore expect reciprocal altruism to have played an important part in human evolution. Trivers goes so far as to suggest that many of our psychological characteristics — envy, guilt, gratitude, sympathy, etc. — have been shaped by natural selection for improved ability to cheat, to detect cheats, and to avoid being thought to be a cheat. Of particular interest are "subtle cheats" who appear to be reciprocating, but who consistently pay back slightly less than they receive. It is even possible that man's swollen brain, and his predisposition to reason mathematically, evolved as a mechanism of ever more devious cheating, and ever more penetrating detection of cheating in others. Money is a formal token of delayed reciprocal altruism.

There is no end to the fascinating speculation which the idea of reciprocal altruism engenders when we apply it to our own species. Tempting as it is, I am no better at such speculation than the next man, and I leave the reader to entertain himself.

PART VII

MORAL BELIEFS IMPOSSIBLE TO JUSTIFY

23

A. J. AYER

∽☯∾

Critique of Ethics

∽☯∾

Introduction

For a critical discussion of the emotive theory of ethics, exemplified by this highly influential selection, see pp. 31–36 of the Introduction.

Reading

THERE IS STILL one objection to be met before we can claim to have justified our view that all synthetic propositions are empirical hypotheses. This objection is based on the common supposition that our speculative knowledge is of two distinct kinds — that which relates to questions of empirical fact, and that which relates to questions of value. It will be said that "statements of value" are genuine synthetic propositions, but that they cannot with any show of justice be represented by hypotheses, which are used to predict the course of our sensations; and, accordingly, that the existence of ethics and æsthetics as branches of speculative knowledge presents an insuperable objection to our radical empiricist thesis.

In face of this objection, it is our business to give an account of "judgements of value" which is both satisfactory in itself and consistent with our general empiricist principles. We shall set ourselves to show that in so far as statements of value are significant, they are ordinary "scientific" statements; and that in so far as they are not scientific, they are not in the literal sense significant, but are simply expressions of

From Sir Alfred Ayer, *Language, Truth and Logic* (London: Victor Gollancz, Ltd., 1947). Reprinted by kind permission of the author and Victor Gollancz, Ltd.

emotion which can be neither true nor false. In maintaining this view, we may confine ourselves for the present to the case of ethical statements. What is said about them will be found to apply, *mutatis mutandis*, to the case of æsthetic statements also.

The ordinary system of ethics, as elaborated in the works of ethical philosophers, is very far from being a homogeneous whole. Not only is it apt to contain pieces of metaphysics, and analyses of non-ethical concepts: its actual ethical contents are themselves of very different kinds. We may divide them, indeed, into four main classes. There are, first of all, propositions which express definitions of ethical terms, or judgements about the legitimacy or possibility of certain definitions. Secondly, there are propositions describing the phenomena of moral experience, and their causes. Thirdly, there are exhortations to moral virtue. And, lastly, there are actual ethical judgements. It is unfortunately the case that the distinction between these four classes, plain as it is, is commonly ignored by ethical philosophers; with the result that it is often very difficult to tell from their works what it is that they are seeking to discover or prove.

In fact, it is easy to see that only the first of our four classes, namely that which comprises the propositions relating to the definitions of ethical terms, can be said to constitute ethical philosophy. The propositions which describe the phenomena of moral experience, and their causes, must be assigned to the science of psychology, or sociology. The exhortations to moral virtue are not propositions at all, but ejaculations or commands which are designed to provoke the reader to action of a certain sort. Accordingly, they do not belong to any branch of philosophy or science. As for the expressions of ethical judgements, we have not yet determined how they should be classified. But inasmuch as they are certainly neither definitions nor comments upon definitions, nor quotations, we may say decisively that they do not belong to ethical philosophy. A strictly philosophical treatise on ethics should therefore make no ethical pronouncements. But it should, by giving an analysis of ethical terms, show what is the category to which all such pronouncements belong. And this is what we are now about to do.

A question which is often discussed by ethical philosophers is whether it is possible to find definitions which would reduce all ethical terms to one or two fundamental terms. But this question, though it undeniably belongs to ethical philosophy, is not relevant to our present enquiry. We are not now concerned to discover which term, within the sphere of ethical terms, is to be taken as fundamental; whether, for example, "good," can be defined in terms of "right" or "right" in terms of "good," or both in terms of "value." What we are interested in is the possibility of reducing the whole sphere of ethical terms to non-ethical terms. We are enquiring whether statements of ethical value can be translated into statements of empirical fact.

That they can be so translated is the contention of those ethical philosophers who are commonly called subjectivists, and of those who are known as utilitarians. For the utilitarian defines the rightness of actions, and the goodness of ends, in terms of the pleasure, or happiness, or satisfaction, to which they give rise; the subjectivist, in terms of the feelings of approval which a certain person, or group of people, has towards them. Each of these types of definition makes moral judgements into a sub-class or psychological or sociological judgements; and for this reason they are very attractive to us. For, if either was correct, it would follow that ethical assertions were not generically different from the factual assertions which are ordinarily contrasted with them; and the account which we have already given of empirical hypotheses would apply to them also.

Nevertheless we shall not adopt either a subjectivist or a utilitarian analysis of ethical terms. We reject the subjectivist view that to call an action right, or a thing good, is to say that it is generally approved of, because it is not self-contradictory to assert that some actions which are generally approved of are not right, or that some things which are generally approved of are not good. And we reject the alternative subjectivist view that a man who asserts that a certain action is right, or that a certain thing is good, is saying that he himself approves of it, on the ground that a man who confessed that he sometimes approved of what was bad or wrong would not be contradicting himself. And a similar argument is fatal to utilitarianism. We cannot agree that to call an action right is to say that of all the actions possible in the circumstances it would cause, or be likely to cause, the greatest happiness, or the greatest balance of pleasure over pain, or the greatest balance of satisfied over unsatisfied desire, because we find that it is not self-contradictory to say that it is sometimes wrong to perform the action which would actually or probably cause the greatest happiness, or the greatest balance of pleasure over pain, or of satisfied over unsatisfied desire. And since it is not self-contradictory to say that some pleasant things are not good, or that some bad things are desired, it cannot be the case that the sentence "x is good" is equivalent to "x is pleasant," or to "x is desired." And to every other variant of utilitarianism with which I am acquainted the same objection can be made. And therefore we should, I think, conclude that the validity of ethical judgements is not determined by the felicific tendencies of actions, any more than by the nature of people's feelings; but that it must be regarded as "absolute" or "intrinsic," and not empirically calculable.

If we say this, we are not, of course, denying that it is possible to invent a language in which all ethical symbols are definable in non-ethical terms, or even that it is desirable to invent such a language and adopt it in place of our own; what we are denying is that the suggested reduction of ethical to non-ethical statements is consistent with the conventions of our actual language. That is, we reject utilitarianism and subjectivism, not as proposals to replace our existing ethical notions by new ones, but as analyses of our existing ethical notions. Our contention is simply that, in our language, sentences which contain normative ethical symbols are not equivalent to sentences which express psychological propositions, or indeed empirical propositions of any kind.

It is advisable here to make it plain that it is only normative ethical symbols, and not descriptive ethical symbols, that are held by us to be indefinable in factual terms. There is a danger of confusing these two types of symbols, because they are commonly constituted by signs of the same sensible form. Thus a complex sign of the form "x is wrong" may constitute a sentence which expresses a moral judgement concerning a certain type of conduct, or it may constitute a sentence which states that a certain type of conduct is repugnant to the moral sense of a particular society. In the latter case, the symbol "wrong" is a descriptive ethical symbol, and the sentence in which it occurs expresses an ordinary sociological proposition; in the former case, the symbol "wrong" is a normative ethical symbol, and the sentence in which it occurs does not, we maintain, express an empirical proposition at all. It is only with normative ethics that we are at present concerned; so that whenever ethical symbols are used in the course of this argument without qualification, they are always to be interpreted as symbols of the normative type.

In admitting that normative ethical concepts are irreducible to empirical concepts, we seem to be leaving the way clear for the "absolutist" view of ethics — that is, the view that statements of value are not controlled by observation, as ordinary empirical propositions are, but only by a mysterious "intellectual intuition." A feature of this theory, which is seldom recognized by its advocates, is that it makes statements of value unverifiable. For it is notorious that what seems intuitively certain to one person may seem doubtful, or even false, to another. So that unless it is possible to provide some criterion by which one may decide between conflicting intuitions, a mere appeal to intuition is worthless as a test of a proposition's validity. But in the case of moral judgements, no such criterion can be given. Some moralists claim to settle the matter by saying that they "know" that their own moral judgements are correct. But such an assertion is of purely psychological interest, and has not the slightest tendency to prove the validity of any moral judgement. For dissentient moralists may equally well "know" that their ethical views are correct. And, as far as subjective certainty goes, there will be nothing to choose between them. When such differences of opinion arise in connection with an ordinary empirical proposition, one may attempt to resolve them by referring to, or actually carrying out, some relevant empirical test. But with regard to ethical statements, there is, on the "absolutist" or "intuitionist" theory, no relevant empirical test. We are therefore justified in saying that on this theory ethical statements are held to be unverifiable. They are, of course, also held to be genuine synthetic propositions.

Considering the use which we have made of the principle that a synthetic proposition is significant only if it is empirically verifiable, it is clear that the acceptance of an "absolutist" theory of ethics would undermine the whole of our main argument. And as we have already rejected the "naturalistic" theories which are commonly supposed to provide the only alternative to "absolutism" in ethics, we seem to have reached a difficult position. We shall meet the difficulty by showing that the correct treatment of ethical statements is afforded by a third theory, which is wholly compatible with our radical empiricism.

We begin by admitting that the fundamental ethical concepts are unanalysable, inasmuch as there is no criterion by which one can test the validity of the judgements in which they occur. So far we are in agreement with the absolutists. But, unlike the absolutists, we are able to give an explanation of this fact about ethical concepts. We say that the reason why they are unanalysable is that they are mere pseudo-concepts. The presence of an ethical symbol in a proposition adds nothing to its factual content. Thus if I say to someone, "You acted wrongly in stealing that money," I am not stating anything more than if I had simply said, "You stole that money." In adding that this action is wrong I am not making any further statement about it. I am simply evincing my moral disapproval of it. It is as if I had said, "You stole that money," in a peculiar tone of horror, or written it with the addition of some special exclamation marks. The tone, or the exclamation marks, adds nothing to the literal meaning of the sentence. It merely serves to show that the expression of it is attended by certain feelings in the speaker.

If now I generalise my previous statement and say, "Stealing money is wrong," I produce a sentence which has no factual meaning—that is, expresses no proposition which can be either true or false. It is as if I had written "Stealing money!!"—where the shape and thickness of the exclamation marks show, by a suitable convention, that a special sort of moral disapproval is the feeling which is being expressed. It is clear that there is nothing said here which can be true or false. Another man may disagree with me about the wrongness of stealing, in the sense that he may not have the same feelings about stealing as I have, and he may quarrel with me on account of my moral sentiments. But he cannot, strictly speaking, contradict me. For in saying that a certain type of action is right or wrong, I am not making any factual statement, not even a statement about my own state of mind. I am merely expressing certain moral sentiments. And the man who is ostensibly contradicting me is merely expressing his moral sentiments. So that there is plainly no sense in asking which of us is in the right. For neither of us is asserting a genuine proposition.

What we have just been saying about the symbol "wrong" applies to all normative ethical symbols. Sometimes they occur in sentences which record ordinary empirical facts besides expressing ethical feeling about those facts: sometimes they occur in sentences which simply express ethical feeling about a certain type of action, or situation, without making any statement of fact. But in every case in which one would commonly be said to be making an ethical judgement, the function of the relevant ethical word is purely "emotive." It is used to express feeling about certain objects, but not to make any assertion about them.

It is worth mentioning that ethical terms do not serve only to express feeling. They are calculated also to arouse feeling, and so to stimulate action. Indeed some of them are used in such a way as to give the sentences in which they occur the effect of commands. Thus the sentence "It is your duty to tell the truth" may be regarded both as the expression of a certain sort of ethical feeling about truthfulness and as the expression of the command "Tell the truth." The sentence "You ought to tell the truth" also involves the command "Tell the truth," but here the tone of the command is less emphatic. In the sentence "It is good to tell the truth" the command has become little more than a suggestion. And thus the "meaning" of the word "good," in its ethical usage, is differentiated from that of the word "duty" or the word "ought." In fact we may define the meaning of the various ethical words in terms both of the different feelings they are ordinarily taken to express, and also the different responses which they are calculated to provoke.

We can now see why it is impossible to find a criterion for determining the validity of ethical judgements. It is not because they have an "absolute" validity which is mysteriously independent of ordinary sense-experience, but because they have not objective validity whatsoever. If a sentence makes no statement at all, there is obviously no sense in asking whether what it says is true or false. And we have seen that sentences which simply express moral judgements do not say anything. They are pure expressions of feeling and as such do not come under the category of truth and falsehood. They are unverifiable for the same reason as a cry of pain or a word of command is unverifiable — because they do not express genuine propositions.

Thus, although our theory of ethics might fairly be said to be radically subjectivist, it differs in a very important respect from the orthodox subjectivist theory. For the orthodox subjectivist does not deny, as we do, that the sentences of a moralizer express genuine propositions. All he denies is that they express propositions of a unique non-empirical character. His own view is that they express propositions about the speaker's feelings. If this were so, ethical judgements clearly would be capable of being true or false. They would be true if the speaker had the relevant feelings, and false if he had not. And this is a matter which is, in principle, empirically verifiable. Furthermore they could be significantly contradicted. For if I say, "Tolerance is a virtue," and someone answers, "You don't approve of it," he would, on the ordinary subjectivist theory, be contradicting me. On our theory, he would not be contradicting me, because, in saying that tolerance was a virtue, I should not be making any statement about my own feelings or about anything else. I should simply be evincing my feelings, which is not at all the same thing as saying that I have them.

The distinction between the expression of feeling and the assertion of feeling is complicated by the fact that the assertion that one has a certain feeling often accompanies the expression of that feeling, and is then, indeed, a factor in the expression of that feeling. Thus I may simultaneously express boredom and say that I am bored, and in that case my utterance of the words, "I am bored," is one of the circumstances which make it true to say that I am expressing or evincing boredom. But I can express boredom without actually saying that I am bored. I can express it by my tone and gestures, while making a statement about something wholly unconnected with it, or by an ejaculation, or without uttering any words at all. So that even if the assertion that one has a certain feeling always involves the expression of that feeling, the expression of a feeling assuredly does not always involve the assertion that one has it. And this is the important point to grasp in considering the distinction between our theory and the ordinary subjectivist theory. For whereas the subjectivist holds that ethical statements actually assert the existence of certain feelings, we hold that ethical statements are expressions and excitants of feelings which do not necessarily involve any assertions.

We have already remarked that the main objection to the ordinary subjectivist theory is that the validity of ethical judgements is not determined by the nature of their author's feelings. And this is an objection which our theory escapes. For it does not imply that the existence of any feelings is a necessary and sufficient condition of the validity of an ethical judgement. It implies, on the contrary, that ethical judgements have no validity.

There is, however, a celebrated argument against subjectivist theories which our theory does not escape. It has been pointed out by Moore that if ethical statements were simply statements about the speaker's feelings, it would be impossible to argue about questions of value. To take a typical example: if a man said that thrift was a virtue, and another replied that it was a vice, they would not, on this theory, be disputing with one another. One would be saying that he approved of thrift, and the other that *he* didn't; and there is no reason why both these statements should not be true. Now Moore held it to be obvious that we do dispute about questions of value, and accordingly concluded that the particular form of subjectivism which he was discussing was false.

It is plain that the conclusion that it is impossible to dispute about questions of value follows from our theory also. For as we hold that such sentences as "Thrift is a virtue" and "Thrift is a vice" do not express propositions at all, we clearly cannot hold that they express incompatible propositions. We must therefore admit that if Moore's argument really refutes the ordinary subjectivist theory, it also refutes ours. But, in fact, we deny that it does refute even the ordinary subjectivist theory. For we hold that one really never does dispute about questions of value.

This may seem, at first sight, to be a very paradoxical assertion. For we certainly do engage in disputes which are ordinarily regarded as disputes about questions of value. But, in all such cases, we find, if we consider the matter closely, that the dispute is not really about a question of value, but about a question of fact. When someone disagrees with us about the moral value of a certain action or type of action, we do admittedly resort to argument in order to win him over to our way of thinking. But we do not attempt to show by our arguments that he has the "wrong" ethical feeling towards a situation whose nature he has correctly apprehended. What we attempt to show is that he is mistaken about the facts of the case. We argue that he has misconceived the agent's motive: or that he has misjudged the effects of the action, or its probable effects in view of the agent's knowledge; or that he has failed to take into account the special circumstances in which the agent was placed. Or else we employ more general arguments about the effects which actions of a certain type tend to produce, or the qualities which are usually manifested in their performance. We do this in the hope that we have only to get our opponent to agree with us about the nature of the empirical facts for him to adopt the same moral attitude towards them as we do. And as the people with whom we argue have generally received the same moral education as ourselves, and live in the same social order, our expectation is usually justified. But if our opponent happens to have undergone a different process of moral "conditioning" from ourselves, so that, even when he acknowledges all the facts, he still disagrees with us about the moral value of the actions under discussion, then we abandon the attempt to convince him by argument. We say that it is impossible to argue with him because he has a distorted or undeveloped moral sense; which signifies merely that he employs a different set of values from our own. We feel that our own system of values is superior, and therefore speak in such derogatory terms of his. But we cannot bring forward any arguments to show that our system is superior. For our judgement that it is so is itself a judgement of value, and accordingly outside the scope of argument. It is because argument fails us when we come to deal with pure questions of value, as distinct from questions of fact, that we finally resort to mere abuse.

In short, we find that argument is possible on moral questions only if some system of values is presupposed. If our opponent concurs with us in expressing moral disapproval of all actions of a given type t, then we may get him to condemn a particular action A, by bringing forward arguments to show that A is of type t. For the question whether A does or does not belong to that type is a plain question of fact. Given that a man has certain moral principles, we argue that he must, in order to be consistent, react morally to certain things in a certain way. What we do not and cannot argue about is the validity of these moral principles. We merely praise or condemn them in the light of our own feelings.

If anyone doubts the accuracy of this account of moral disputes, let him try to construct even an imaginary argument on a question of value which does not reduce itself to an argument about a question of logic or about an empirical matter of fact. I am confident that he will not succeed in producing a single example. And if that is the case, he must allow that its involving the impossibility of purely ethical arguments is not, as Moore thought, a ground of objection to our theory, but rather a point in favour of it.

Having upheld our theory against the only criticism which appeared to threaten it, we may now use it to define the nature of all ethical enquiries. We find that ethical philosophy consists simply in saying that ethical concepts are pseudo-concepts and therefore unanalysable. The further task of describing the different feelings that the different ethical terms are used to express, and the different reactions that they customarily provoke, is a task for the psychologist. There cannot be such a thing as ethical science, if by ethical science one means the elaboration of a "true" system of morals. For we have seen that, as ethical judgements are mere expressions of feeling, there can be no way of determining the validity of any ethical system, and, indeed, no sense in asking whether any such system is true. All that one may legitimately enquire in this connection is, What are the moral habits of a given person or group of people, and what causes them to have precisely those habits and feelings? And this enquiry falls wholly within the scope of the existing social sciences.

It appears, then, that ethics, as a branch of knowledge, is nothing more than a department of psychology and sociology. And in case anyone thinks that we are overlooking the existence of casuistry, we may remark that casuistry is not a science, but is a purely analytical investigation of the structure of a given moral system. In other words, it is an exercise in formal logic.

When one comes to pursue the psychological enquiries which constitute ethical science, one is immediately enabled to account for the Kantian and hedonistic theories of morals. For one finds that one of the chief causes of moral behaviour is fear, both conscious and unconscious, of a god's displeasure, and fear of the enmity of society. And this, indeed, is the reason why moral precepts present themselves to some people as "categorical" commands. And one finds, also, that the moral code of a society is partly determined by the beliefs of that society concerning the conditions of its own happiness — or, in other words, that a society tends to encourage or discourage a given type of conduct by the use of moral sanctions according as it appears to promote or detract from the contentment of the society as a whole. And this is the reason why altruism is recommended in most moral codes and egotism condemned. It is from the observation of this connection between morality and happiness that hedonistic or eudæmonistic theories of morals ultimately spring, just as the moral theory of Kant is based on the fact, previously explained, that moral precepts have for some people the force of inexorable commands. As each of these theories ignores the fact which lies at the root of the other, both may be criticized as being one-sided; but this is not the main objection to either of them. Their essential defect is that they treat propositions which refer to the causes and attributes of our ethical feelings as if they were definitions of ethical concepts. And thus they fail to recognise that ethical concepts are pseudo-concepts and consequently indefinable.

As we have already said, our conclusions about the nature of ethics apply to æsthetics also. Aesthetic terms are used in exactly the same way as ethical terms. Such æsthetic words as "beautiful" and "hideous" are employed, as ethical words are employed, not to make statements of fact, but simply to express certain feelings and evoke a certain response. It follows, as in ethics, that there is no sense in attributing objective validity to æsthetic judgements, and no possibility of arguing about questions of value in æsthetics, but only about questions of fact. A scientific treatment of æsthetics would show us what in general were the causes of æsthetic feeling, why various societies produced and admired the works of art they did, why taste varies as it does within a given society, and so forth. And these are ordinary psychological or sociological questions. They have, of course, little or nothing to do with æsthetic criticism as we understand it. But that is because the purpose of æsthetic criticism is not so much to give knowledge as to communicate emotion. The critic, by calling attention to certain features of the work under review, and expressing his own feelings about them, endeavours to make us share his attitude towards the work as a whole. The only relevant propositions that he formulates are propositions describing the nature of the work. And these are plain records of fact. We conclude, therefore, that there is nothing in æsthetics, any more than there is in ethics, to justify the view that it embodies a unique type of knowledge.

It should now be clear that the only information which we can legitimately derive from the study of our æsthetic and moral experiences is information about our own mental and physical make-up. We take note of these experiences as providing data for our psychological and sociological generalisations. And this is the only way in which they serve to increase our knowledge. It follows that any attempt to make our use of ethical and æsthetic concepts the basis of a metaphysical theory concerning the existence of a world of values, as distinct from the world of facts, involves a false analysis of these concepts. Our own analysis has shown that the phenomena of moral experience cannot fairly be used to support any rationalist or metaphysical doctrine whatsoever. In particular, they cannot, as Kant hoped, be used to establish the existence of a transcendent god.

24

R. M. HARE

Ethics in a New Key

Introduction

R.M. Hare is a Fellow of Corpus Christi College, Oxford. He was formerly White's Professor of Philosophy at the University of Oxford, and is now Graduate Research Professor of Philosophy at the University of Florida at Gainesville. Among his best known books are *The Language of Morals, Freedom and Reason*, and *Moral Thinking*. He is one of the most distinguished of contemporary moral philosophers.

This passage is too lucid to need further exposition from me. For some remarks about imperativism, to which Richard Hare's views bear a close affinity, the reader is referred to pp. 31–35 in the introduction.

Reading

MOST OF THE MAIN problems which occupy ethical thinkers at the present time arise from the complexity of the meaning of moral terms, which combines two very different elements.

(1) *The evaluative or prescriptive meaning* (these more non-committal terms are now often preferred to Stevenson's "emotive meaning"). It is not necessary, and probably false, to attribute to moral judgments, as such, any impulsive or causative force or power to *make* or *induce us to* do what they enjoin; but even descriptivists sometimes admit that moral judgments have the function of *guiding* conduct. It is indeed fairly evident that in many typical cases we ask, for example, "What

From *The Language of Morals* by R. M. Hare (1952). Reprinted by permission of Oxford University Press.

ought I to do?" because we have to decide what to do, and think that the answer to the "ought" question has a bearing on our decision greater and more intimate than that possessed by answers to questions of non-moral fact. To take another example, it is fairly evident that there is an intimate connexion between thinking A better than B, and preferring A to B, and between the latter and being disposed to choose A rather than B. This intimate connexion is emphasized in the old tag (whose substance goes back to *Socrates*): "Whatever is sought, is sought under the appearance of its being good." It would follow from this that to call a thing good is thereby to offer guidance about choices; and the same might be said of the other moral terms. Descriptivists, however, refuse to admit that this feature is part of the *meaning* of moral terms.

Their principal opponents, who may be called "prescriptivists," hold that it *is* part of the meaning. Moral judgments, on this view, share with imperatives the characteristic that to utter one is to commit oneself, directly or indirectly, to some sort of precept or prescription about actual or conceivable decisions or choices. In typical cases, disagreement with a moral judgment is displayed by failure to act on it — as when someone has told me that the right thing to do is such and such, and I immediately do the opposite. Such a view does not like the emotive theory, make moral argument impossible; for according to some prescriptivists logical relations may hold between prescriptions as well as between ordinary statements.

Prescriptivists have to face, like Socrates, the difficulty that in cases of so-called "weakness of will" we may choose to do something which we think bad or wrong. The most promising line for prescriptivists to take in answer to this objection is to point out that in such cases either the chooser is *unable* to resist the temptation (as is indicated by the expression "*weakness* of will"; cf. also St Paul, Romans 7, 23); or else he thinks the thing bad or wrong only in some weaker, conventional sense, having the descriptive meaning of "bad" or "wrong" but lacking their prescriptive force.

(2) *The descriptive meaning.* The second main feature of moral judgments is that which distinguishes them from imperatives: whenever we make a moral judgment about, for example, an act, we must make it because of *something about* the act, and it always makes sense to ask what this something is (though it may be hard to put a reply into words). This (although it has been denied by some recent thinkers) follows from the "consequential" character of moral "properties." To every particular moral judgment then, there corresponds a universal judgment to the effect that a certain feature of the thing judged is, so far as it goes, a reason for making a certain moral judgment about it. For instance, if I say that a particular act is good because it is the act of helping a blind man across a road, I seem to be adhering thereby to the universal judgment that it is good to help blind people across roads

(and not merely this particular blind man across the particular road). Those who accept this argument may be called "universalists"; and their opponents, who do not, may be called "particularists." A universalist is not committed to the view that, if it is a good act to help a blind man across a road on this occasion, it would be a good act on all occasions (for example, it would not be a good act if the blind man was known to be hopelessly lost and his destination lay on this side of the road); he is committed only to the view that it would be a good act in the absence of something to make a difference between the two acts — something more than the mere numerical difference between the acts.

The universalist thesis is closely connected with the thesis that moral judgments, besides their function as prescriptions, have also a descriptive meaning. On this view, in calling an act, for example, good, we are commending it (the prescriptive element in the meaning), but commending it because of something about it. These two elements are well summarized by the *Oxford English Dictionary*'s first definition of "good": "The most general adjective of commendation, implying the existence in a high, or at least satisfactory, degree of characteristic qualities which are either admirable in themselves or useful for some purpose." The word "characteristic" is important; it draws attention to the fact that the word which follows "good" makes a difference to the qualities which a thing has to have in order to be called good (for example, a good strawberry does not have to have the same qualities as a good man). In the case of some words (for example, "knife"), if we know what they mean, we know some of the conditions that have to be fulfilled before we can call a thing of that kind good. Some philosophers (for example *Plato* and Aristotle) have held that the same is true of all words — that, for example, if we could determine "the nature of man" we should therefore be able to say what makes a man a good man. But this type of argument may be based on a false analogy between words like "man" and words like "knife."

A more promising way of bringing the universalist thesis to bear on moral arguments (and thus to some extent satisfying those who insist that ethical studies should be relevant to moral questions) is that exemplified by the "Golden Rule" and worked out in some detail (though obscurely) by *Kant* and his followers. In certain cases it may be a powerful argument, if a man is contemplating some act, to ask what it is about the act which makes him call it right, and whether, if some other act possessed the same features, but his own role in it were different, he would judge it in the same way. This type of argument occurs in two famous passages of Scripture (2 Samuel 12, 7 and Matthew 18, 32). It has been held that a judgment is not a *moral* judgment unless the speaker is prepared to "universalize his maxim." But this raises the vexed question of the criteria for calling judgments "moral judgments" a question which is beyond the scope of this article.

25

BERTRAND RUSSELL

Is There an Absolute Good?

Introduction

Bertrand Arthur William Russell (1872–1970), the third Earl Russell, benefited from coming from an aristocratic family, starting life as a mathematician, and having long periods when he did not hold a professional teaching post. He was jailed for his pacifism and (later) noted for his opposition to nuclear weapons. He was the author of about forty books and some two thousand articles! The books include *Principia Mathematica* (with Alfred North Whitehead), works on logical atomism, *The Principles of Mathematics, An Introduction to Mathematical Philosophy* (which makes the philosophy of mathematics read like a novel), *The Problems of Philosophy, Mysticism and Logic,* and *Our Knowledge of the External World.* He also published a small amount of fiction. His work made what many people consider to be enormous contributions to mathematical philosophy and epistemology, but his scope was much wider than that. The selection included here is historically interesting, as it marks a transition between the ethical objectivism of the early Russell and his later ethical subjectivism.

The reader is again referred to the remarks on the error theory in the Introduction (p. 31–32). But Russell should have drawn from his premise — that there is no such predicate as goodness — the conclusion that moral sentences are *meaningless*, rather than that moral judgments are *false*. If I say that something has a predicate, and it lacks this predicate, then my judgment is false, but a thing cannot lack a predicate if there *is* no predicate for it to lack. For example, if I judge that *A, B,* and *C* are all slithy, and there is no predicate for which the word "slithy" stands, then my remark that *A, B,* and *C* are *not* slithy will make as little sense as the judgment that they *are* slithy. That moral sentences are all meaningless is difficult to believe.

Reading

WHEN THE GENERATION to which I belong were young, Moore persuaded us all that there is an absolute good. Most of us drew the inference that *we* were absolutely good, but this is not an essential part of Moore's position, though it is one of its most attractive parts.

Moore's position, in essence, is this: When we judge (say) "pleasure is good," the word "good" has a meaning, and what it means is a certain simple and unanalysable predicate. I wish to leave out of account the question whether the predicate "good" is simple, which is of minor importance; my point is that the word "good" does not stand for a predicate at all, but has a meaning only in the sense in which descriptive phrases have meaning, i.e. in use, not in isolation; further that, when we define it as nearly as possible in accordance with the usage of absolutists, *all* propositions in which the word "good" has a primary occurrence are false.

Moore is right, I think, in holding that when we say a thing is good we do not *merely* mean that we have towards it a certain feeling, of liking or approval or what not. There seems to me no doubt that our ethical judgments claim objectivity; but this claim, to my mind, makes them all false. Without the theory of incomplete symbols, it seemed natural to infer, as Moore did, that, since propositions in which the word "good" occurs have meaning, therefore the word "good" has meaning; but this was a fallacy. And it is upon this fallacy, I think, that the most apparently cogent of Moore's arguments rest.

I conceive the genesis of the notion of "good" as follows: We have emotions of approval and disapproval. If A, B, C, . . . are the things towards which we have emotions of approval, we mistake the similarity of our emotions in the presence of A, B, C, . . . for perception of a common predicate of A, B, C,. . . . To this supposed predicate we shall give the name "good." It may be that A, B, C, . . . will have several common predicates, but the irrelevant ones can be eliminated by the rule that the predicate "good" is not to belong to anything of which we *dis*approve. Thus the process is as follows:

A, B, C, . . . are things of which we approve; X, Y, Z, . . . are things of which we disapprove. We judge: "There is a predicate possessed by A, B, C, . . . but not by X, Y, Z. . . ." To this supposed predicate, so described, we give the name "good." Thus when we judge "M is good," we mean: "M has that predicate which is common to A, B, C, . . . but is absent in X, Y, Z. . . ." It will be seen that the emotions of approval and disapproval do not enter into the meaning of the proposition "M is good", but only into its genesis. The fundamental proposition of ethics, according to the theory I am advocating, is: "There is a predicate common to A, B, C, . . . but absent from X, Y,

From "Is There an Absolute Good?" *Collected Papers of Bertrand Russell*, Volume 9. Reprinted by permission of Routledge.

Z. . . ." I believe this proposition to be false. It follows that, if I am right, all ethical propositions are false. Their falsehood is of the same kind as the falsehood of the proposition: "the present King of France is bald"; except that what is described in an ethical proposition is the predicate, not the subject.

Why believe this theory?

(1) It is not considered by Moore, and the arguments which he brings against the rival theories he does consider do not apply against it.

(2) It seems to be an empirical fact that the things people judge good are the same as those towards which they have an emotion of approval, while the things they judge bad are those towards which they have an emotion of disapproval.

(3) The emotions of approval and disapproval influence our actions, whereas purely theoretical judgments do not. Therefore in so far as ethics is concerned with what people actually do, or with how to influence action, the emotions suffice without the help of the predicates "good" and "bad."

(4) Since people disagree in their judgments of good and bad to just the same extent to which they differ in their feelings of approval and disapproval, the objectivity secured by ethical predicates is only theoretic, and does nothing to mitigate ethical disputes in practice.

(5) Since the facts can be accounted for without the predicates "good" and "bad," Occam's razor demands that we should abstain from assuming them.

Apart from logical arguments, there is a mass of what one may call sentiment which leads me to entertain emotions of disapproval towards absolute good, i.e. to judge that good is bad. But I will not waste your time by developing these sentimental considerations.

26

J. L. MACKIE

A Refutation of Morals

Introduction

J. L. Mackie (1917–1981) held chairs at Otago (New Zealand) and York University before going to University College, Oxford, (U.K.), and becoming Reader in Philosophy at Oxford University. Mackie is the author of *Problems from Locke; The Cement of the Universe; Truth, Probability and Paradox; Ethics: Inventing Right and Wrong* (from which this excerpt is taken); *The Miracle of Theism;* and *Hume's Moral Theory.*

Reading

[IN THIS PAPER I do not pretend to be advancing any particularly new ideas: hardly any of the arguments are original, and indeed most are the stock instruments of all modern discussions of morals. But I think I am justified in offering this re-statement of them, because it is seldom realised how they may be brought together and interrelated, or how radically destructive they are of all common views of morality, when this is done.]

We all have moral feelings: all of us find that there are human actions and states of affairs of which we approve and disapprove, and which we therefore try to encourage and develop or to oppose. (This emotion of approval is different from liking, one difference being that its object is more general. If someone stands me a pint, I like it: if someone stands an enemy of mine a pint, I dislike it: but I should approve of a state of society which provided free beer all round. So if I hear of someone whom I have never met and to whom I am personally indifferent being stood a pint, I should not say that I like it, for I am not directly affected, but I may well approve of it, because it is an instance of the sort of thing I want to see everywhere. A thorough distinction of approval from liking and other relations would require further discussion, but perhaps this will serve to indicate a contrast between classes with which we are all in fact acquainted. I shall suggest later a possible source of these generalised emotions.) But most of us do not merely admit that we have such *feelings*, we think we can also *judge* that actions and states are right and good, just as we judge about other matters of fact, that these judgments are either true or false, and that the qualities with which they deal exist objectively. This view, which almost everyone holds, may be crudely called "believing in morals." A few sceptics, however, think that there are only feelings of approval, no objective moral facts. (Of course the existence of a feeling is an objective fact, but not what is commonly called a moral fact.) One of their main arguments is that moral facts would be "queer," in that unlike other facts they cannot be explained in terms of arrangements of matter, or logical constructions out of sense-data, or whatever the particular theorist takes to be the general form of real things. This argument is not in itself very strong, or even very plausible, for unless we have good *a priori* grounds for whatever is taken as the basic principle of criticism, the criterion of reality, the mere fact that we seem to observe moral qualities and facts would be a reason for modifying that principle. Their other main argument, which is both older and more convincing, though not logically conclusive, is that although at any one time, in a particular social group, there is fairly complete agreement about what is right, in other classes, other countries, and above all in other periods of history and other cultures, the actual moral judgments or feelings are almost completely different, though perhaps there are a few feelings so natural to man that they are found everywhere. Now feelings may well change with changing conditions, but a judgment about objective fact should be everywhere the same: if we have a faculty of moral perception, it must be an extremely faulty one, liable not only to temporary illusions, as sight is, but to great and lasting error. Of course it may be that every society except our own is mistaken, that savages are morally backward because they lack our illuminating experience of the long-term effects of various kinds of action, and so on. But this complacent view (not indeed very popular now) is shaken by the observation that the variations in moral feelings can be explained much more plausibly not as being due to mistakes, but as reflections of social habits. This moral relativity would be less alarming if we could say that the varying judgements were not ultimate, but were applications to different circumstances of a single principle or a small number of principles, which were every-where recognised — for example, that whatever produces pleasure is good, that whatever society commands is right, or, at the very least, that we should always do what we believe to be right. But these principles are not commonly laid down first, and the particular judgements deduced from them: rather the particular judgements are made by ordinary people, whereas the principles are later invented by philosophers and manipulated in order to explain them. In any case there is just as little agreement about principles as about particular judgements.

We find on further enquiry that most, perhaps all, actual moral judgements are fairly closely correlated with what we may call social demands: any society or social group has regular ways of working, and, in order to maintain these, requires that its members should act in certain ways: the members — from whatever motive, perhaps mainly habit, which has compelled them to adapt their desires to the estab-lished customs — obey these requirements themselves and force their fellows to do so, or at least feel obliged to obey and approve of others obeying. They call "right" and "good" whatever accords with these ways of working. Moreover as the science of social history develops, it is more and more strongly suggested that ways of working and institu-tions have their own laws of growth, and that the desires or moral views of individuals do not so much control the history of society as arise out of it.

Belief in the objectivity of moral qualities is further undermined when we remark that whenever anyone calls an action or activity or state of affairs right or good (unless he is speaking in an ironical tone or puts these words in inverted commas) he himself either has a feeling of approval, or desires that the action should be done or the activity pursued or the state of affairs come into existence. (Only one of these alternatives is necessary, but they are often found together.)

None of these considerations is conclusive, but each has a certain weight: together they move the moral sceptic (who is often of a scien-tific and inductive turn of mind, and less devoted than some others to the clear light of intuition or the authority of reason) to conclude that in all probability we do not recognise moral facts, but merely have feel-ings of approval and disapproval, which arise in general from social demands and therefore vary from one society to another. This view I intend to examine and re-state, and to advance what I regard as decisive arguments for one of its more important aspects.

The simplest formulation of this view is that when someone says "this act is right" he means merely "I approve of this act." The well-known reply simply leaps into the reader's mind: when one person says that an act is right, another that the same act is wrong, they would not on this theory be disagreeing, whereas in fact they think they are. It will not do to say, with Stevenson,[1] that there is a disagreement in attitude, but not in belief: they think, at any rate, that they disagree in belief. Nor does one mean that "society approves of this act," since we frequently meet people who say "I know society approves of this, but it is wrong all the same." But there is no need for argument: direct introspection shows that when we use the terms "right," "good," and the rest, we never intend merely to state that there are feelings of approval. An improved formulation of the sceptical view is that in saying "this is right," and so on, we are not *stating* any approval, but only *expressing* one, that words like "right" and "wrong," "good" and "bad" are to be compared not with "red" and "square" but with exclamations or ejaculations like "ow!", "boo!", and "hurray!" This is certainly nearer the truth, and avoids the previous difficulties, but is, in another way, just as unplausible. For we do not think that we are merely ejaculating when we talk in moral terms. If we did, and if someone disagreed with us, we should merely disapprove of his approvals, and either try to coax him into a different emotional attitude, or if he proved obstinate, knock him down. In fact we reason with him. These facts, and the logical tangles that we get into when we try to re-state fairly complex moral situations in the "boo-hurray" language, prove that we think, at least, that we are not merely expressing our emotions but are describing objective facts, and therefore that the meaning of moral terms is not parallel with that of ejaculations. Many refutations of the "boo-hurray" theory have been worked out, but they all depend upon and illustrate the fact that we *think* that we are doing things of quite different sorts when we say "right" and when we say "ow!" Now if philosophy could do no more than elucidate the meaning of the terms of common speech, remove confusions and rationalise the thought of ordinary men, there would be nothing more to be said. Moral terms do mean objective qualities, and everyone who uses them does so because he believes in objective moral facts. But if the very terms of common speech may include errors and confusions within themselves, so that they cannot be used at all without falsity, if, we may add, philosophy may be permitted to enquire into these errors by observing a few facts for itself and founding inductive conclusions on them, the moral sceptic need not be so soon disheartened.

But we must modify his view again, and say that in using moral terms we are as it were objectifying our own feelings, thinking them into qualities existing independently of us. For example, we may see a plant, say a fungus, that fills us with disgust, but instead of stating that we have this feeling, or merely expressing and relieving it by an exclamation, we may ascribe to the fungus a semi-moral quality of foulness, over and above all the qualities that a physical scientist could find in it.

---

[1] *Ethics and Language*, Chapter 1.

Of course, in objectifying our feelings we are also turning them inside out: our feeling about the fungus is one of being disgusted, while the foulness we ascribe to the fungus means that it is disgusting. The supposed objective quality is not simply the feeling itself transferred to an external object, but is something that would inevitably arouse that feeling. (No one would say, "That fungus is foul, but I feel no disgust at it.") The feeling and the supposed quality are related as a seal or stamp and its impression.

This process of objectification is, I think, well known to psychologists and is not new in philosophy. I believe that it resembles what Hume says we do when we manufacture the idea of necessary connection out of our feeling of being compelled, by the association of ideas, to pass from cause to effect, though here the process of turning inside out does not occur.

There are strong influences which might lead us thus to objectify moral feelings. As I have mentioned, our moral judgments seem to arise from approvals borrowed from society, or from some social group, and these are felt by the individual as external to himself. It is for this reason that they are universal in form, applying equally to himself and to others. They are thus formally capable of being objective laws, in contrast to the "selfish" desires of the individual. This generality or universality, which I mentioned as characteristic of the emotion of approval, is reflected in Rousseau's doctrine that the general will and therefore law must be general in their object, and in Kant's criterion of the possibility of universalisation of a moral law. Since we inevitably tend to encourage what we approve of, and to impose it upon others, we want everyone to adopt our approvals, and this will most surely come about if they have only to perceive a genuinely existing objective fact, for what we feel is in general private, what we perceive may be common to all. Suppose that we approve of hard work: then if as well as a feeling of approval in our own minds there were an objective fact like "hard work is good," such that everyone could observe the fact and such that the mere observation would arouse in him a like feeling of approval, and even perhaps stimulate him to work, we should eventually get what we want done: people would work hard. And since what we want does not exist in fact, we naturally construct it in imagination: we objectify our feelings so thoroughly that we completely deceive ourselves. I imagine that this is the reason why our belief in moral objectivity is so firm: we much more readily admit that the foulness of a fungus is an objectification than that the depravity of people who break our windows is. If moral predicates were admitted to be what the moral sceptic says they are, we should never be able to extol a state of affairs as good in any sense which would induce people to bring it about, unless they already wanted it, though we might point out that this state had features which in fact they did desire, though they had not realised this: we should never be able to recommend any course of action, except in such terms as "if you want to be rich, be economical"; nor could we give commands by any moral authority, though we might again advise "if you don't want a bullet through your brains, come quietly"; and we should never be able to lecture anyone on his wickedness — an alarming prospect. The temptations to objectify feelings of approval, and to retain our belief in morals, are clearly strong ones.

This process of objectifying our feelings is, then, neither impossible nor improbable: there is also abundant evidence that it is just what has occurred. It is commonly believed by moralists that good means desirable in a sense such that the mere recognition that a thing is good makes us desire it, and similarly the conclusion of the practical syllogism is both "this is right" and the performance of the action. This is what we should expect if "right" were the objectification of a tendency to compel or command the kind of act so described, and "good" of desire and approval. This is again indicated by the use of the term "value" which is clearly borrowed from spheres like economics where value is created by demand — in fact a quality manufactured in imagination out of the relation of being demanded by someone, the abstraction being the easier because the demand is not essentially that of a single buyer, but of an indeterminate crowd of potential buyers: the analogy with the objectification of moral feelings, aided by their generality, is very plain. Anderson has pointed out (in "The Meaning of Good," published in the Journal for September, 1942) that whenever anyone argues "Y is good, X is a means to Y, therefore X is good" he must be using "good" in an economic sense, as relative to some demand: now this is one of the commonest forms of argument in ordinary moral thought. There is nothing inconsistent in saying that "good" is the objectification of both desire and approval: its meaning is not quite fixed, and approval both is a development from liking and desiring, and attains its end when its object is generally desired. Further evidence is given by the categorical imperative, which looks very much like an abstraction from the commonplace hypothetical imperative, "if you want this, do that," and which may be described as the making objective and so absolute of advice which is properly relative to the condition of the presence of the desire. "Naturalistic" theories of ethics, which seem so absurd to a logician like G. E. Moore, who insists on the objective-quality aspect of moral terms, represent as it were partially successful attempts at objectification. "The good is the desired" and suchlike statements, which recur with remarkable persistence in philosophic history, plainly betray the emotional origin of moral terms. But there is no need to multiply examples: almost every moral term and style of moral thought may be seen to be borrowed from less lofty spheres, and in the course of the transfer objective qualities have appeared where only emotions were previously recognised.

In attempting to give an account of the origin of moral terms in this process of objectification, I do not, of course, claim that it is complete or precise in all respects. It is still open to discussion and correction on empirical grounds. We might go on to consider this process as a psychological process, investigating its causes, its similarities and contrasts with other mental processes, and the steps of which it is made up. We might ask whether "objectification" or some other name is really the most suitable, and also what are the precise motives objectified: we might consider, for example, Westermarck's argument[2] that "ought" normally expresses a conation, is sometimes but not necessarily or essentially imperative, and has its origin in disapproval rather than approval.

My discussion in this paper is intended to open the way for such discussions, not to settle them once and for all. What I am concerned to establish is simply the logical status of moral terms, not the psychological details of their origin; in effect I am asserting only that there are no facts of the form "this is right," that when we use such words the only fact is the existence of some feelings in ourselves or in others or in both, but that in using these terms we are falsely postulating or asserting something of the simple, objective form "this is right."

I am not, of course, disagreeing with the point mentioned several times by Anderson (for example in "The Meaning of Good", p. 120) that "I like this," "I approve of this," "this society approves of this," are all statements of objective fact and would in any particular case be true or false. But they are all of a different form from statements like "this is right," the latter attributing a predicate to a subject, the former asserting a relation between two or more things. When I say that we objectify, I mean that we believe in the truth of statements of the subject-predicate form.

This re-statement does away with the logical difficulties previously encountered by moral scepticism. Nor are there, I think, any non-logical difficulties in the way of our accepting this view, except the persistence of the belief that moral facts are objective. It might be claimed that this firm belief is based on an intuition, but it has no further arguments to support it, and we have indicated social and psychological causes which would produce such a belief even if it had no foundation. However firm the belief may be, therefore, it is not valid evidence for the existence of moral facts. But the true moralist will not be deterred by lack of evidence: he will perhaps be compelled to admit that moral judgements are evolved, historically, by objectification of feelings. But none the less, he will maintain, when evolved they *are* valid. But now we remind him of their variability, their correlation with social demands. Actual moral judgements, en masse, cannot be valid, since they are mutually contradictory: in fact all the evidence suggests that not

[2] *The Origin and Development of the Moral Ideas*, Chapter VI.

only are moral judgements derived from feelings, but there are no objective moral facts: the feelings are *all* that exists. We may now legitimately be influenced by the "queerness" of the alleged moral facts, their striking differences from most of the other objects of knowledge and belief. But we must not be over-emphatic. We have only attained probability. Even when our assumptions and observations are accepted it is still possible that there may be facts of the forms "this act is right," "this activity or state of affairs is good," though our recognition of them is very much confused by desires and approvals. We have seen that a great deal of so-called moral judging is really the objectifying of feelings, but perhaps not all of it is. (This leaves the field open for a positive system of ethics like that upheld by Anderson.) But this concession will give the moralist no pleasure when we add that we can show, by a different line of argument, that that part of morals to which moralists are most devoted, which is absolutely essential to their purpose, is certainly not objectively valid, and is therefore to be explained in terms of objectification. I mean everything connected with the notice of obligation.

The demonstration is merely a re-enactment of the drama in which moral thinkers of opposing schools have shown that both determinism and indeterminism are absolutely required by (and may be deduced from) our common views about obligation. We begin with the principle that "ought implies can". It is obvious that if we meet someone who is clearly not in a fit state to be wandering about the streets and say to him "you ought to go home" we are assuming that it is physically possible for him to go home, if he wants to. This kind of freedom no one will deny. But suppose that we know that he has a strong and inflexible determination not to go home, and in fact are certain that he will not go, can we still say that he ought to go? Not, I think, in the full sense of "ought." We may feel regretfully that it is a pity, that going home is the act that would have produced most good, or something like that, but we no longer say he ought to go. (I have seen it suggested that the phrase "he ought not to have done it" shows that we do not restrict obligation to what is undetermined, since we speak of a present obligation about a past act. But this phrase results merely from the perversity of the English language, and we should be speaking more accurately, as well as translating more literally the learned tongues, if we said "he didn't ought to do it." It is then clear that the alleged obligation existed before the act was performed, when it might still be regarded as undetermined.) In the case described, we should probably change our ground, and say that he ought to want to go, or that, given his present unreasonably obstinate nature, he ought to set himself to change it. (We may, of course, go back in time to a point at which the determination began, saying, for example, that now the man is drunk we cannot expect him to do anything but what he does, but he ought not to have started drinking. But we cannot go back indefinitely; we must fix on a moment at which the man might have acted in either of two opposite ways, and if the way in which he acted was determined by his character and circumstances, we must say that he ought not to have this character, or rather, since this is at present an inescapable fact, that he ought to set about reforming himself.) That is to say, if we assume that motives and circumstances fully determine action, we shift the obligation from the external act to its motives. In doing this, we assume that motives themselves are not determined, for clearly we cannot both say "it is right that the man should have such motives" and realise that it was inevitable that he should have them, or should not have them, whichever happens to be true. Now in fact our common practical judgement is that human actions, like physical events, follow discoverable laws: this is only an inductive conclusion, but a well-supported one; in fact we are in the habit of tracing even how men's motive are produced by circumstances and by previous practices: we regard the "empirical self" as determined and postulate behind it a metaphysical self which is a true originator of action, to be the subject of moral judgements. This is indicated when we say "you ought to set about improving your character" for if it was the empirical self we were speaking of, it would *be* that character, though admittedly if one part of the character were already good it might set about reforming the rest. If we then start to regard the metaphysical self as determined, we must postulate a third self, and so on. When we say "you *ought* to go home" we imply that at some level in the series of selves a process which would determine the going home may or may not arise: this is a genuine origination of motion, not determined by anything else. An ultimate freedom, in this sense, is absolutely required for the full meaning of obligation: to see this we need only meditate on the common use of "ought." Now it may be argued that we are not absolutely certain that such freedom does not exist.

But now we turn to the other group of speakers. Even if such freedom did exist, it would be useless for morals. We say not only "you *ought* to go home" but also "*you* ought to go home." We ascribe the obligation to a person, and hold him responsible for acting or failing to act. From this point of view, we are not satisfied with a process that "just happens," which begins or does not begin by pure chance. The action must belong to the person, and this may be accounted for in either of two ways. There may be a self, an entity with some determinate character (which may be unknowable, but that does not matter) such that given that character the process "flows from it" inevitably: but this contradicts the previous requirement, that the action should be possible but not inevitable, and we are faced with an infinite regress, at no point in which can we stop and say "you (meaning a determinate character) ought to (implying can) go home." Alternatively the process may not "flow from" a self, but may be one of a group of originations of motion which together make up a self; the action belongs to the person as part to whole. Then either the different originations that occur as time passes are quite independent of one another, so that any one may be different and the rest unchanged — in which case there is no unity of the self, no real "you" to be held responsible — or else they exhibit a more or less unified character, and follow some kind of determinate law or mode of reaction to external stimulus, and again they are not true originations, but each one, given the rest, could not have occurred in any other way. In all this discussion there is no need for the determination to be causal or "mechanical": the argument may be applied to any form of determination that is postulated. Nor is it of any use to mix them, to suggest that we deny one kind of determination in our notion of obligation and assert another in our notion of responsibility. The *kind* of determination does not matter: the essential point, which our common notions both affirm and deny, is that the act is determined, that given the self and the circumstances, the act just will occur. The notion of obligation thus implies both freedom, and, through responsibility, which is a vital part of the notion, the negation of freedom, and cannot be objectively valid. We may wonder how it can even persist as a feeling; but it is easy not to attend to all aspects of the notion at once, and in any case we may well go on wanting what we know to be unattainable, we may regret what is past repair, whereas we cannot maintain as objective fact that these things ought or ought not to be. This demonstration leaves it possible that obligation in an attenuated sense, may exist objectively. If we reject determinism, we may hold that certain events ought to happen, but it will be purely a matter of chance whether they do or not: it is nobody's business to bring them about. I am afraid that this concession will not satisfy the moralists, and that anyone who comes as far as this with us will abandon obligation altogether. But is should be noted as a logical possibility.

We may now sum up the progress that we have made. We have discovered how we can state the traditional view of moral sceptics without logical contradiction or denial of the observable facts of moral thinking, by saying that we have only moral feelings, but objectify these and think we are recognising objective facts and qualities. But we were not sure how much of our moral thought was made up of these objectifications, whether there might not be, say, an objective quality of goodness, with which these objectifications have been confused. We have shown that obligation, as we commonly use the term, cannot be an objective fact, but our notion of it must be derived from objectification. The same is true of everything necessarily connected with it, the terms "should," "duty," and "right." Exhortation and recommendation can have no absolute validity when obligation is removed: we can only advise people how to attain what they already desire. With these we

place those notions that bear plainly the marks of the process of objectification or of their emotion origin: the notion of value, the notion that
goodness, if there is such an objective quality, has any necessary relation to desire, or to happiness and pleasure, since it is through desire
that it is connected with these. Also, if there is such a quality, it will be
such that we can recognise it without feeling impelled to approve of it
or to pursue it. In fact, without going into further detail we may say that
there may be an objective quality which we have confused with our
objectifications of moral feelings, but if so it has few of the relations and
other features that we have been in the habit of associating with goodness. But in any case we have shown that the great mass of what is
called moral thought is, not nonsense, but error, the imagining of
objective facts and qualities of external things where there exists nothing but our feelings of desire and approval.

27

JONATHAN HARRISON

A Refutation of Mackie

Reading

Gallant hero of romantic film, who has just killed his equally gallant antagonist in a duel: "Was I wrong, father?" Father (Yul Brynner): "You were *both* wrong; and you were both right, too."

DAVID HUME, SPEAKING of moral sceptics, once said "And as reasoning is not the source, whence either disputant derives his tenets; it is in vain to expect, that any logic, which speaks not to the affections, will ever engage him to embrace sounder opinions."[1] I am guilty of an inconsistency of *some* kind in quoting the above passage from Hume with approval for, though everything Hume wrote ought to be quoted with approval, it is inconsistent to approve of advice, and then immediately to disregard it. I am also guilty of an inconsistency of another kind. Once upon a time I myself defended a version of moral scepticism,[2] but I can say in mitigation of this deplorable act that my tongue was partly in my cheek at the time, which is where one's tongue should be on the occasion of addressing the Joint Session of the Mind Association and the Aristotelian Society.

From "Mackie's Moral Scepticism" by Jonathan Harrison. Reprinted with permission of the Royal Institute of Philosophy. From *Philosophy*, © 1982.

[1] *An Enquiry Concerning the Principles of Morals*, L. A. Selby-Bigge (ed.), revised by P. H. Nidditch (Oxford: Oxford University Press, 1975), 170.

[2] In "Moral Scepticism," *Proceedings of the Aristotelian Society, Supplementary Volume* XLI (1967). A more detailed discussion of some of the points I make in this article will be found in my *Our Knowledge of Right and Wrong* (London: George Allen and Unwin, 1971).

Though Mr. Mackie describes his own epistemological view[3] as a form of scepticism (a term which he is inclined, wrongly, to use interchangeably with "subjectivism") it may be doubted whether this is a correct description of his own theory. Philonous, arguing with Hylas, disclaims the epithet "sceptic" on the ground that he does not profess not to know whether there is matter or not. He roundly asserts that there is not any. Hence he is not suspended between two alternative answers to a question which he thinks he will never be able to resolve. Similarly, Mackie does not profess not to know whether anything is wrong or not. He asserts that nothing is.

However, with a slightly different definition of "sceptic" (suggested by G. E. Moore in "Four Forms of Scepticism[4]") both Mackie and Philonous can be described as sceptics, for the one claims that no one knows that matter exists, and the other that no one knows that anything is wrong: both these statements, indeed, follow from the fact that, if Mackie and Philonous are right, there *is* no matter, and *nothing* is right. (Whether Philonous would claim that he *knew* that matter did not exist, and Mackie that he *knew* that nothing was wrong, is another matter.)

Mackie believes that moral statements are neither true nor false. He presumably also believes that the statement that killing people is not wrong is a moral statement. From these two things it follows that it is not true that killing people is wrong. From this it further seems to follow that killing people is not wrong. (It *would*, for example, follow from the fact that it is not true that the cat is on the mat that the cat is not on the mat.) Mackie, however, does not appear to wish to maintain that killing people is not wrong. Indeed, it would seem to be his view that killing people *is* wrong. How is he to make these two views, that it is not true that killing people is wrong, and that killing people is wrong, consistent with one another?

I can think of three ways of resisting the passage from "It is not true that killing people is wrong" to "Killing people is not wrong."

(1) One way would be to maintain that the words "Killing people is wrong" do not express a statement at all, but rather a command, like "Let us not kill people," or the expression of a wish, like "Would that men killed people much less often than they do." Without wishing to go into the question, I myself can see nothing to be said for a view such as this. But whether you regard such a view as plausible or not, it would at least enable its holder to maintain that moral sentences did not enable the person using them to say something true, and at the same time enable him to say the very thing which, he is maintaining, cannot assert something true. For example, a person who holds such a theory could consistently maintain both that what someone who says "Eating people is wrong" is saying is not something which is true, and also that

[3] In *Ethics: Inventing Right and Wrong* (Harmondsworth: Penguin Books, 1978).
[4] In *Philosophical Papers* (London: George Allen and Unwin, 1959).

eating people is wrong. He could do this just as he could maintain that the words "Let us now praise famous men" do not say anything which is true, without having, in consistency, to refuse to say "Let us now praise famous men." The trouble with this view, however, is that the consistency of maintaining that it is not true that killing people is wrong and nevertheless maintaining that killing people is wrong, is purchased at too high a cost. It is bought at the price of having to hold that you cannot *maintain* (or, alternatively, assert, say when "say" simply means assert, hold, contend, think, believe, argue in favour of, produce reasons for thinking, think it likely) that killing people is wrong at all. For if it were the case that one could not do any of these things, this would make nonsense of the business of first order morality, which does consist precisely in producing reasons for maintaining or believing one statement about morality rather than its opposite. This view, indeed, shows such insensitivity to the English language, and has been so adequately and frequently[5] refuted, that it surprises me very much that there are still moral philosophers who continue to hold it. But, as I say, we need not concern ourselves with it, since it is not Mackie's. Mackie does not think that we can consistently assert that what a moral sentence expresses is not true, without having to stop saying such things as that killing people is wrong, on the ground that such sentences do not assert propositions. They do, according to Mackie, assert propositions, but propositions which are neither true nor false (as he says in some places) or are all false (as he says in others). Indeed, Mackie describes his theory as an error theory, which implies that moral judgments are capable of being true or false, for if they were not capable of being true or false, they could not be false; error concerning them would then be impossible, and Mackie could not consistently hold an error theory.

(2) It may also be possible to deny the entailment which appears to hold from "It is not true that p" to "Not-p" in other cases. For example to deny that "It is not true that all her sins were little ones" entails "Not all her sins were little ones" on the ground that, if she had not sinned, the former will be true, but the latter neither true nor false. But this cannot possibly be the reason for resisting the entailment from "It is not true that killing people is wrong" to "Killing people is not wrong." For the reason why one is prepared to say that it is not true that all her sins were little ones, without being prepared to say that not all her sins were little ones, is that she has not sinned. The same reason would not explain the fact, if it is one, that one is prepared to say that it is not true that killing people is wrong, but not prepared to say that killing people is not wrong, for this fact, if it is one, has nothing to do with consideration of whether or not there are any cases of killing people.

---

[5]For example, by Alan White in *Truth* (London and Basingstoke: Macmillan, 1971).

(3) Many philosophers have held that it is possible consistently to maintain both that it is not true that there will be a sea battle tomorrow, and also to maintain that, nevertheless, there will be a sea battle tomorrow.

But the reason why the alleged fact that it is *not true* that killing people *is* wrong does not entail that killing people is *not* wrong cannot be similar to the reason why the alleged fact that it is *not true* that there *will* be a sea battle tomorrow does not entail that there will *not* be a sea battle tomorrow. For Mackie again describes his theory as an error theory. And it is clear, by what he says in many places, that the error he has in mind is not simply the error of supposing that it *is true* that killing people is wrong (though, for all that, killing people may nevertheless be wrong). This would be analogous to the error, if it is an error, of supposing that it is *true* that there will be a sea battle tomorrow (though, for all that, there may *be* a sea battle tomorrow). The alleged fact that it is not *true* that there will be a sea battle tomorrow is not supposed to be due to the person asserting that there *will* be a sea battle tomorrow's being in error when he asserts this. The reason why some philosophers think that it is a mistake to say that this is true have nothing to do with the reasons for thinking that there will not be a sea battle tomorrow, that the wind will be too high, for example. Indeed, there may not be any such reasons. Mackie, nevertheless, claims that his is an error theory, and the reasons he gives for calling it an error theory are reasons for thinking that actions cannot have the "characteristic" (if it can properly be called that) which people ascribe to them when they describe them as wrong. No philosopher deduces the fact, if it is one, that it is not true that there will be a sea battle tomorrow from the nautical fact that there cannot be a sea battle tomorrow (nor, as I have said, do they deduce that there will not be a sea battle tomorrow from the fact, if it is a fact, that it is *not true* that there *will* be a sea battle tomorrow). The only reasons Mackie has, however, for thinking that it is not true that killing people is wrong are reasons for thinking that killing people cannot have the "characteristic" that is ascribed to it when it is said that killing people is wrong. The reasons which Mackie gives for thinking that it is not true that killing people is wrong (and, also not true that killing people is right) have nothing to do with the purely "academic" reasons for thinking that it is not true that there will be a sea battle tomorrow. That it is not true (and also not false) that there will be a sea battle tomorrow need give one not the slightest discouragement over one's attempt to find out whether there will be one tomorrow or not. Mackie, however, in saying that it is not true (and also not false) that killing people is wrong, does say these things as a result of producing reasons which certainly ought to discourage people from attempting to find out whether killing people has or does not have what Mackie regards as the "phoney" characteristic of being wrong.

If Mackie is right, not only is it not true that killing people is wrong, it is not false either. Barring cases like the ones I have just mentioned, which are not here relevant, "It is not false that p" entails "p." "It is not false that killing people is wrong" entails "Killing people is wrong." Hence I cannot see why Mackie does not have to hold both that killing people is not wrong (because this is entailed by "It is not true that killing people is wrong") and also that "Killing people is wrong" (because this is entailed by "It is not false that killing people is wrong"). Obviously, however, it cannot both be true that killing people is wrong, and also true that killing people is not wrong.

Though Mackie does not explicitly say so, if judgments asserting that a thing is wrong are not true or false, then judgments asserting that a thing is right are not true or false either. By moves precisely analogous to the ones we have just made, we can deduce both that it is right and that it is not right to kill people. We can therefore conclude that it is both wrong and not wrong to kill people, and also that it is both right and not right to kill people. If Mackie is right, then talking about morality would, if people were rational, be a completely pointless business. Since all moral judgments and their contradictories could be asserted on purely epistemological grounds, there would never be any point in finding out anything about the facts of any matter. One could assert any moral judgment at all without any such knowledge being necessary. The omnivorous nature of Mackie's moral epistemology deprives it of any bite. For, since moral judgments are all true and all false, any given moral judgment, as far as Mackie's epistemological views are concerned, must be both true and false. Hence Mackie's views, since they always cancel out any substantive conclusions that they might seem to lead to, are rendered totally innocuous. Indeed, so far from describing his theory as an error theory, Mackie might with equally good reason have described it as a truth theory, for on Mackie's view moral judgments are just as much all true as all false.

Mackie's view that there are no "objective" moral qualities is partly arrived at because he has an over-simple view about what it is to be objective. He has a similar kind of view to those people who used to deny that there was a "realm of values." I suspect, however, that it is as misplaced to deny that there is a realm of values as it is to assert that there is one. It is to put values in the wrong category to suppose that it would even make sense to suppose that there was a "realm" "out there." Similarly, it would be to put moral "qualities" in the wrong category to do what Mackie does, and say that there cannot be objective qualities in the thing judged of, because there is nothing to exist out there. Let us take, for example, the hypothetical imperative that, if one wants to win a game of chess, one must move one's bishop to QR4. This is absolutely objective, in that it is so whatever one feels about it, or, indeed, whatever one thinks about it, or even whatever one wants.

But it would be a great mistake to look for some "Oughtness" out there, clinging inescapably to the board, or to the move which one would make, if one moved one's bishop to QR4. Turn the board, or the move, on all sides, one does not come across any such quality. One comes across black and white squares, wooden pieces, intentional or unintentional arm movements, etc., and there is no peculiar characteristic, physical or otherwise, to be found belonging to any of these. Nevertheless, it is quite certainly an objective fact, which anyone can work out with apodeictic certainty, that I must move my bishop, if I want to win, since this is the only move which I can make and still win.

I have, of course, been talking here about a hypothetical imperative, but why should the case be any different with categorical imperatives? At the very least, it will not follow from the fact that we cannot find any wrongness out there that wrongness is not an objective characteristic, because, as I have said, the same thing does not follow in the case of hypothetical imperatives. Because inspection does not reveal anything which is the wrongness of a wrong move at chess, when someone has made a move which he hypothetically ought not to have made, the fact that inspection does not reveal anything like an objective characteristic, wrongness, answering to the rather peculiar description Mackie gives of it (e.g. 38f.) when we do something which we *categorically* ought not to do, does not show that (categorical) wrongness is not something objective.

Though Mackie *says* that moral "judgments" are statements which are neither true nor false, it is fairly clear that it is his preferred view that they are statements which are all false. This is what is suggested, for example, by his describing his theory as an "error theory" (35), and by his comparing wrongness with secondary qualities like yellowness, which, I think he thinks, it is a mistake to suppose material objects have in the way in which ordinary people suppose that they have them. That it is his view that moral judgments are all false is also suggested by some remarks of his about what he calls "factual analysis". I do not think there is such a thing as factual analysis myself, but in mentioning it Mackie is quite properly drawing our attention to the fact that there is a distinction between analytic questions, such as "What are we asserting when we say that something is yellow?", and factual questions, such as "What *really is* the difference between an object which is commonly supposed to be yellow and one which is not?" — though why Mackie should describe the latter question as a question of factual analysis I cannot see. It would be an analytic question whether, when we said that something was yellow, we *meant to assert* no more than that it had the power to arouse sensations of yellow in normal observers, and would actually arouse these sensations if they cast their eyes in its direction, or whether we *meant to assert* instead a categorical proposition to the effect that yellowness is spread evenly all over the surface of the object, sides, back and front, in some non-hypothetical sense. It would be a factual question whether, whatever we *meant to assert* when we said that an object was yellow, yellowness *was* spread evenly over its surface, or whether, instead, all that was true of the object was that it had a disposition to produce sensations of yellowness in normal observers.

These two questions can be answered in any of four logically possible combinations. Firstly, we can say that we *do* mean to assert that yellowness is spread over the back of the object, and that it *is* so spread. Second, we can maintain that we *do* mean to assert that it is so spread, but it is *not*. Thirdly, we can maintain that we *do not* mean to assert that yellowness is spread over the back of the object (but to attribute to the object only a disposition to produce sensations) and that yellowness is *not* so spread. Fourthly, we can maintain that, though we do *not* mean to assert that yellowness is so spread (but only that it has the disposition) in fact yellowness *is* spread over the object in some categorical sense. (Lots of things we do not intend to assert are nevertheless true.) In the second case, all colour judgments would have to be false. In all the other cases, they could be true.

Phenomenalism gives us another example. It may be asked, firstly, whether, when we assert that material objects exist, we are asserting the existence of anything over and above minds and their sensations. And it may, secondly, also be asked whether there *is* anything in the world over and above minds and their sensations. Again, affirmative and negative answers to these two questions can be held in any combination. It is possible to combine the view that, when we say that there are material objects, we *are* asserting categorically the existence of things over and above our sensations, firstly, with the view that there *are* in fact things over and above our sensations, or secondly, with the view that there is *not* anything over and above sensations. (In the first case what we were saying would be true; in the second it would be false.) On the other hand we can maintain that we are *not* asserting the existence of anything over and above our sensations, with the assertion that, thirdly, there *are*, or that fourthly, there are not things over and above our sensations. In the third case it will be a true *synthetic* proposition that material objects are things over and above our sensations, a possibility which phenomenalists never seem to consider. Mackie, though he has different views about different moral judgments in different places, often takes an analogous view of "wrong." That is to say, he maintains two things. First of all, as a question of ordinary analysis, he maintains that when we assert that something is wrong, we are asserting that it has some objective characteristic (rather like the tertiary qualities of eighteenth-century philosophy) and further that actions do not (and, indeed *cannot*) have characteristics such as these, since these are false projections of our sentiments on to the thing itself.

Of course, if Mackie is right in thinking that when we say that something is wrong we are attributing an "objective" property to it, and if he is also right in thinking that no actions can possess this objective property, what follows is that all such attributions are false, and that, whenever we say that something is wrong, we are making a statement which is false, not one which is neither true nor false, as Mackie says at other times. From this it should follow that nothing is wrong. Whether Mackie's view also leads to the conclusion that every-thing is right (because nothing is wrong) or to the conclusion that nothing is right *and* nothing is wrong (because that something is right is just as much a moral judgment as that it is wrong) I do not know. There are reasons for thinking either of these two things. For one thing, if that something is right and that something is wrong are contradictories (and not just contraries) and nothing can be wrong, it would seem to follow that everything must be right. On the other hand, if "right" is defined in terms of "wrong," as it will be if "right" simply means "not wrong," then right should be as defective as wrong is; in which case it should follow that actions are as little capable of being right as they are of being wrong. Though the view that nothing is wrong or impermissible sounds a daring and important one, the view that nothing is right or permissible sounds just silly. Yet I cannot think of any logical differ-ences that should make the one more plausible than the other. (Perhaps it is just that one is naturally more attracted by the thought that nothing is impermissible than that nothing is permissible.)

It is possible that Mackie can answer the objection that, since right and wrong are contradictories, every action must be one or the other. One wants to say, for example, that "Slithy toves gyre" is the contradic-tory of "Slithy toves do not gyre"; one could perfectly well do exercises in elementary logic with examples like this. Hence "Slithy toves gyre" and "Slithy toves do not gyre" are, though not contradictories, at any rate pseudo-contradictories; for logical purposes they behave just as if they were contradictories, and would be contradictories if the words in the sentences expressing them made sense. Mackie could, I suppose, say the same about moral judgments, but only at the cost of maintaining that "Promise-breaking is wrong" is meaningless in the same way in which "Slithy toves gyre" is meaningless. This cost, to my mind, is too high. In any case it *ought* to be Mackie's view that moral *judgments* are erroneous, not that moral *sentences* are meaningless, and so do not express moral judgments at all.

If Mackie thought that killing people was not wrong because of some reasons which applied exclusively to killing people, then this might be an immoral doctrine; it might, too, cut some ice, if any there were to pay any attention to it. But if he holds that eating people is not wrong because nothing is, and then adds that nothing is right, either, then his doctrine ceases to be immoral because it also ceases to be serious. It becomes "philosophical" in the worst sense. It is not serious in the sense that it does not have any practical consequences, though it ought to have some. If someone holds that nothing is wrong, and then adds, in case we regard the news as cheering, that nothing is right, either, then his words are devoid of any practical import, and this not just because of men's inertia, which would be the reason why the fact that believing nothing was wrong because everything was right would have no practical consequences. It is for this reason that Mackie can, as he does — inconsistently, one would suppose — go on to make moral judgments himself without the force of his words being undermined by what he has previously said about moral epistemology, for what he says about moral epistemology, since it points in all directions at once, has not got any practical force to *be* undermined by his subsequently pointing in one direction rather than another.

This, however, does not prevent Mackie from being inconsistent in another way. If one holds that *all* moral judgments are false, one is guilty of a kind of inconsistency in later asserting some of them. It is not that what one asserts is inconsistent with what one has previously asserted, for, in asserting them, one is not asserting that they are true. It is that, if what one has previously asserted is true, what one is now doing would be an irrational thing to do, unless one has a desire to deceive, rather than a desire to educate (as Mackie has). For, though to assert a moral judgment is not to assert that it is true, it would be irrational to assert it (again assuming one does not wish to deceive) if one did not think it was true, and Mackie, if he believes what he has himself said, presumably does think that it is not true, for, according to him, no moral judgments are true. For example, if one has put forward the view that nothing is wrong, and that all moral judgments are false, though it is not actually logically inconsistent to say as Mackie does "As the world is, wars and revolutions cannot be ruled to be morally completely out of the question. The death penalty, I believe, can" (195), it is a very peculiar thing to do. (The three propositions "No moral judgments are true," " 'Capital punishment is wrong' is a moral judgment," and "That capital punishment is wrong is true" would be inconsistent, but Mackie does not assert that it is true that capital punishment is wrong; he simply asserts that capital punishment is wrong.) If the reason why Mackie asserts that capital punishment is wrong is that he thinks it *is* wrong, and if, if he thinks that it is wrong, he must think that anyone (including himself) saying that it is wrong is saying what is true, then it follows that Mackie is being inconsistent. He is being inconsistent in the sense that he thinks or believes something which he ought not to think or believe if what he himself says is the case. Mackie's reply, however, might be that to say that capital punishment is wrong because one thinks that it *is* wrong is different from saying that capital punishment is wrong because one thinks that it is *true* that it is wrong.

This reply would amount to saying that there is a class of statements which are such that, though things may be as these statements say they are, one could not express the fact that one thinks things are as these statements say they are by saying that these statements are true.

It seems to be very unlikely that there should be a class of statements which (a) are such that they say how things are, but (b) which are not true even if things are as these statements say they are. (This does not mean that there is not a class of statements which are sometimes neither true nor false; but then, of course, if we assert one of these statements, and things are as it says they are — which, when it *is* neither true nor false, things cannot be — then it is true. For example, that her sins were scarlet may be neither true nor false if she committed no sins, but this does not mean that, if her sins were scarlet, anyone *saying* that they were scarlet is not saying what is true.)

Propositions about the future are sometime alleged to be an exception. It has been held that, though I may say that she is going to be late, and she *is* going to be late, it does not follow that it is true that she is going to be late. I think this is a mistake, but a natural one. Though if I were to say that she was going to be late I would, if she *was* going to be late, be saying what was in fact true, it would be improper for me to *say* that it was true that she was going to be late, because my saying this would have contextual implications which were misleading. If someone comes up to me and says "Are you engaged to be married?" it is quite proper (if it is true that I am so engaged) to reply that I am. Furthermore, if someone comes up to me and says "I hear that you are engaged to be married. Is that true?" it is also quite proper for me to reply, that, yes, it is true. But if he adds "Is it also true that you are going to be happily married" I shall be at a loss what to say, even though I may firmly believe that I am going to be happily married. Though I can without impropriety express the view that I will be happily married, I cannot, without impropriety, express the view that it is true that I will be happily married.

The reason for this is that though I am in a better position than most other people to give an authoritative opinion on the question whether or not I am engaged, I am only very slightly, if at all, in a better position than anyone else to give an opinion on the question whether or not I will be happy. I cannot, however, without implicitly claiming to be in such a position, say that it is true that I will be happy. And since, in the great majority of cases, no one is in such an authoritative position where propositions about the future are concerned, this is the reason why, though it is not improper barely to assert such propositions, it is improper to say that they are true. I can properly assert them on worse evidence than I need properly to assert that they are true. Usually, when I say that something is true, I am pronouncing judgment upon something someone else has already said, and this I usually cannot do when what I am asked to pronounce upon is the truth of a proposition about the future. Better evidence is needed to assert that a proposition is true than is needed to assert it, which is why I often cannot assert that a proposition is true, even when I believe that it is, and even though, were I to say that it is true, I would be right. "p," indeed, entails "It is true that p"; if there are occasions on which I can assert the former without asserting the latter, this is because their contextual implications are different.

What I have just said about propositions about the future applies as well, if not better, to moral judgments. We are all amateurs when it comes to morality. Hence, though someone could come to me and say "David thinks suicide is not wrong. Do you agree?", it would be absurd for someone to come up to me and say "David says that suicide is not wrong. Is what he says true?", for this person would be revealing that he supposed, wrongly, that I had some secure way, better than his way, or than most other people's way, of arriving at the truth on such a matter. If I were to reply that it was true, I would be implicitly claiming that I thought the same. The reason, then, why I cannot say that moral judgments are true is not that they are not true, but that, were I to say that they were true, I would be claiming to be an expert witness in a sphere of knowledge where, because it is a matter of judgment rather than of science, to have experts is impossible. Hence, though if I say that promises ought to be kept, and they ought to be kept, what I say must *in fact* be true, I cannot *say* that it is true that they ought to be kept without claiming to be in an authoritative position on this matter, and, from the nature of the subject, I cannot *be* in such a position.

What I have just said, of course, rebuts only an argument designed to show that moral judgments are neither true nor false. But Mackie's view, despite his own account of it, is only occasionally that moral judgments are neither true nor false; his more usual view is that they are false. Mackie, of course, though he holds that all moral judgments are in general false, is very unlikely to want to assert of every *given* moral judgment that it is false. He may be quite happy to assert, because all moral judgments are false, that it is not the case that killing people is wrong, but less happy to assert, because all moral judgments are false, that killing people is not wrong (as it must be, if it is not true that killing people is wrong). The reason for this, presumably, is that anyone hearing Mackie say that killing people is not wrong would not only infer that Mackie thought that it was not true that killing people was wrong, but also that Mackie lacked an antagonistic attitude to killing people which, I imagine, he does not lack. When I say that killing people *is* wrong, I am not only saying something about killing people, from which it follows that it is true that killing people is wrong if killing people is wrong, as I say it is. I am evincing an attitude of disapproval towards killing people. If, on the other hand, Mackie were to say that killing people is wrong, he would, on his own view, be saying something which was false, but nevertheless contextually implying that he disapproved of killing people, which let us suppose he does. He is thus impaled upon the horns of a dilemma, between saying what is true, and contextually implying what is false, or saying what is false, in order contextually to imply what is true. When he says that capital punishment is wrong, and when he says similar things, as he does on a large number of other occasions, he very sensibly plumps for the latter alternative. He is rather in the position of a man who thinks he ought not to say that anything is disgusting, because he thinks that to say that something is disgusting is to say that it essentially or in itself possesses an attribute which is in fact merely a projection on to it of our own sentiments of disgust, but by refusing to say such things is continually giving the impression that nothing disgusts him, and that he expects nothing to disgust anybody else. It would seem to me to be more sensible for such a person to say that some things are disgusting, and for Mackie to say that some things are wrong, though both, by doing so, are implying that their epistemological theories, about the nature of disgustingness or wrongness, are wrong.

As I have said, although Mackie holds that all moral judgments are false, he himself asserts numerous moral judgments during the course of the book. Not all of these moral judgments are clothed in normal moral terminology, as is his judgment (195) that capital punishment would in all circumstances be wrong, but it is fairly clear when you look at them that they are moral judgments. The key to an explanation of this apparent inconsistency (it is inconsistent in some form, though not necessarily in the way of holding two incompatible views) may lie in what Mackie says about inventing right and wrong. Unfortunately, his views on the nature of the invention of right and wrong are obscure. One of his views, which I am quite sure is absolutely right, is that our present moral sentiments and the direction they take have come about in order to solve certain practical problems. For example my wife, who is an ardent feminist, and I agree to share our expenses by each paying for half of anything bought by the other. It is now to my interest to buy as many things as it would be if they were being offered at only half price (since she pays for the other half) and the same is true of her. If either of us acts on this principle without the other, the one who so acts is the gainer, but if we both act on it, the consequences are financially disastrous. Hence it is greatly to the advantage of both of us that there should grow up and become effective some moral sentiments condemning such outrageous—or what will then come to seem outrageous—behaviour, regardless of any consideration of whether it is individually to our interest to indulge in it. The fact that man has a sense of duty may be nature's answer to practical problems like this. But this does not mean that anyone has invented this solution. It has come about, I dare say, as the result of a process of natural selection, but this does not mean that someone thought it up deliberately, any more than does the fact that the eye is another of nature's solutions to a practical problem mean that someone invented the eye.[6]

The most natural interpretation to put on the claim that human beings invented right and wrong, when it is considered that it is juxtaposed with the claim that all moral judgments are false, is that moral judgments are both false and invented falsehoods. On such a view (which has been held by some Greek philosophers, but not, I think, by Mackie) that we have a duty to our country, or to its king, or to the ruling classes, or to our creditors, or to our parents, is something which was invented by some members of these heterogenous classes of people, who perceived that it was in their own interest that the common run of people should believe such things as this. On this view, morality would be invented in the sense in which a mother invents a story about bogymen to encourage her children to be better behaved. But this view, interesting (and implausible) though it is, is not Mackie's. The view that is Mackie's, I think, is something more like this. It is impossible to discover what things are right and what things are wrong, for such a quest would presuppose that rightness and wrongness were essential non-projected characteristics of things, which view is a delusion produced by man's innate tendency wrongly to project his sentiments on to those things which arouse them. Since none of the things on to which we project these qualities actually have the qualities so projected, all moral judgments are false. But this very fact, that none of the things which we describe as right or wrong can possibly have the projected characteristics which we attribute to them, when we do describe them, means that we are not tied (and Mackie thinks that this is a good thing: though whether a moral sceptic ought to think that anything is a *good* thing is another matter) to describing as right those things which actually are right. *Nothing* actually is right. Hence we can describe as right (or wrong) anything we like, and among the things to which we attribute being right (or wrong) there will be some things which no one has regarded as being right (or wrong) before. This is a good thing because we are now able to modify our existing moral code to meet new needs, abandon those parts of it which are out of date, and invent moral rules to solve quite new problems.

I entirely agree with Mackie that these things are good things to be able to do, though I think we can change existing moral beliefs for the worse as well as for the better. But there are two important points on which I disagree with him. Could we not have changed our moral codes anyway, even if we did not subscribe to his view that all moral judg-

---

[6]See my *Our Knowledge of Right and Wrong*.

ments are false? Further, given that one holds that all moral judgments *are* false, can we change moral codes for the better at all?

The most natural way of interpreting the fact that we need new views about what is right and wrong, to respond to increasing knowledge and changing needs, is to say that some of the things we formerly believed to be wrong were, because our beliefs were based on inadequate information, never wrong at all, and others, because circumstances have changed, are wrong no longer. Either our beliefs were incorrect, because we were misinformed about the facts, or they have become incorrect, because circumstances have altered. This process in no way implies that all moral judgments are false; indeed, it suggests that some moral judgments are true, for how can something be wrong no longer unless it really was wrong once? On the other hand, if Mackie is right, and no moral judgment are true, is the process I have described even possible? If we are freed from the delusion that anything is right at all, we are, of course, freed from the delusion that our traditional moral beliefs are incapable of being changed for the better because they are true. If, however, as Mackie maintains, it is not just that it so happens that the moral beliefs we have now are false, but that all moral beliefs, future ones as well as past ones, are false (because of the aforementioned false projection) then it must also be a delusion that we can replace the moral beliefs we have now by anything better. We certainly, if all moral beliefs are false, cannot replace the ones we have now by ones which are true, for none of them *can* be true.

This difficulty could in part by met if it were supplemented by a doctrine of degrees of truth, which Mackie himself does not have. Though all moral beliefs, old and new alike are false, the new ones might, I suppose, be more true (or less false) than the old. I shall say more about this later.

Another possibility, which I think might be the one Mackie actually thinks obtains, is that, though all moral beliefs are false, it is better that men believe some of these falsehoods than others. It is neither true, for example, that patriotism is a duty, nor true that it is not one, but, when the dreadful consequences of war with modern weapons are considered, it is much better that men should think that it is not a duty than that they should think that it is. (Here I agree with him.) One can then set about persuading people to believe those moral judgments which have good effects instead of those which have bad effects, and it really does not matter that we are thus inducing people to have beliefs which are useful, rather than beliefs which are true, because whatever they believe would be false anyway. But this view, which might be Mackie's, has the difficulty that it seems to imply that it is true that the consequences of believing that patriotism is a duty are *better* than the consequences of believing that it is not. (There would not be much point in asserting it if one did *not* think that it was true.) Hence it implies that, though certain kinds of moral "judgment," e.g. those asserting that certain things are right or wrong, cannot be true or false, there are other moral "judgments," e.g. those asserting that certain things are good or bad, which can be.

I suspect that one reason why Mackie thinks that right and wrong are invented, however, is quite different from any that I have hitherto suggested. I think he thinks that there are various practical difficulties which can be solved, or which can best be solved, only by having rules, as Hume, for example, thought that the practical difficulty created by the fact that I have no inducement to help you with your crop today unless some means be found of compelling you to help me with mine tomorrow, if I help you today, is solved by the invention of the human institution of promising, and the rules which enforce promise-keeping. Here, however, Mackie is confused in a way in which Hume was not. Mackie thinks that the fact that we invent promising and the rules which regulate it, as well as a large number of other useful rules, means that we invent morality. This is a mistake. Hume is quite clear — sometimes, at any rate — on the fact that, though we invent the rules, we do not invent the morality of the rules (any more than we invent their usefulness). A given society, for example, collectively if not individually, can help whether or not it has a rule prescribing monogamy. This rule is a human invention, and one which might or might not have been made. But, given that it has such a rule, whether this rule is a good rule, whether its invention solves the problem it was intended to solve, whether it has useful consequences, whether or not it is fair, are not things which anyone invents. Men invent machines, but they do not invent the goodness or badness or usefulness or efficiency of the machines they invent. And though men invent rules, they do not, and cannot, invent such things as whether the rules to be obeyed. Sometimes they ought to be obeyed, sometimes they ought not. Whether they ought to be obeyed or not will depend to a very large extent, if not entirely, upon whether or not they are fair and useful. If they are fair and useful, men do not invent this fact, and, if they ought to obey these rules for this reason, then this is not something they invent either. Similarly, though men invent theories, they do not invent their truth; though men invent new ways of doing things, they do not invent the success of these ways. To emphasize the point, though the rules are invented, the truths to the effect that the rules ought to be obeyed, if they ought to be obeyed, are not.

A large number of other contentions which Mackie makes, and questions which he asks, also turn out to be rather peculiar if we take seriously his own view that all moral judgments are false. For example, he maintains that the universalization principle is true, that is to say, that if of two otherwise exactly similar actions, one is right (or wrong) then the other must be right(or wrong) also. This would have to be prefaced by the further if-clause, to make a double if-clause, "*If* any actions ever were right (or wrong), then *if* of two exactly similar actions, one is right. . . . " Mackie also raises questions about the relations between religion and morality and between law and morality, and about the bearing of the truth or falsity of determinism on morality. These three questions, if all moral judgments are false, all take on a very extraordinary aspect, which Mackie does not even notice. The question of the relation between theology and morals concerns (crudely) questions about the bearing of the truth of theological judgments upon the truth of moral judgments. An example would be, "Would any moral judgment be true if there were no God?" On Mackie's view this question would take a highly idiosyncratic twist because, since moral judgments are all false anyway, the only question that can be asked about them is whether they would *still* be false, if there were no God, or whether, if there were no God, they might somehow turn out to be true. (Or, if there *is* no God, then the question would be "Would moral judgments still be false if there were a God?" On a view like Mackie's I am sure that the answer would be that they *would* still be false.) The question of the bearing of law upon morality is in fact a whole complex of questions, such as "Can something be made morally wrong by the legitimate law-making authority passing a law prohibiting it?" And if Mackie's view is taken seriously, the answer must be that nothing this law-making body can do can make any difference; no actions were wrong before any laws were passed, and it will continue to be the case that no actions are wrong, after the passing of whatever laws are passed. On the question of the relation between determinism and morality the same paradoxical result follows. For the question of the relation between determinism and morality is (again put crudely) this: "Would the truth of determinism entail that any or all of the moral judgments we ordinarily make are false?" And though the fact that all moral judgments, according to Mackie, are false anyway would not entail that determinism did not entail that they are false, it would, at the very least, deprive this question of almost all its interest.

The fact that Mackie himself can discuss such questions, quite oblivious of the rather obvious conclusions which I have just pointed out, suggests to me that, when he discusses them, he is again thinking of those moral judgments which, though false, are more true than the others. Though it is both false that killing people is wrong and also false that killing people is not wrong, it is, on Mackie's view, I suppose, more false that it is not wrong than that it is wrong. His questions about the relation between theology and morals, between law and morals and between determinism and morals, presumably then become "Would any moral judgments remain *as true as they are*, if determinism is true?" and "Would any moral judgments remain *as true as they are*, if there were not a God?" and "Would the passing of a law demanding that one wear a crash helmet turn it from being entirely and completely false that a Sikh ought to wear a crash helmet to being more nearly true that a Sikh ought to wear a crash helmet, than it was before this law was passed?"

Absolute Idealists, who held that everything short of the whole and complete truth was false, naturally had to bolster up their theory with a doctrine of degrees of truth. It may be false, since it is short of the complete truth, that the battle of Hastings was fought in 1066, but it is at least more true that it was fought in that year than that it was fought in any other year. Similarly anyone who held that time was unreal could deprive his views of a great deal of their sting — though, alas, also of a great degree of their interest and importance — if he held that, though it was false that I had my breakfast before my lunch, it was at least more true that I had my breakfast before my lunch than that I had it after it. Again, if one thinks that to say that roses are red and violets are blue is to assert that this redness and this blueness are spread evenly over the surfaces of these objects, back as well as front, in the dark as well as in white light, and this belief is false, then all assertions describing the colours of objects will be false. But some will be more false than others. If God could reveal to us in a dream that colours were not so spread over objects' surfaces, it would be absurd for this reason to stop making statements describing the colours of things. It might be false that roses were red, because redness was not spread evenly all over them, but nevertheless it would be much less false that they were red than that they were blue or colourless. And it is quite obvious that we would go on describing objects as having the colours they have now. It would be extremely misleading to our hearers if we did not do this, much more misleading than it would be if we truly said that they were not of the colours that we had previously taken them to be, and that roses are *not* red and violets are *not* blue.

Again, if God revealed to us in another dream that all the world contained was minds and their experiences, and we accepted on similar impeccable authority that Phenomenalism did *not* give us a correct analysis of the meaning of material object statements, and that in consequence such statements were all false, I think it quite obvious that we would nevertheless go on talking of material objects exactly as we do now. Though it would then be false that there is an unobserved magnet in my pocket, one would somehow wish to avoid drawing the conclusion that there is not an unobserved magnet in my pocket, for the "hypothesis" that there is explains the phenomena of apparent compass needles pointing to my apparent pocket much better than the hypothesis that there is *not* a magnet in my pocket, and enables me to predict the course of my future experience much better. Although that there is a magnet in my pocket, and that there is a ferret in my pocket, are both false, if there are no material objects at all, it is at least nearer the truth that there is a magnet in my pocket than it is that there is a ferret in it, and nearer the truth that I have a pocket than that I do not have a pocket.

Though it is Mackie's view that all moral "judgments" are false, for much the same reason as that all colour judgments would be false on the view I have just outlined, he ought, nevertheless, to hold that some must be more false than others, to make his view even moderately plausible. For he is at some pains to refute utilitarianism, as well as a number of other commonly accepted moral views, and this, when it is considered that he holds what he himself describes as an error theory of right and wrong, according to which there is no possibility of finding a moral view which is *not* incorrect, would be an absurd thing to do. For if all moral judgments are false, then the only reason for introducing, as Mackie does, special arguments against some of them is that some are more false than others. (And as Mackie also *asserts* some moral "judgments," this must presumably be because some of them are more true than others.) If, however, you do fall back on saying that some moral judgments are more true than others, it is difficult to see how you have not simply given way to the curious philosophical vice of taking away with one hand what you have given with the other (or giving with one hand what you have taken away with the other) and that you are not back precisely where you started from. All you need do is to say "For 'true' read 'more true than false'" and you can go on talking exactly as you did before.

It does seem to me that there is a simpler explanation than Mackie gives of how it is that *sometimes* we come to say that certain things are wrong when they are not wrong, which does not suffer from the disadvantage that, if it were the correct explanation of why we do this, it would turn out that all actions whatsoever were wrong. If we have been brought up to think that it is wrong to eat pork, or beans, or horse meat, or human flesh, or anything but vegetables, then it may very easily come about that we regard it as being unthinkable that we should eat any of these things. The idea of eating them fills us with horror and disgust. And the horror and disgust, so to speak, seem to cling inescapably and essentially to the action as, to take as an analogous example what used to be called the phenomenon of complication, tactual coldness seems to cling inescapably and essentially to the visual impression of ice. To say that this action is wrong is not, however, as Mackie supposes, to say, falsely, that the sentiments of disapproval which we project on to the action cling inescapably to it. If we were to say of one moral judgment that it was wrong for this reason, we would have to say this of them all, and *no* actions would be wrong. It is *because* we believe, falsely, that certain things are inherently and inescapably morally disgusting that we (irrationally) believe that they are wrong. Our conclusion that such things are wrong, however, *could* be true, although the reason we have for it is false. When we come to the same conclusion in other cases, there is no reason why what we believe, in those cases, should not be true.

That moral judgments assert the existence of a false projection of our sentiments on to the actions judged is not the only theory of the nature of moral judgment put forward by Mackie in *Ethics*. Sometimes he holds that moral judgments are false because they assert that the actions which we say are wrong are contrary to law, when there is (assuming that there is not a God) no law for them to be contrary to. At other times he holds that moral judgments are false because they say that certain actions categorically ought to be done, whether the agent wants to do them or not. Since there are no wants which such imperatives realize, as there cannot be if they are *categorical* imperatives, such judgments are bound to be wrong. Though both these theories lead to the conclusion Mackie wants, that moral judgments are false, only a moment's reflection is necessary to see that these two views are incompatible with Mackie's original theory, and with one another.

In fairness to Mackie I ought to point out — and I do not think that the judgment that I *ought* to do this is in any way defective — that there is a great deal more to Mackie's book than the view about the nature of moral judgment that I have been criticizing, and that, leaving aside whether he ought to be doing what he is doing in the second part of his book if what he says in the first part of his book is true, I agree with a great deal of it. But even in the first part of his book there is something of the very greatest importance with which I also agree. That is that people making moral judgments *are* making assertions (though Mackie thinks they are making assertions that are false). To put the matter very very simply, I think — and I also think that this is obvious — that, when I enunciate some fairly elementary moral truth, such as that burning babies alive is wrong, I say this because I think that it *is* wrong. I also, incidentally, think that it would be wrong, even if I did *not* think that it was wrong, even if the agent did not think that it was wrong, and even if no one else at all thought it was wrong. And I most certainly do not think that I can change it to being right by doing anything (say, taking drugs) to alter my attitude to it, nor do I think that I can make it right by altering other people's attitudes to it. I, like most other people, say that it is wrong because I think it *is* wrong. It is possible, logically possible, that I might be mistaken. The fact that I believe that something is wrong does not entail that it is wrong. But in this case I think that most certainly I am *not* mistaken. But if I say, as I do, that burning babies alive is wrong because I think it is wrong, then I ought to think, if I think it is wrong, that what I think is true. And if Mackie thinks, as he does, that it is not true that burning babies alive is wrong, then I do not see how he can consistently refuse to say that it is not wrong.

These last steps, I concede, are tricky ones, which is a good reason for feeling disquiet about the redundancy theory of truth. Perhaps, although burning babies alive *is* wrong, it is not *true* that it is wrong. The trouble with Mackie's arguments, however, is that they would not just show that it is not *true* that burning babies alive is wrong. I might be perfectly happy to accept this, provided that I am allowed to go on believing that burning babies alive *is* wrong. I dare say a sea-captain would not care very much whether or not it is *true* that there will be a sea battle tomorrow, so long as there is one. But what Mackie's arguments show is that burning babies alive is not wrong (though, of course, it may be that they also show that burning babies alive is not right, either). After all, if, when we say that burning babies alive is wrong we are attributing to this act a characteristic which it cannot have, what other conclusion can one come to?

It is possible, as I have said, that what makes Mackie think that it cannot be true that it is wrong to burn babies alive is a rather naive view about what it is to make a statement true. And I wish I could put forward a more sophisticated theory of truth, which would not lead to this error. At the moment I am unable to do this. But the fact that one cannot do what philosophers from time immemorial have failed to do, and hit upon a satisfactory theory of truth, does not mean that one is justified in saying for this reason that certain judgments are *not* true. Philosophy is not yet far enough advanced to enable philosophers to set aside whole classes of judgments such as that burning babies alive is wrong, because they cannot fit them into a theory of truth, or a theory of the meaning of the word "wrong," which only a little experience of the history of philosophy will tell us is very unlikely itself to be true anyway.

28

ALASDAIR MACINTYRE

Taboo Epistemology

Introduction

Alasdair MacIntyre holds a chair of philosophy at Notre Dame. His books include *The Unconscious, A Short History of Ethics*, and *After Virtue*, from which this excerpt is taken.

In this reading MacIntyre parodies the efforts of modern moral philosophers to give a correct account of the meaning of the word "right" by comparing them with imaginary attempts of native epistemologists to give a similar account of "taboo." What are the implications of these remarks for "right" and "wrong"? I leave the reader to decide for himself.

Reading

IN THE JOURNAL of his third voyage Captain Cook records the first discovery by English speakers of the Polynesian word *taboo* (in a variety of forms). The English seamen had been astonished at what they took to be the lax sexual habits of the Polynesians and were even more astonished to discover the sharp contrast with the rigorous prohibition placed on such conduct as that of men and women eating together. When they enquired why men and women were prohibited from eating together, they were told that the practice was *taboo*. But when they

From Alasdair MacIntyre, *After Virtue*, Gerald Duckworth & Co Ltd., London, 1981. By permission of Gerald Duckworth & Co Ltd.

enquired further what *taboo* meant, they could get little further information. Clearly *taboo* did not simply mean *prohibited*; for to say that something — person or practice or theory — is *taboo* is to give some particular sort of reason for its prohibition. But what sort of reason? It has not only been Cook's seamen who have had trouble with that question; from Frazer and Tylor to Franz Steiner and Mary Douglas the anthropologists have had to struggle with it. From that struggle two keys to the problem emerge. The first is the significance of the fact that Cook's seamen were unable to get any intelligible reply to their queries from their native informants. What this *suggests* is — and any hypothesis is to some degree speculative — that the native informants themselves did not really understand the word that they were using, and this suggestion is reinforced by the ease with which Kamehameha II abolished the taboos in Hawaii forty years later in 1819 and the lack of social consequence when he did.

But could the Polynesians come to be using a word which they themselves did not really understand? It is here that Steiner and Douglas are illuminating. For what they both suggest is that taboo rules often and perhaps characteristically have a history which falls into two stages. In the first stage they are embedded in a context which confers intelligibility upon them. So Mary Douglas has argued that the taboo rules of Deuteronomy presuppose a cosmology and a taxonomy of a certain kind. Deprive the taboo rules of their original context and they at once are apt to appear as a set of arbitrary prohibitions, as indeed they characteristically do appear when the initial context is lost, when those background beliefs in the light of which the taboo rules had originally been understood have not only been abandoned but forgotten.

In such a situation the rules have been deprived of any status that can secure their authority and, if they do not acquire some new status quickly, both their interpretation and their justification become debatable. When the resources of a culture are too meagre to carry through the task of reinterpretation, the task of justification becomes impossible. Hence perhaps the relatively easy, although to some contemporary observers astonishing, victory of Kamehameha II over the taboos (and the creation thereby of a moral vacuum in which the banalities of the New England Protestant missionaries were received all too quickly). But had the Polynesian culture enjoyed the blessings of analytical philosophy it is all too clear that the question of the meaning of taboo could have been resolved in a number of ways. *Taboo*, it would have been said by one party, is clearly the name of a non-natural property; and precisely the same reasoning which led Moore to see *good* as the name of such a property and Prichard and Ross to see *obligatory* and *right* as the names of such properties would have been available to show that *taboo* is the name of such a property. Another party would doubtless have argued that "This is *taboo*" means roughly the same as "I disapprove of this; do so as well"; and precisely the same reasoning which led Stevenson and Ayer to see "good" as having primarily an emotive use would have been available to support the emotive theory of *taboo*. A third party would presumably have arisen which would have argued that the grammatical form of "This is taboo" disguises a universalizable imperative prescription.

Bibliography

Part I: The Impossibility of Altruism

Broad, Charlie Dunbar. "Egoism as a Theory of Human Motives," in *Ethics and the History of Philosophy*, London, Routledge, 1952; "Butler," in *Five Types of Ethical Theory*, London, Kegan Paul, 1930.

Butler, Joseph. "Fifteen Sermons (especially Sermons II and III), *Butler's Works*. Vol. 1, edited by W. E. Gladstone, Oxford, England, Oxford University Press, 1897; "Dissertation of the Nature of Virtue," in *The Analogy of Religion*, London, Everyman's Library, 1936.

Dawkins, Richard. *The Selfish Gene*, especially Chapter 10, Oxford, England, Oxford University Press, 1978.

Hume, David. *An Enquiry Concerning the Principles of Morals*, edited by L. A. Selby-Bigge, revised by P. H. Nidditch, Oxford, England, Oxford University Press, 1975, Appendix II, "Of Self-Love."

La Rochefoucauld, Francois VI, duc de. *Maxims*, translated by L. W. Tancock, Harmondsworth, England, Penguin Books, 1967.

Lorenz, Konrad. *On Aggression*, London, Methuen, 1966.

Nagel, Thomas. *The Possibility of Altruism*, Princeton, NJ, Princeton University Press, 1970.

Part II: Virtue Does Not Pay

Brandt, R. B. *A Theory of the Good and the Right*. Oxford, Clarendon Press, 1979.

Butler, Joseph, "Fifteen Sermons."

Dawkins, Richard, *Selfish Gene*.

Harman, Gilbert. *The Nature of Morality*, Oxford, England, Oxford University Press, 1977.

Harrison, Jonathan. "Kant's First Formulation of the Categorical Imperative," *The Philosophical Quarterly*, Vol. 7, 1953; "Duty and Interest," *The Australasian Journal of Philosophy and Psychology*, Vol. 49, 1953, "Utilitarianism, Universalisation and Our Duty to be Just," in *Aristotelian Society Proceedings*, 1952–53; "Rule Utilitarianism and Cumulative Effect Utilitarianism," *Canadian Journal of Philosophy*, Supplementary Vol. V; "Be Ye Therefore Perfect," *Religious Studies*, Vol. 53, 1985; *Hume's Theory of Justice*, especially Chapter 11, Oxford, England, Oxford University Press, 1981.

Hume, David. *A Treatise of Human Nature* (especially Book III, Part II), edited by L. A. Selby-Bigge, revised by P. H. Nidditch, Oxford, England, Oxford University Press, 1978.

Machiavelli, Niccolo. *The Prince*, translated by George Bull, Harmondsworth, England, Penguin Books, 1961.

Nagel, Thomas. *The Possibility of Altruism*, Oxford, England, Oxford University Press, 1970.

Parfitt, Derek. *Reasons and Persons*, Oxford, England, Oxford University Press, 1984.

Plato. *Gorgias*, in *The Dialogues of Plato*, translated by B. Jowett. Oxford, Oxford University Press, 1871.

Prichard, H. H. "Does Moral Philosophy Rest on a Mistake?" in *Moral Obligation*, Oxford, England, Oxford University Press, 1949.

Taylor, Paul. *The Principles of Ethics*, Belmont, CA, Wadsworth, 1975.

Ullman-Margalit, Edna. *The Emergence of Norms*, Oxford, England, Oxford University Press, 1977.

Part III: Virtue Not Within Our Power

Aquinas, Thomas. "Of Predestination," in *Summa Theologica*, London, Blackfriars with Eyre and Spottiswood, and New York, McGraw-Hill, 1912–38, 1a, 23, i.

Augustine. "On Free Will," in *Augustine: Earlier Writings*, translated by John A. S. Burleigh, London, S.C.M. Press, 1953.

Austin, J. L. "Ifs and Cans," in *The Collected Papers of J. L. Austin*, Oxford, England, Oxford University Press, 1961.

Ayer, A. J. "Freedom and Necessity," in *Philosophical Essays*, London, Macmillan, 1954.

Ayers, M. R. *The Refutation of Determinism*. London, Methuen, 1968.

Boethius, Ancius. *The Consolations of Philosophy*, Harmondsworth, England, Penguin Books, 1969.

Broad, Charlie Dunbar. "Determinism, Indeterminism and Libertarianism," in *Ethics and the History of Philosophy*, London, Routledge, 1952.

Campbell, C. A. *In Defence of Free Will*, London, George Allen and Unwin, 1967.

Chaucer, Geoffrey. "The Nonne's Priest's Tale," *The Canterbury Tales*, translated by David Wright, Oxford, England, Oxford University Press, 1985.

Davidson, Donald. "Freedom to Act," in *Essays on Actions and Events*, Oxford, England, Oxford University Press, 1980.

Dennett, Daniel. *Elbow Room*, Oxford, England, Oxford University Press, 1984.

Edwards, Paul. "Hard and Soft Determinism," in *Determinism and Freedom in the Age of Modern Science*, edited by Sidney Hook, New York, Collier, 1961.

Geach, P. T. "Omnipotence," *Philosophy*, Vol. 48, 1973; "Can God Fail to Keep Promises?", *Philosophy*, Vol. 52, 1977.

Harrison, Jonathan. "Foreknowledge, Will and Fate," University of Nottingham, 1967; "Tom and Jerry, or What Price Pelagius?" in *A Philosopher's Nightmare*, Nottingham University Monographs, 1985; "Some Difficulties with Hypothetical Accounts of Freedom of the Will," *Cogito*, Vol. 2, 1985; "Geach On God's Inability to do Evil," *Philosophy*, Vol. 51, 1976; "Geach on Harrison on Geach on God," *Philosophy*, Vol. 52, 1977.

Hobart, R. E. "Free Will as Involving Determination and as Inconceivable Without It," *Mind*, 1934.

Honderich, Ted (Ed.). *Essays on Freedom of Action*, London, Routledge, 1973; *A Theory of Determinism, The Mind, Neuroscience and Life Hopes*, Oxford, England, Oxford University Press, 1988.

Hook, Sidney (Ed.). *Determinism and Freedom*, New York, Collier, 1961.

Hume, David. *Treatise of Human Nature*, Book II, Part III, Sections 1 and 2.

Ingwagen, Peter van. *An Essay on Free Will*, Oxford, England, Oxford University Press, 1983.

Kant, Immanuel. "The Fundamental Principles of the Metaphysics of Morals," Part III, in *The Moral Law*, translated by H. J. Paton, London, Hutchinsons, 1948.

Kenny, Anthony. *Free Will and Responsibility*, London, Routledge, 1978.

Locke, John. *An Essay Concerning Human Understanding*, Chapter XXI, Book II, edited by P. H. Nidditch, Oxford, England, Oxford University Press, 1970.

Lucas, John. *The Freedom of the Will*, Oxford, England, Oxford University Press, 1970.

Moore, G. E. *Ethics*, especially Chapter 6, London, Williams and Norgate, 1912.

Nowell-Smith, Patrick. *Ethics* (especially Chapters 19 and 20), Harmondsworth, England, Penguin Books, 1969.

Ockham, William. *Predestination, God's Foreknowledge and Future Contingents*, translated by Marylin McCord Adams and Norman Kretzmann, New York, Appleton Century Crofts, 1969.

Rée, Paul. "Determinism and the Illusion of Moral Responsibility," translated by Stefan Bauer-Mengelberg, in *A Modern Introduction to Philosophy*, 3rd ed., edited by P. Edwards and A. Rap, New York, Macmillan, 1973.

Skinner, B. F. *Beyond Freedom and Dignity*, Harmondsworth, England, Penguin Books, 1973.

Spinoza, Benedict. *Ethics*, translated A. Boyle, with an introduction by George Santayana, London, Everyman's Library and J. M. Dent and Sons Ltd., 1910.

Strawson, Galen. *Freedom and Belief*, Oxford, England, Oxford University Press, 1988.

Strawson, P. F. "Freedom and Resentment," in *Freedom and Resentment*, London, Methuen, 1974.

Taylor, Richard. *Metaphysics*, Chapters 4 and 5, Englewood Cliffs, NJ, Prentice-Hall, 1963.

Williams, Bernard. *Moral Luck*, Cambridge, England, Cambridge University Press, 1981.

Part IV: Goodness Not Demanded by God

Anscombe, G. E. M. "Modern Moral Philosophy," *Philosophy*, Vol. 33, 1958.

Ayer, A. J. *The Central Questions of Philosophy*, (especially Chapter X), London, Weidenfeld and Nicholson, 1973.

Barnes, Hazel. *An Existentialist Ethics*. New York, Vintage, 1971.

Bayle, Pierre. *The Great Conflict of Faith and Reason*, translated by Karl C. Sandberg, New York, Frederick Ungar, 1963.

Butler, Joseph. *The Analogy of Religion*, Dissertation II, "Of the Nature of Virtue," "Fifteen Sermons."

Freud, Sigmund. *The Future of an Illusion*, translated by W. Robson Scott, London, Hogarth, 1953.

Geach, P. T. *God and the Soul*, London, Routledge and Kegan Paul, 1969.

Harrison, Jonathan. "Can I Have a Duty to Believe in God," *Philosophy*, Vol. 33, 1957; *Our Knowledge of Right and Wrong*, London, George Allen and Unwin, 1971; "Some Reflections on the Ethics of Knowledge and Belief," *Religious Studies*, Vol. 23, 1987; "Utilitarianism and Toleration," *Philosophy*, Vol. 62, 1987.

Helm, Paul (Ed.). *Divine Commands and Morality*, Oxford, England, Oxford University Press, 1981.

Mitchell, Basil. "Law, Morality and Religion," in *Secular Society*, Oxford, England, Oxford University Press, 1970.

Quinn, Philip L. *Divine Commands and Moral Requirements*, Oxford, England, Oxford University Press, 1978.

J. M. Robertson. *A Short History of Christianity*, London, The Thinkers' Library, Watts and Co., 1931.

Sartre, J. P. *Existentialism and Humanism*, translated by Philip Mairet, London, Methuen, 1948.

Voltaire. *Philosophical Dictionary*, Harmondsworth, England, Penguin Books, 1972, article on "Atheist, Atheism."

Warnock, Mary. *Existentialism*, Oxford, England, Oxford University Press, 1970.

Part V: Being Good Involves Being the Dupe of Someone Else

Cohen, G. A. *Karl Marx's Theory of History*, Oxford, England, Oxford University Press, 1978; *History, Labour and Freedom, Themes from Marx*, Oxford, England, Oxford University Press, 1988.

Danto, Arthur C. *Nietzsche as Philosopher*, New York, Macmillan, 1965.

Kropotkin, Petr Aléxievich. *Mutual Aid, a Factor in Evolution*, Allen Lane, London, 1972; *Modern Science and Anarchism*, London, Freedom Press, 1923.

Lukes, Steven. *Marxism and Morality*, Oxford, England, Oxford University Press, 1985.

Mandeville, Bernard. *An Enquiry into the Nature of Virtue*, in *Mandeville: The Fables of the Bees*, edited by Philip Harth, Harmondsworth, England, Penguin Books, 1970.

Marx, Karl (with Friedrich Engels). *Manifesto of the Communist Party: Capital* (three volumes), Harmondsworth, England, Penguin Books, 1977–81.

Monro, D. H. *The Ambivalence of Bernard Mandeville*, Oxford, England, Oxford University Press, 1975.

Nietzsche, Friedrich, *Thus Spake Zarathustra*, translated by A. Tille, revised by M. M. Bozman, London, J. M. Dent and Son, 1933; *Beyond Good and Evil*, translated with a commentary by Walter Kaufman, London, Random House, 1966.

Plato. "Republic," Book III.

Russell, Bertrand. "Is There an Absolute Good?," *Collected Papers of Bertrand Russell*, edited by Alan Ryan, Vol. 9, London, Routledge, 1988.
Stirner, Max. *The Ego and His Own*, translated by John Carroll, London, Jonathan Cape, 1971.
Tennyson, Alfred Lord. "The Charge of the Light Brigade," *Poems*, Oxford, England, Oxford University Press, 1911.

Part VI: Moral Beliefs: The Irrational Products of Evolution

Caplan, Arthur L. (Ed.). *The Sociobiology Debate*, London, Harper and Row, 1978.
Dawkins, Richard. *The Blind Watchmaker*, London, Longman, 1986.
Flew, Antony. *Evolutionary Ethics*, London, Macmillan, 1971.
Harrison, Jonathan, *Our Knowledge of Right and Wrong*, Chapter XI, "Evolution and Ethics", London: George Allen & Unwin, 1971.
Huxley, Julian. *Evolutionary Ethics*, Oxford, England, Oxford University Press, 1943.
Huxley, Thomas. *Evolution and Ethics*, London, Macmillan, 1993.
Lorenz, Konrad. *On Aggression*, Methuen and Company Ltd., London, 1966.
Midgley, Mary. *The Beast in Man*, London, Methuen, 1980; *Evolution as a Religion*, London, Methuen, 1985.
Ruse, Michael. *Sociobiology: Sense or Nonsense?*, Dordrecht, The Netherlands, D. Reidel, 1979; *Taking Darwin Seriously*, Oxford, England, Blackwell, 1987; *Readings in the Philosophy of Biology*, New York, Macmillan, 1989.
Singer, Peter. *The Expanding Circle*, Oxford, England, Oxford University Press, 1983.
Wilson, E. O. *Sociobiology, the New Synthesis* (especially Chapter 26), Cambridge, MA, Harvard University Press, 1975; *On Human Nature*, Cambridge, MA, Harvard University Press, 1978.

Part VII: Moral Beliefs, Impossible to Justify

A. The Variability of Moral Judgments

Durkheim, Emile. *Sociology and Philosophy*, translated by D. F. Pocock, London, Cohen and West, 1953.
Gibbart, Allan. *Wise Choices, Apt Feelings: A Theory of Normative Judgment*. Oxford, Clarendon Press, 1990.
MacIntyre, A. C. *After Virtue*, London, Duckworth, 1981.
Westermarck, Edward. *Ethical Relativity*, London, Routledge and Kegan Paul, 1932; *The Origin and Development of the Moral Ideas*, London, Macmillan, 1917–24.
Sextus Empiricus. "Against the Ethicists," *Works*, translated by R. G. Bury, London, Loeb, 1933–53.

B. Subjectivism and Relativism

Harman, Gilbert. "Moral Relativism Defended," *The Philosophical Review*, 1975.
Harrison, Jonathan. *Our Knowledge of Right and Wrong*, Chapters VI and X.
Hume, David. *A Treatise of Human Nature*, Book III, Part I; *An Enquiry Concerning the Principles of Morals*, Section I and Appendix I, edited by L. A.

Selby-Bigge, revised by P. H. Nidditch, Oxford, England, Oxford University Press, 1975.

Kraus, Michael, and Jack Meiland (Eds.). *Relativism, Cognitive and Moral*, Notre Dame, IN, University of Notre Dame Press, 1982.

Lyons, David. "Ethical Relativism and the Problem of Incoherence," in *Ethics*, The University of Chicago Press, 1976.

Moore, G. E. *Ethics*, Chapters 3 and 4.

Stevenson, Charles. "Moore's Arguments Against Certain Forms of Ethical Naturalism," *The Philosophy of G. E. Moore*, edited by P. A. Schilpp, Evanston, New York, Tudor Publishing Co., 1942.

Williams, Bernard. *Morality*, New York, Harper and Row, 1972; "The Truth in Relativism," in *Proceedings of the Aristotelian Society*, 1974–75; *Ethics and the Limits of Philosophy*, London, Fontana Paperbacks, 1985.

C. The Emotive Theory

Ayer, A. J. *Language, Truth and Logic* (especially Chapter VI), London, Victor Gollancz, 1947; "Are There Objective Values?" *Freedom and Morality*, Oxford, England, Oxford University Press, 1984.

Barnes, W. H. F. "Ethics Without Propositions," in *Supplementary Proceedings of the Aristotelian Society*, 1947.

Edwards, Paul. *The Logic of Moral Discourse*, Glencoe, IL, Free Press, 1955.

Harrison, Jonathan. "Can Ethics Do Without Propositions?" *Mind*, 1952.

Stevenson, Charles. *Ethics and Language*, New Haven, CT, Yale University Press, 1944.

Urmson, J. *The Emotive Theory of Ethics*, London, Hutchinson, 1968.

White, Alan. *Truth*, Chapter 3, Section b, London, Macmillan, 1970.

D. Imperativism

Carnap, Rudolf. *Philosophy and Logical Syntax*, London, Kegan Paul, Trench Trubner & Co., 1935.

Geach, P. T. "Imperative and Practical Reasoning," *Logic Matters*, Oxford, England, Basil Blackwell, 1972.

Hare, Richard. *The Language of Morals*, Oxford, England, Oxford University Press; *Freedom and Reason*, Oxford, England, Oxford University Press, 1963; *Practical Inferences*, London, Macmillan, 1971; *Moral Thinking*, Oxford, England, Oxford University Press, 1981.

Harrison, Jonathan. "When Is a Principle a Moral Principle?" in *Supplementary Proceedings of the Aristotelian Society*, Vol. 28, 1952; "Ethics and the Archangelic Spectator," *Cogito*, Vol. 1, 1985; "Imperative Logic and Deontic Logic," in *Logic and Ethics*, edited by P. T. Geach, Dordrecht, The Netherlands, Kluwer Academic Publishers, 1991; "Pure Morality and Impure Truth," *The Philosophical Quarterly*, Vol. 32, 1983.

MacDonald, G. F. *Perception and Identity, Essays Presented to A. J. Ayer and His Replies to Them.* London, Macmillan, 1979.

Rescher, Nicholas. *The Logic of Commands*, London, Routledge, 1966.

Smart, J. J. C. *Ethics, Persuasion and Truth*, London, Routledge, 1984.

Williams, Bernard. "Imperative Inference," in *Problems of the Self*, Cambridge, England, Cambridge University Press, 1973.

E. Modern Moral Nihilism

Bambrough, Renford. *Moral Scepticism and Moral Knowledge*, London, Routledge, 1979.

Edwards, Paul. *Logic of Moral Discourse*, chapter 3.

Harrison, Jonathan. "Scepticism About Morals," in *The Supplementary Proceedings of the Aristotelian Society*, 1967; *Our Knowledge of Right and Wrong*, Chapter I.

Hinckfuss, Ian. *The Moral Society, Its Structure and Effects*, Australian National University, 1987.

Honderich, Ted (Ed.). *Morality and Objectivity, Essays in Honour of J. L. Mackie*, London, Routledge, 1985.

Mackie, John. "The Refutation of Morals," *The Australian Journal of Philosophy and Psychology*, 1946; *Ethics: Inventing Right and Wrong*, Harmondsworth, England, Pelican Books, 1977.

Nozick, Robert. *Philosophical Explanations*, Part V, Oxford, England, Oxford University Press, 1981.

Williams, Bernard. *Ethics and the Limits of Philosophy*, London, Fontana Press and William Collins, 1985.

F. INTUITIONISM

Harrison, Jonathan. "Desert Island Deontology," in *Time Travel for Beginners and Other Stories*, Philosophy Department, Nottingham University, 1990; *Hume's Moral Epistemology* (especially Chapter V), Oxford, England, Oxford University Press, 1981.

Hudson, W. D. (Ed.). *The Is/Ought Gap*, London, Macmillan, 1969.

Hume, David. *A Treatise of Human Nature*, Book III, Part I, Section 1.

Price, Richard. *Review of the Principal Questions of Morals* (especially Chapter 1), edited by D. D. Raphael, Oxford, England, Oxford University Press, 1939.

Ross, David. *The Foundations of Ethics* (especially Chapter 8), Oxford, England, Oxford University Press, 1948.